THE SEXUALITY DEBATE
IN
NORTH AMERICAN CHURCHES,
1988-1995

Controversies, Unresolved Issues, Future Prospects

Edited by

John J. Carey

Symposium Series
Volume 36

The Edwin Mellen Press
Lewiston/Queenston/Lampeter

Library of Congress Cataloging-in-Publication Data

Carey, John Jesse.
  The sexuality debate in North American churches, 1988-1995 :
controversies, unresolved issues, future prospects / [edited] by
John J. Carey ; with an appendix on "Homosexual practices in
biblical perspectives" by Victor Paul Furnish.
     p.   cm.
  Includes bibliographical references.
  ISBN 0-7734-9111-2
  1. Sex--Religious aspects--Christianity--History of
doctrines--20th century. 2. Protestant churches--North America-
-Doctrines--History--20th century. 3. Homosexuality--Biblical
teaching. 4. North America--Church history--20th century.
I. Furnish, Victor Paul. II. Title.
BT708.C37   1995
241'.66'0973--dc20   94-38866
                                                                CIP

This is volume 36 in the continuing series
Symposium Series
Volume 36 ISBN 0-7734-9111-2
SS Series ISBN 0-88946-989-X

Assessments of:
  The Presbyterian Church (U.S.A.)   The Evangelical Lutheran Church in America
  The Episcopal Church   The United Church of Canada
  The United Methodist Church

Essays in Part II and the Appendix Copyright, 1995 by their respective authors.

A CIP catalog record for this book is available from the British Library.

The Edwin Mellen Press   The Edwin Mellen Press
     Box 450   Box 67
Lewiston, New York   Queenston, Ontario
USA 14092-0450   CANADA L0S 1L0

The Edwin Mellen Press, Ltd.
Lampeter, Dyfed, Wales
UNITED KINGDOM SA48 7DY

Printed in the United States of America

DEDICATION

This book is dedicated to
Charles G. "Gary" Stephens

—in appreciation for thirty-five years of friendship

TABLE OF CONTENTS

Part One: The Presbyterian Experience

Part Two: Ecumenical Experiences and Reflections

Part Three: The Future of the Debate

ACKNOWLEDGEMENTS

Grateful acknowledgement is given for permission to reprint the following copyrighted material:

"Waiting on the Spirit: Episcopalians and Homosexuality," by Ephriam Radner and George Sumner, Jr. Copyright 1991, Christian Century Foundation. Reprinted by permission from the October 9, 1991 Issue of *The Christian Century*.

Excerpt from *Theology for the Third Millennium*, by Hans Küng. Copyright 1988, Doubleday; citation from p. 244.

PREFACE

In December 1991, the Religious Newswriters Association of America voted the debate over sexuality in America's churches as the leading religious news story of 1991. The debate seemed to peak as a media event in the summer of 1991 with the meetings of the Presbyterian General Assembly in Baltimore and the Episcopal House of Deputies in Phoenix. It continued, however, with the Methodist General Conference in the summer of 1992 and with the appointment of various local and regional church committees to pursue study of sexuality issues. Editors of *The Christian Century* regarded the continuing debate over homosexuality as the third leading religious story of 1992, and issues of sexual abuse ranked as number four. Leading scholarly professional organizations, such as the Society of Christian Ethics, The American Academy of Religion, and the Society of Biblical Literature, sponsored special discussions in 1992 and 1993 on themes, problems, and consequences of this debate. Throughout 1994 and 1995, various denominations have prepared study materials for use at the congregational or regional levels of church life, and the various issues of sexuality — gay and lesbian ordination, clergy sexual misconduct, sex and singleness, family and child abuse, the AIDS controversies — continue to draw national attention.

This book seeks to tell the story of what has happened, what issues have emerged, what this debate tells us about North American churches, and what the iv

debate of the future may look like. I served as Chair of the Presbyterian Special Committee on Human Sexuality, and have spent much of the past seven years traveling around the country speaking to churches, presbyteries, professional associations, colleges, universities, and seminaries about these matters. I have learned much from these experiences about the national church, and about the levels of pain and perplexity surrounding human sexuality in American culture.

As I watched this debate evolve, I increasingly felt that this was a story that needed to be analyzed and clarified, for I knew we were living through a remarkable event in American Protestantism. The Presbyterian Report has sold over 100,000 copies and is still selling. Clearly this debate has touched some deep nerves in our churches. I felt that there was a need for two books: one to analyze the Presbyterian experience, and one to consider the broader concerns and experiences of the other churches that have been involved in the sexuality debate. Although I followed the debates and reports of other churches carefully, I was not sure that I had the expertise or sensitivity to analyze their experiences for a national audience. I finally decided to invite colleagues who were leaders and shapers of those other denominations to do chapters describing their experiences, and in the interest of depth and balance, I invited three of my colleagues from the Presbyterian Committee — Marvin M. Ellison, Janet Fishburn and Sylvia Thorson-Smith to contribute essays on the Presbyterian experience as they saw it. I have assumed the responsibility for the organization of the material, the broad assessment of the Presbyterian story, and have written most of the chapters concerning the future of this debate. As valuable as the contributions of my colleagues are to this book, none of them bear any responsibilities for its shortcomings or limitations. Those are mine alone.

The chapter by Ephriam Radner and George Sumner, Jr., was originally published in the October 9, 1991 issue of *The Christian Century* and is reprinted here with the permission of that journal and the authors. The Appendix by Victor Funish was originally prepared as a study document for the Methodist Committee on Sexuality, and is published here in abbreviated form. I am grateful to Professor Furnish for allowing me to include his essay in this book. Inasmuch as the denominations focused their deliberations solely on the issue of homosexuality, and how we interpret the Bible is critical for that discussion, his essay adds a special dimension to this book.

Four observations should be made about this book and the American church sexuality controversies. The first is that this book is not structured to provide a series of "pro" and "con" reactions in the sexuality debate. The country, in my judgment, has already been overwhelmed with negative, emotional, and confusing news stories about churches and sexuality issues. This book, for the most part, brings together reflections of persons who have been involved in the sexuality debate from the constructive side: i.e., persons who felt that it is timely and important for the churches to re-think a number of assumptions about the Christian life, Christian ethics, and the role of the Churches in society. This is the perspective that has not been communicated to church members and to the American public.

The second observation is that it is only with optimism that I entitle this book "The Sexuality Debate in North American Churches." In fact the emotionalism which was aroused very early across the country precluded much serious debate in many churches, especially the Presbyterian Church (U.S.A.). If "debate" implies serious discussions where at least two viewpoints listen to each other and try to understand each other, that is more of a hope than a past experience. Perhaps this book will be a means to that end.

The third observation pertains specifically to the Presbyterian (U.S.A.) report. Although as Chair of the Committee my name quickly became associated with the report, and I was thrust into a role of explaining and defending the report, it needs to be stressed that the report was the result of the combined efforts and concerns of a committee of seventeen people. All members of the committee agreed on the range of topics to be included in the report. All members served on sub-committees for research on specific topics and on sub-committees for the drafting of various chapters. Four members of the committee dissented from the majority report and prepared a minority report, but at all times members showed a cordiality and openness towards those with whom they disagreed. In light of the gathering storm clouds In the Presbyterian Church (U.S.A.), the final support of the majority report was an act of faith and courage by eleven committee members. In addition to my three colleagues who have contributed to this volume, I want to pay special tribute to Thelma Burgonio-Watson, now on the staff of the Center for the Prevention of Sexual and Domestic Violence in Seattle, Washington; Robert H. Fernandez, Executive Presbyter of the Presbytery of San Fernando in the greater Los Angeles area; William T. Hancock, Pastor of the Northminster Presbyterian Church of Dellwood, Missouri; Elizabeth Johnson, Associate Professor of New Testament Studies at the Reformed Theological Seminary in New Brunswick, New Jersey; Grace Kim, who teaches sex education in the public schools of Davis, California; Bernadine McRipley, now serving as Interim Associate of the Presbyterian Church (U.S.A.) Washington office; and Daniel E. Smith, Pastor of the West Hollywood Presbyterian Church in West Hollywood, California. It was a privilege to work with them all.

The fourth observation relates to the landslide Republican victories in the November, 1994 elections. Although there were clearly many issues related to the Republican triumph, the election signaled an emerging conservative consensus in American in social and cultural issues. That same trend is reflected in North

American churches, as evidenced in the negative theological reaction to the Women's Re-Imaging Conference held in Minneapolis in November of 1993. Whether this new conservative mood will lead to a rejection of efforts to reappraise sexuality issues in our culture, or whether it will lead to a new way of framing issues, remains to be seen. It is clear, however, that the new mood of conservatism in 1995 makes it harder for the historic mainline churches to play a prophetic role in our culture. Social change, we have learned, comes hard, and all calls for change create a backlash.

It is a pleasure for me to acknowledge several people who have helped me in different ways as this manuscript was taking shape. James B. Nelson of the United Theological Seminary of the Twin Cities has been a friend since our student days at the Yale Divinity School. His pioneering studies in Christian ethics and human sexuality have opened new vistas for all ethicists working in the field. William B. Kennedy of Union Theological Seminary in New York, also a close friend since our student days, has illumined me on many nuances of Presbyterian polity and politics. Beverly W. Harrison of Union Theological Seminary in New York has been an example to many of us over many years of how Christian ethics might explore other paradigms, and I am indebted to her for her many ethical insights.

Mary Charlotte McCall, my wife, a lawyer and sometime (1988-94) Vice-Chair of the Presbyterian Committee on Social Witness Policy, was a valuable dialogue partner at all stages of my work, and provided me with computer data from PRESBYNET about the church's continuing debates on sexuality issues. I have been inspired by her courage as she herself works on many of these issues, and I am indebted to her in ways far beyond what I can acknowledge here. Joyce Brescia, faculty secretary at Agnes Scott College, used her word processing skills to bring order to various drafts of this manuscript and her editorial eye caught numerous convolutions in the text. Without her assistance this manuscript would never have seen the light of day.

Finally, my five daughters — Sarah, Mary Lynn, Beth, Joanna and Jessica — once little girls and now mature young women, have been encouraging at all stages of my work and have helped me with their good humor. They have knowingly and unknowingly given me insights into what it means to grow up female in our society. I hope that in some modest way this book can help our society become a safer and healthier place for them and others of their generation.

John J. Carey

Decatur, Georgia
February 1, 1995

INTRODUCTION

In the last several years a number of Protestant denominations in North America have undertaken studies of human sexuality: the United Church of Christ, the United Church of Canada, the Episcopal Church, the Presbyterian Church (U.S.A.), the United Methodist Church, and the Evangelical Lutheran Church in America. Both the actions taken by these denominations and the studies published by them — particularly the studies done by the Presbyterian Church (U.S.A.) and the Evangelical Lutheran Church in America — have received much attention in the secular media. The Presbyterian report in fact became a "media event" in the months before the Presbyterian General Assembly meeting in Baltimore in June of 1991. The church debates over sexuality have produced much confusion and acrimony. They have also illumined special problems in the consciousness of predominantly middle class American Christians, and have reminded scholars and denominational leaders that debates about sexuality take place within a broader cluster of cultural values and interests.

Other American churches watched the sexuality debate but never really entered into it. The Roman Catholic Church has had a dialectical relationship to the debate. At the level of foundational theology or moral theology it has resisted any major reappraisals of sexual practices and norms. Pressures and confusions among lay people required some perspective on the emerging issues, however, so the United States Catholic Conference Committee on Education published a book in 1990 entitled *Human Sexuality: A Catholic Perspective for Education and Lifelong Learning*. This volume, however, is more of an exposition of traditional Catholic moral teaching than a reconsideration of the adequacy of Catholic moral teaching. Although some of the contemporary issues are acknowledged (sexuality of single persons, homosexuality, the AIDS crisis), the traditional norms are affirmed, viz., that "genital sexual union is only legitimate if a definite community of life (i.e., marriage) has been established between the man and the woman" (p. 53), and that "homosexual activity...is morally wrong" (p. 55). Unfortunately, as Charles Curran has noted, "Catholic moral teaching is still based on the neoscholasticism of the pre-Vatican II manuals of moral theology."[1] The Roman Catholics therefore never really entered into the sexuality debate as this book describes it. Individual Catholic ethicists have creatively probed aspects of sexuality issues (one thinks of Lisa Sowle Cahill, Daniel C. Maguire, Richard A. McCormick, and Margaret Farley) but Charles Curran himself is a sad example of what happens to Catholic ethicists who object in print to Vatican dogmatic standards for human sexuality. The norms of heterosexual marriage, the primary role of sexual union for procreation, the admonitions against birth control, and the prohibitions against divorce have not been seriously challenged in Catholic ethical reflection.

At the level of practical experience and pastoral theology, however, the Catholic church has been painfully dragged into a critical aspect of this debate: the issue of sexual abuse by priests. The scandals of Fr. James Porter in Boston received national attention by the media. More and more cases across the country have come into public view. Cardinal Joseph Bernadin of Chicago set a precedent by forming a commission to review clergy files for allegations made about sexual abuse in the Chicago Archdiocese over the last 25 years, and established a "hot line" to the Chancery office for sexual abuse complaints. Jason Berry published a major study on this problem (*Lead Us Not Into Temptation* [Doubleday, 1992]), but that seemed to trigger various defensive responses that the problem is probably not as bad as the public has been led to believe, and that in fact the problem is now under control. In a recent startling article in the national Jesuit periodical *America*, however, Andrew Greely, America's foremost Catholic sociologist, has estimated (on the basis of data from the Archdiocese of Chicago) that the number of priests in America guilty of sexual abuse is somewhere from 5% to 10%. Nationally this projects to 2,000 to 4,000 priests.[2] He does not think that sexual abuse has become more frequent, but rather that parents and survivors have become more willing to come forward with charges. The Archdiocese of Chicago has admitted that it spent $1.8 million in 1992 for settlements and legal costs; on a national basis, Greely suggests that costs to the Catholic church are "$50 million a year and rising." Sadly, he notes, most priests and priest councils are still in a posture of denial about the scope and pain of this problem.

There are unresolved issued raised by this data, such as whether or not celibacy is a factor; whether or not abusers are homosexuals (it seems not, since young girls have been abused as well); and what the role of seminaries is (or should be) in the solution of this problem. Future studies and commissions of the Catholic church will monitor all of these problems. As 1993 has unfolded there have been more and more accusations about sexual abuse by priests. A scandal has developed around the molestation of 34 boys by 11 monks at the St. Anthony's Franciscan Seminary in Santa Barbara, California and in October 1993, there were allegations involving Cardinal Bernadine himself. Greeley has revised his earlier estimates to suggest that perhaps 100,000 children have been victimized by priests over the past 20 years.

It is beyond our interests here to consider this problem in greater detail. For our purposes it is sufficient to note that the Catholic church has been drawn into the sexuality debate at one of its most painful points. The sexuality debate is more than a pan-Protestant discussion.

Southern Baptists held their annual national meeting in Atlanta in June 1991 while the Presbyterian Church (U.S.A.) was meeting in Baltimore. The prevailing literalist-fundamentalist mentality of the Convention was expressed through resolutions and warnings to other denominations "not to forsake Biblical norms" and not to repudiate clear Biblical authority in their deliberations. I participated on the *Today* show on June 4, 1991 with a Baptist representative, and I believe the discussion demonstrated that the Baptists felt sure that they both knew the right questions and had the right answers, whereas Presbyterians (some, at least!) felt that the questions were changing and that we were groping in faith for new answers. The most dramatic actions taken by the 1991 Baptist National Convention were to expel the two North Carolina churches (Pullen Memorial in Raleigh and Binkley Memorial in Chapel Hill) that had ordained self-acknowledged homosexual men to the ministry, and to revise the by-laws of the Convention to make crystal clear that no homosexuals were to be admitted to membership, yet alone ordained.[3] In April of 1993 the Nashville-based Baptist Sunday School Board launched a campaign towards teenagers entitled "True Love Waits." This is being implemented through some 1,000 youth ministers. Young people are invited to take a public pledge of abstinence until marriage and to give testimonies about the benefits of abstinence during youth rallies.

In June of 1992 the General Board of the American Baptist Churches approved a statement that declared that homosexuality is incompatible with Christian teaching. That vote was a follow-up to a "Statement of Concern" that was expressed in the 1991 Biennial Meeting of American Baptist Churches. In the aftermath of the 1992 vote the Office of the General Secretary of the Convention has prepared a list of resources for local congregations which want to study sexuality issues, but it has not taken any advocacy positions.

The sexuality debate in American churches, therefore, has taken place within those denominations that have some theological flexibility. The conservative churches generally have sat this one out, looking on with varying degrees of bewilderment and hostility. The debate, after all, opened up for consideration a number of issues that conservative Christians felt had been long established by divine decree.

Although this book is basically concerned with the experience of different denominations, we should note that there has been one major ecumenical component to the debate: the vote on November 12, 1992 in the National Council of Churches over whether or not to grant "official observer" status to the Universal Fellowship of Metropolitan Community Churches, the only denomination in America organized to minister primarily to gay and lesbian persons. The Council rejected that request by a vote of 90-81, with the mainline church delegations being generally supportive and the smaller pietistic churches, the Afro-American churches, the Korean churches, and the Orthodox church being overwhelmingly negative. The status of the M.C.C. with the National Council of Churches has been under discussion for nearly a decade, but the November 12, 1992 vote seems to have finally resolved it. It reflects the high emotion about gays and lesbians even in high circles of church leadership; we must note in passing that Jews, Muslims, and Unitarians all have "official observer" status with the N.C.C. The United Church of Christ, the United Methodist Church, and the Swedenborgian Church all filed formal dissents to the N.C.C. decision.[4]

This volume brings together the reflections of a number of people who have been leaders in these debates in various denominations. Most of the contributors have spoken about these issues around the country. Several of us had an opportunity to talk among ourselves at the Society of Christian Ethics meeting in Philadelphia in January 1992, and five of us participated in a panel discussion at the American Academy of Religion meeting in San Francisco in November of 1992. This seems to be an appropriate time to share with the broader public some of our perspectives on this debate, as well as our reflections on the lessons that have been learned, and prospects for future ethical reflection.

This book does not offer a detailed synopsis of the various sexuality reports prepared by denominational committees. As such it is not a substitute for these documents, which are obtainable through the Presbyterian (U.S.A.) headquarters in Louisville, the ELCA headquarters in Chicago, and the Methodist headquarters in Nashville.[5] Our focus here is to reflect on the variety of the issues involved, how these issues were distorted by the media, and what the different denominations experienced in their debates over sexuality issues. A bibliography of extended literature on the various topics involved is found at the end of the Presbyterian (U.S.A.) report, pages 89-97 of the second printing.

Of the various denominations which have addressed sexuality issues, five (The United Church of Christ, The United Church of Canada, The Episcopal Church, The American Baptist Churches, and The United Methodist Church) limited their considerations to the vexing issue of whether or not self-acknowledged and sexually active gay and lesbian persons should be eligible for ordination to the ministry. Even when technically this is the only issue to be faced, it inevitably has opened up broader issues of ecclesiology, crises about church leadership, the tension between national policies and local congregational life, and the theological foundations of the denomination. Two denominations — The Presbyterian Church (U.S.A.) and The Evangelical Lutheran Church in

America — undertook broader studies. The Presbyterians identified ten major issues, but the Lutherans limited their initial study to three topics: sexual abuse, gay and lesbian relationships, and genital sexual relationships outside of marriage. A second Lutheran document, revised and recast based on responses to the 1991 study, was published in October 1993 under the title "The Church and Human Sexuality." This document, which is discussed in more detail in Chapter XIV, broadens the range of issues but looks more in depth at the church's concerns for gay and lesbian persons.

Part I of this book focuses on aspects of the Presbyterian debate; Part II contains chapters on the experiences of the United Church of Canada, the Episcopal Church, the Evangelical Lutheran Church in America, and the United Methodist Church. Part III reminds us that there are still more complex issues about sexuality to be considered by the churches, and offers some reflections on both lessons learned and future prospects for the debate.

The United Church of Canada led the way among North American Churches with their 1988 decision that sexual orientation should not be a factor in the evaluation of candidates for ordination. There were many dire predictions that this would lead to the splintering and eventual financial disaster of that denomination, but in fact the Church weathered the consequences fairly well. In the United States, the Presbyterian Report, entitled "Keeping Body and Soul Together: Sexuality, Spirituality, and Social Justice" was the first published church study on the broader ramifications of sexuality and contemporary culture. It drew the most attention and attracted the most heat. The story of the Presbyterian Report and the controversies it raised are treated in Chapters I-III of this book; how it was treated in the media is described by Janet Fishburn in Chapter IV. Four contributors to this volume (Marvin M. Ellison, Janet Fishburn, Sylvia Thorson-Smith and myself) were members of the Presbyterian Committee and were on the editorial subcommittee which gave that report its final form. The Lutheran experience is analyzed by Karen Bloomquist, the Director of the ELCA's Commission for Church in Society and the Chair of the ELCA Committee. The Methodist debate is reported by Victor P. Furnish, University Distinguished Professor of New Testament Studies at the Perkins School of Theology in Dallas, and a member of the Methodist Committee. Thomas G. Bandy is Director of the Office of Congregational Mission and Evangelism of the United Church of Canada and lives in Guelph, Ontario. Ephriam Radner and George R. Sumner, Jr. are both Episcopal priests who are doing doctoral studies in theology at Yale.

All of the denominational studies and discussions have taken place in the context of America's main-line denominations losing membership and facing various financial crises. Some of the strong reaction to new perspectives on sexuality was triggered by fear of losing members and thereby of decreased financial support. Presbyterians in particular also faced the political pressure that their report was due at the precise time when congregations faced the deadline time of when they could withdraw from the Presbyterian Church (U.S.A.) and retain their property.[6]

Most of the contributors to this book are familiar with and have utilized the analysis of American culture and church life done by James Davison Hunter in his book *Culture Wars* (San Francisco: Basic Books, 1991). Hunter argued that the major religious divisions in American life are not found "vertically" by denominational lines but "horizontally" in groups identified as "Progressive" and "Orthodox." These terms are broadly synonymous with what might be called "Liberal" and "Conservative" world views. They cut across denominations, and have very different value systems, and ways of conceiving truth and morality. They lead to different theological views and to different positions on public policy on matters pertaining to families, education, media and the arts, the law, and electoral politics. Progressives in various denominations have more in common with each other than they have with the "Orthodox" members of their own traditions. (The same is true, of course, for those in the "Orthodox" camp.) Similar observations have been made about the polarization of American churches by Princeton sociologist Robert Wuthnow, in his books *The Restructuring of American Religion* (Princeton, 1988) and *The Struggle for America's Soul* (Eerdmans Publishing Company, 1989).

Hunter is not the only person, of course, to use the metaphor of "culture wars" to describe different ideological-political-theological views in America. Pat Buchanan used this term in his televised speech at the 1992 Republican National Convention; he used it, however, to warn Republicans that they are literally at war with the competing powers of secularism, humanism, and socialism. Avery Dulles, S.J., the distinguished Roman Catholic theologian, was quoted in national newspapers in the fall of 1992 to the effect that Christians of all kinds are engaged in a "culture war" against the powers of materialism and secularism. It is unfortunate that he did not acknowledge the positive theological vision of those who oppose dogmatic conservatism. The metaphor is often extended in the political realm to mean whether or not we will have a "Christian nation" — a favorite theme of religious and political conservatives.

As helpful as the "culture wars" metaphor is, it needs to be utilized cautiously because it has the potential to over-simplify what the sexuality debate has been about. It too easily enables people of both sides to develop a "children of light" versus a "children of darkness" mentality. It needs to be said that not all people who dissented from the Presbyterian sexuality report are reactionary or uncaring people. Many supported the broad vision but had concerns about the language and tone of particular sections of the report. Some moderates were troubled about the timing of the report. Some wanted to proceed on many fronts but to do so more cautiously than our report seemed to advocate. "To be right," cautioned one seminary president, "is not always to be wise." Some theological leaders supported the analysis and recommendations but felt that to be effective the report needed to utilize a more traditional starting point and methodology. There are problems and issues described in the report (e.g., how to deal with teenagers, how to deal with clergy sexual abuse, how the church should respond to the AIDS crisis) on which people of good faith can disagree. Many of my good friends felt that the Report needed to be fine-tuned in one section or another. Some nuancing, therefore, and some charity are called for from both sides of the debate. Persons who were most negative might acknowledge that advocates of the report were moved by compassion and justice, and were not trying to destroy the Presbyterian Church (U.S.A.).

At any rate, to note the symbolic quality of the metaphor "culture wars" is to recognize that the sexuality debate in America's churches tapped into a deep reservoir of emotion, and come to symbolize religious and cultural issues far deeper than just sexuality.

Although I have not polled my colleagues on all these points, I expect we would have a consensus on the following observations:

1. The sexuality debate in America's churches has not been about truth and error, right or wrong, orthodoxy or heresy despite the attempts of many to frame it that way. It is rather about differing visions of the Christian life and of the Christian community. It is about two different models of ethics. It is a debate about where to begin, how to prioritize, and how to nuance Christian concerns. Unfortunately Christian people (like all others) often have a tendency to describe the best in themselves and the worst in their opponents, so these debates have usually lacked charity. In this debate people of righteousness have been

confronted by people of purity. When that is the case it is hard to hear others and ascribe decent motives to them. For nearly two thousand years Christians have argued as to how to understand and be engaged with the cultures in which they find themselves. There have always been debates about continuity and change. Views of the Christian life are different for those who are comfortable in a society and for those who are oppressed or marginalized. It is therefore wise to see this intense debate in America's churches in a broader historical context.

2.   It is unfortunate that the issues in the debate were initially named by the conservative side. Janet Fishburn in Chapter IV reviews the role of *The Presbyterian Layman* and the newsletter of Presbyterians for Renewal as shrilly denouncing the Presbyterian Committee and creating a furor even before the report was published. Those interpretations were picked up by the secular media and the theological climate quickly became colored for other denominational committees as well. This polarized the debate at an early stage and made thoughtful dialogue very difficult. I have often said that three of the great metaphysical questions of our time are who sets the agenda, who stays till the end, and who cleans up. The conservative side named the issues, set the agenda, and stayed till the end. The progressives would have named the issues differently but never really had a public chance to do so. The major parallel to this experience, of course, would be national political campaigns, where parties name the issues differently and have different ways of describing what an election is about. Moderates were squeezed out almost from the beginning, and all churches paid a price for that.

3.   None of the problems of human sexuality in our culture is confined to any particular denomination. The broad sweep of issues identified in the Presbyterian (U.S.A.) report, including violence and coercive sexuality; clergy sexual misconduct; special sexual problems of older adults, handicapped persons, and

young people; problems relating to AIDS; problems of sexuality and singleness; and the special problems of gay and lesbian people — all extend across the board in American society. That is why many denominations have had to cope with issues of sexuality, and to face, whether they want to or not, the many painful aspects of sexuality in our culture. This helps us also to understand why Reform Jews and Conservative Jews have likewise undertaken studies of sexuality.

4.   It is far more difficult to work with a denominational committee on sexuality issues than to do an independent study of one's own on sexuality. Virtually all denominational committees are appointed to be broadly representative of theological viewpoints, gender, geographical regions, racial ethnic minority constituencies, laity and clergy, and parish as well as specialized ministry perspectives. Just as the nation is divided on how to understand and cope with sexuality issues, so are our denominations. The critical tasks for denominational committees, therefore, are in establishing trust levels, agreeing on methodologies and the scope of an agenda, and in learning how to reach consensus. No one denominational document is ever exactly as any one person would write it. (Thus is the fate, I suppose, of all committee reports.) The receiving audience, of course, is far wider and more diverse than the audience which responds to scholarly papers. The stakes are higher, and the theological heritage of the denomination becomes a major issue. (A critical related issue is who defines what this theological heritage is and what it means.)

5.   All denominational studies and the debates related to them were only partially about sexuality. They are also about the authority and interpretation of the Bible; about power in the society and in the church; about church politics; about styles of leadership; and about diverse views about how the church should be related to the society at large. Some segments of the church population (predominantly male, white, middle-class clergy) have in previous times set the

agenda for church reflections on sexuality. In a theological climate that is new and struggling with the meaning of diversity and inclusivity, there are major differences of opinion of where to begin, what to assume, and what should be regarded as authoritative for Christian reflection. Those differences are found within denominations, not just across a denominational spectrum.

6.   In the broad range of human sexuality, most Protestant churches in America have traditionally addressed only a narrow spectrum of concerns. The assumptions of our denominations (probably mirroring their constituencies) have generally assumed that participants in this discussion should be of age, married, and healthy. The strong Christian affirmation of marriage has excluded much sensitivity to special problems of single people of any age. Vast dimensions of sexuality which are of interest to sociologists, psychologists, anthropologists and home and family specialists have not had much priority in Christian discussion. What serious students of human sexuality know, of course, is that sexuality is a multi-faceted human phenomenon, and that sexual experience means different things to different people in different contexts. There is a whole realm of sexual experience related to the youth culture and "hard body" sex that understands sexuality as pleasure and fun; this was at one time referred to as "the Playboy philosophy." (Whatever else that meant, it was clearly an attempt to offer an alternative to the negative views of sexuality so often expressed by religious communities.)

There is a whole world of sexuality related to lonely, hungry, isolated and needy people, where sexuality is an expression of many other human needs. There is a domain of sexuality tied to Freud's work (and others) which understands sexuality as a basis for human motivations, behavior, repression, and fantasy. There is a sub-culture that uses sexuality for economic rewards; this thrives off of advertising, innuendo, and pornography. This explains much of the sexual saturation of our culture. "Sex sells," as they say. There are special problems with family structures and sexual behaviors in lower socioeconomic levels and racial ethnic communities, where women often do not have permanent partners, child care is difficult, and life is essentially a matter of survival.

To most of these diverse and complicated expressions of sexuality our churches have turned a deaf ear. Our theological and ideological biases have led churches to prioritize social stability, married life, and heterosexual values. There are reasons for that, of course, but any person who has worked in the field is bound to be concerned that our historic Christian interests in sexuality have been narrow and parochial. The final section in this book points to complex areas of sexuality which up to this point have not been considered by churches at all. Part of the controversy which has emerged from these newer sexuality studies is related to the attempt to open the debate into broader dimensions, and to point the majority culture to the voices who have not previously been a part of church discussions on sexuality.

7.   Finally, we would agree that as important as human sexuality is, it is not the primary factor in the life and identity of a Christian person. It is at best a penultimate concern. The main goal in the life of a Christian person is to be a faithful disciple of the Lord Jesus Christ. That entails many related components: compassion, sensitivity to others, a recognition of our own shortcomings, charity, the capacity to forgive, a concern for justice in the social order, and a concern for what the Bible calls "the least of these." A prolonged and intensive debate over sexuality tends to distort our perspective on where it fits in the larger scheme of Christian personhood. That is why reflections on sexuality from the standpoint of Christian ethics are different from doing sociological or psychological studies for the Sex Information Council in the United States or for the Kinsey Institute. Christian concerns about sexuality are not limited just to

techniques of love making or how to enrich our relationship with a person we love. Our sexuality is a part of our broader personhood, our calling as Christians, and that is why human right-relatedness — justice — is also a part of the discussion.

Let us now, however, turn to the voices of those who have been on the front lines of these discussions. We begin with an appraisal of aspects of the Presbyterian debate: the findings of the Special Committee, the theological foundations of the Report, the actions of the 1991 General Assembly, the role of the media in distorting the issues in the debate, and the way that sexuality issues have continued to impact on the denomination into 1995.

ENDNOTES

[1]"Roman Catholic Sexual Ethics: A Dissenting View," in James B. Nelson, ed., *Sexual Ethics and the Church* (Chicago: The Christian Century Foundation, 1989), p. 52.

[2]See Greely's article, "How Serious is the Problem of Abuse by Clergy?," *America*, March 20/27, 1993, pp. 6-10. Greely's estimate of the total number of priests involved has been challenged by other Catholic scholars as too high; see the critiques by Philip J. Murnion and William J. Sherzer in *America*, April 17, 1993, pp. 21-22. *Commonweal* has editorially agreed with Greely's assessment of the seriousness of the problem; see their editorial of November 20, 1992.

[3]From a theological and sociological point of view, the Southern Baptist Convention is a special story in American Protestantism. Interested readers may wish to consult Nancy T. Ammerman, ed., *Southern Baptists Observed: Multiple Perspectives on a Changing Denomination* (Knoxville: University of Tennessee Press, 1993).

[4]See the news report on this vote in *The Christian Century*, December 2, 1992, p. 1097.

[5]I have described the major themes and emphases of the Presbyterian report in my article "Body and Soul: Presbyterians on Sexuality," *The Christian Century*, May 8, 1991, pp. 516-520. The Lutheran Report, entitled "Human Sexuality and the Christian Faith" has gone out of print but has been replaced by a second document entitled "The Church and Human Sexuality: A Lutheran Perspective. "The Presbyterian Report is now available in a document entitled *Presbyterians and Human Sexuality, 1991.* This includes both the majority and minority reports, along with the official actions taken at the Baltimore General Assembly. It eliminated, however, the 48 recommendations which were in the original report.

[6]Under Presbyterian polity, the property of local churches is owned by the presbytery, the regional administrative unit. Under the terms of the 1983 merger of the former northern and southern streams of the church, local congregations who entered the new church had an eight year trial period to "test" the new denomination, and anytime within that time could withdraw with their property. This was basically a political concession to southern conservatives. The withdrawal deadline and the submission of the sexuality report unfortunately coincided.

PART ONE:

THE PRESBYTERIAN EXPERIENCE

CHAPTER I

THE PRESBYTERIAN CHURCH (U.S.A.) AND ITS SEXUALITY REPORT

Prolegomena: A Few Words about American Presbyterianism

Because of the complexities of Presbyterian history and the existence of various Presbyterian denominations in America, we should clarify where the Presbyterian Church (U.S.A.) fits into the American scene. The Presbyterian Church (U.S.A.) was formed in 1983 with the merger of the United Presbyterian Church in the United States of America (UPCUSA. the "northern" stream) and the Presbyterian Church in the United States (PCUS, the "southern" stream). At the time of the merger the UPCUSA outnumbered the PCUS by about three to one. The PCUS was formed originally in 1863 as the result of the secession of southern parishes during the Civil War. The reunion of these two churches formed a reunited mainstream of American Presbyterianism. This church is ecumenically active in the National Council of Churches, the World Council of Churches, and the World Alliance of Reformed Churches. It sponsors eleven seminaries and has a membership of about 2.9 million people. It is what most other Christians mean when they speak of "The Presbyterian Church".

Several other smaller Presbyterian bodies need to be distinguished from the Presbyterian Church (U.S.A.). The Evangelical Presbyterian Church (EPC) is itself a merger of two earlier dissenting movements. One group was organized in 1937 as the Bible Presbyterian Church; the other was formed by dissidents who opposed the 1983 merger of the UPCUSA and PCUS. This group is theologically conservative. There are also smaller conservative bodies known as the Associate Reformed Presbyterian Church, the Cumberland Presbyterian Church (an outgrowth of the nineteenth century revival movements), the Orthodox Presbyterian Church (founded by J. Gresham Machen of Princeton in 1936 as an outgrowth of the modernist/fundamentalist controversy) and The Presbyterian Church in America, founded in 1973 as a conservative alternative to both the UPCUSA and the PCUS.

None of these smaller bodies have been involved in the Presbyterian sexuality debate. All the shouting, as we say, has been within the Presbyterian Church (U.S.A.).

INTERNAL TENSIONS IN THE PRESBYTERIAN CHURCH (U.S.A.)

The preceding analysis of Presbyterian splinter groups might imply that conservative Presbyterians have gone their own way and allowed the Presbyterian Church (U.S.A.) to express the views of centrist Presbyterians. Such, however, is not the case. There has remained within the P.C.(U.S.A.) a residual element of conservatives, not exactly of the same mind and spirit of fundamentalists, but shaped by a distinct evangelical heritage. They believe in propositional revelation, and the core truth of the ten historical Presbyterian Confessions. They take a high view of the authority of Scripture (somewhat akin to the theological views of Karl Barth), and have generally opposed church union, the church's involvement in social policy issues, the ordination of women, and the church's commitment with peacemaking ministries. Much of that mentality flared in the modernist controversy of the 1920s and 1930s; this group lost these struggles, went underground, but never really left the church.[1] These church members have organized in various groups and collectively all opposed the sexuality report. They have influenced the church disproportionately to their numerical strength.

The Presbyterian Church (U.S.A.) is in trouble on three other fronts. The two streams which created it in 1983 lost 28% of their membership from 1965 to 1985; church leaders lament that but disagree as to why this has happened and what should be done about it. There has been a continuing decline in membership since 1985 as well. (This is, of course, a part of the broad decline in membership in virtually all main-line Protestant denominations.)[2] A second crisis related to that is financial; auditors have predicted an eight million dollar budget shortfall for the 1993-94 fiscal year. That has triggered a major restructuring plan for the church, which will eliminate many staff positions and program agencies, and realign administrative power in the church.

Like most denominations, the P.C. (U.S.A.) embraces a wide variety of people, values, and viewpoints. It is not a homogeneous constituency. There are Democratic and Republican Presbyterians, urban and rural Presbyterians, large and small church mentalities, a few blacks, Hispanics, Koreans, but mostly (95%) are middle-class white people. The church copes with strong conservative sectionalism in the Pacific northwest, southern California, the southeast, and western Pennsylvania. The General Assembly, which meets annually in early June, tends to be more progressive than most local churches and even presbyteries; that adds another internal tension in the church — i.e., suspicion of national offices, Committees, and leaders. This reinforces the desire for more localism, and disparages the work of national committees and policy-shaping groups. It makes many Presbyterians sound more like Baptists than Presbyterians!

This is the church that met in Biloxi, Mississippi in June of 1987, and did three momentous things: (1) it elected Dr. Isabel Rogers, a nationally known ethicist on the faculty of the Presbyterian School of Christian Education in Richmond, Virginia as Moderator for 1987-88; (2) it voted to move the national headquarters of the church to Louisville, Kentucky (in spite of a committee recommendation to go to Kansas City); and (3) it voted to undertake a new study of human sexuality. With that, our story begins.

THE FORMATION OF THE SPECIAL COMMITTEE ON HUMAN SEXUALITY

Why did Presbyterians and other denominations decide to undertake fresh studies in human sexuality from 1987-1992? In the decade from 1970 to 1980 most denominations issued some kind of study paper on human sexuality; Presbyterians interestingly enough issued seventeen such documents. Yet at the Presbyterian General Assembly in Biloxi, Mississippi, in June of 1987, commissioners voted to undertake yet another study. Why was that? Among other things the commissioners were aware that theological, ethical, and medical perspectives were changing in America, and that many of these new factors impact significantly on the Christian understanding of human sexuality.

One of these was the feminist critique of theological assumptions that had shaped earlier church documents. Feminists pointed to the predominantly male language and approaches to the Bible which had been so influential in previous studies. Commissioners were also aware of the rising AIDS epidemic in America; it was pointed out that no previous church document on sexuality had taken the AIDS phenomenon into account. Physicians pointed out that there had been a number of new developments in reproductive technologies that had not previously been included in church studies. Data from sex educators indicated a dramatically increasing percentage of sexual activity on the part of young people. Virtually everyone who had been reading the newspapers or watching television was aware of a national movement by gays and lesbians to assure their human rights and legal rights in a pluralistic society. Those pressures were felt not just in the society but also inside the churches. Virtually every denomination has some organization that is committed to gay and lesbian concerns. Pastors knew that there had been some significant changes in what we would call the "nuclear family," and recognized the church had to have some broader categories to understand diverse living units. For all of these reasons the Presbyterians voted to have a new study on human sexuality and charged that committee to study "the trends, issues and movements pertaining to sexuality in American culture during the last decade, and to report back to the church on what those trends, issues and movements might mean for the Presbyterian Church and its institutions."

The Presbyterian committee, however, was appointed amid great controversy. Not all Presbyterians wanted to have such a committee, especially those who were satisfied with the 1978 and 1979 resolutions of the former Northern (UPCUSA) and Southern (PCUS) Churches, which held that self-acknowledged and practicing gay and lesbian persons cannot be eligible for ordination as church officers. Still other Presbyterians felt that controversial studies such as human sexuality do nothing but divide the church: their vision for the church would be to recover a warmer and more evangelical day, when Sunday school enrollment was higher, youth groups were more active, and there were more Bible study groups in the churches. Virtually every administrative unit of the Presbyterian Church wanted to be represented on this committee, so even the naming of an initial committee of sixteen was a major political process. The 1987-88 moderator of the church, Dr. Isabel Rogers, took six months to appoint the committee. Even so there was controversy that the committee was not geographically or theologically representative enough, and the 1988 General Assembly authorized five additional members to insure better geographical and theological representation. Several people had to resign from the committee because of time pressures, so we wound up with a committee of seventeen. The seventeen members included six pastors, five academics (with specializations in theology, ethics, New Testament studies, gender studies, and American church history), two physicians, one nurse, two presbytery executives, and one woman who teaches sex education in the public schools of Davis, California. The committee of seventeen had twelve married persons and five single persons. It also had two blacks, one Filipino, one Hispanic, one Korean, and one pastor of a predominantly gay and lesbian congregation. (According to national Presbyterian policy, all national committees have to be representative of different minority groups within the church.) More than one-third (6 of 17 people) on our committee represented minority constituencies in the church. This presented a political problem for the Presbyterian Church (U.S.A.), which is 95% white and middle to upper middle class. Our Committee was in trouble with the Presbyterian Church even before we held our first meeting.

It was not self evident when we first gathered in January of 1988 just what topics should be included in our report nor how the study should be organized and presented. We first tried to find a consensus on the most important topics, and then organized into sub-committees and research groups to investigate different topics and make reports back to the general committee. We invited national specialists in all of these areas to come and speak to the committee. We held open hearings at General Assembly meetings in 1988, 1989, and 1990, and in every city where we met. We did not begin to finalize chapters of the report until the last six months of our work.

FINDINGS OF THE COMMITTEE

To introduce readers to some of the complexities of sexuality issues, let me propose an exercise. Imagine that you received a call from the moderator of the Presbyterian Church and were asked if you would be able to serve on such a committee. If you decided that you were interested and had the time to invest, what would you find out? What would you come to know in nearly four years of work that you do not know now? Let me list a few of the things that came as surprises to us:

1.   We were surprised to find out the scope of sexual activity in the youth culture. In spite of the fact that most adults would caution young people about sexual involvement and would generally believe that young people are wiser to postpone sexual activity until they are mature, we found out that over fifty percent of fifteen year old girls in America have had sexual experience. By age nineteen, sixty-nine percent of American girls and seventy-eight percent of American boys are or have been sexually active. We recognize that there has been a major communications gap between middle-age culture and the youth culture. They simply do not start at the same place in reflecting on the nature and meaning of human sexuality.

2.   We found out that there are a number of persons in American society whose sexual needs have never been addressed very effectively by church groups. The ethical focus of Presbyterian sexuality studies has been towards persons who are of age, persons who are married, persons who are healthy, and persons who are white. That bias, of course, reflects the homogeneity of Presbyterianism in America. It was sobering to realize that other constituencies in the church had been consistently overlooked or ignored: young people, single people, racial-ethnic people, and persons with disabilities. Changing demographics now require us to be attentive to these groups in a new way. Consider, for example, the "graying" of the Presbyterian Church. The median age of members in the Presbyterian Church is fifty-five. Nearly one-third of all Presbyterians in this country are age sixty-five or older. (That is why we decided to include in our report a chapter on "Sexuality and Older Adults.") Depending on where one considers the beginning age for church membership, somewhere from one-fourth to one-third of all Presbyterians are single. We noted with great concern that none of the previous Presbyterian reports had really addressed the problem of the sexual needs of single people. Racial-ethnic persons face different family situations and their young people grow up with special problems of

poverty and peer pressures. Our studies also clarified for us that persons with various disabilities have special sexual needs, and hence we included in our report a chapter on sexuality and the disabled.

All of this reminded us that main-line churches have tended to mirror the interests and outlooks of white middle-class America, and that we needed to remind the Church of the importance of inclusivity as it seeks to minister to a more pluralistic constituency.

3.   We found out that we have over-romanticized what it means to be a family. Presbyterians at least (and I expect this is true of other mainline churches as well) have been inclined to envision families as being a father who works outside the home, a mother who does not work outside the home but is the primary homemaker and care-giver, and dependent children in the home. We found out that in the United States today only five percent of the living units fall into this traditional category of families. What we have instead in American society are multiple models of bonded units: we have intergenerational families, single parent families, and women who are becoming pregnant because they want to be mothers but who do not wish to be married. In our society and churches there are gay and lesbian couples, there are the blended families that come together in a second or third marriage, and in which parents divide the children by referring to them as "yours," "mine," and "ours." There are special needs and problems in racial ethnic communities related to different models of families.

One of our committee members, Janet Fishburn, has probed this issue thoughtfully in her book *Confronting the Idolatry of Family* (Abingdon, 1991). She notes that much Protestant thinking about the family was shaped in the Victorian period (roughly 1830-1913), and that this has influenced the way Protestants think about moral issues, sexual role models, and even congregational life. Victorians also had a high regard for their own intellectual and moral righteousness, both born of a philosophical assumption that truth is self-evident (pp. 12-13).

The church struggle to come to grips with diverse models of families mirrors a broader societal conflict. The 1980 White House Conference on Families divided sharply over whether we should speak of "the Family" or of plural "families." It was in protest to the pluralist emphasis that conservatives adopted the motto of being "pro-family" — i.e., against variant family life styles, abortion, the Equal Rights Amendment.

Change comes hard for the churches on this point, mostly, as Janet Fishburn points out, because of our romanticized past.

4.   We were stunned by the scope of sexual violence in America. Although many people said to me that in spite of our broad mandate the only issue that was really going to count with the Presbyterian Church would be what we said about gays and lesbians, we came to feel that the problem of sexual violence is a far greater problem for the churches. Unless one has lived close to this problem, one is inclined to think that sexual violence is a problem of lower socioeconomic groups or minority cultures. We found that this problem permeates our society at all socioeconomic levels, and it is a major problem inside and outside the churches. All major churches, we felt, have been silent too long about this issue, but social workers, counselors, and refuge house workers recognize the scope of the problem. We regret to report that time and again we heard that pastors were not helpful to abused women; their convictions about the life-long commitment of marriage led many of them to advise women to remain in abusive situations, since they pledged to love another person "for better or worse." Clearly one implication of our findings is that ministers generally need more training and information about spouse abuse and sexual violence.

5.   We were surprised to realize the scope of the problem of clergy sexual misconduct. This problem presents itself in different ways. In the Presbyterian tradition it is usually the involvement of male ministers who become

sexually involved with female parishioners through a counseling relationship. In the Roman Catholic tradition the problem has focused on child abuse by priests. This issue raises many complex questions for single clergy about their dating or social lives within their own congregations. This problem has become acute in virtually all denominations because of recent court decisions which have indicated that the national ordaining body is financially responsible in any legal actions which are taken on these matters. Most denominations have wanted to minimize the publicity that has occurred when there are charges like these, but current legal situation now forces many of these things to be made public. When we met in Los Angeles we found out that Fuller Theological Seminary has an institute which is tracking reported cases of clergy sexual misconduct. This is a problem far more extensive than most denominations have wanted to acknowledge, but we thought it did have some special implications for theological education and training of ministers. Hence we included in our study a chapter on clergy sexual misconduct.

6.   We studied the gay and lesbian issue at great length. We held open hearings in virtually every city in America where we met, and heard many moving stories of gay and lesbian persons, stories from the parents of gay and lesbian children, and even stories from persons who had been married to a gay or lesbian person. We came to see that there are many myths and stereotypes which the heterosexual culture has about gays and lesbians, and we decided to name those myths in the chapter which we included in our report. Those myths need to be repeated here since they resurface in virtually every discussion of gay and lesbian persons:

Myth #1:   Gays and lesbians are an urban phenomenon.

Myth #2:   Gays and lesbians "recruit" by molesting children.

Myth #3:   Gays and lesbians are mentally ill.

Myth #4:   Gay men hate women: lesbians hate men.

Myth #5:   Gays and lesbians are causing the breakdown of the family.

Myth #6:   The only thing gays and lesbians think about is sex.

Myth #7:   Transvestites and transsexuals are examples of gay and lesbian life.

Myth #8:   Gays and lesbians do not really want to be that way.

Myth #9:   Gays and lesbians can be "reoriented" into heterosexual life styles.

Myth # 10: The Bible consistently and totally condemns homosexuality.[3]

Our report basically concluded that the Presbyterian Church (U.S.A.) should change its policy about gay and lesbian persons, and we recommended that all members of the church, regardless of sexual orientation, should be eligible for consideration for ordination.

We found out many things in the course of our deliberations on this topic. Probably five or six members of our committee changed their minds as we moved on in our work. We came to regard the plight of gay and lesbian persons in America as a justice issue which impacts on many structures and assumptions in American life. With regard to ordination we basically felt that ordination is a matter of spiritual calling and spiritual gifts. Certainly not all gay and lesbian persons possess those qualities and gifts, and not all heterosexual persons possess those qualities and gifts. We did feel, however, that the basic task of church examination committees should be to establish whether persons are spiritually called and have the talents and abilities to fulfill the course of study that is required for the ministry.

One of the things we found out, however, is that the discussion of the gay and lesbian issue is not primarily a theological or intellectual matter. This topic touches deep emotional cords in most persons. Across the nation many people simply closed our report once they saw our recommendation that gay and lesbian persons should be regarded as eligible for ordination. Anger in the church over this issue shaped the attitude of the whole church towards the report. We saw homophobia first hand, and up close.

7.   We also had to come face to face with the chilling facts of the AIDS epidemic in America. We lamented the fact that so many Christians seemed to think that persons with AIDS are the modern counterparts of Biblical lepers. We thought, by contrast, that the AIDS epidemic has special implications for the church's ministry and its historic senses of compassion and hospitality. We reminded Presbyterians that people contact AIDS through other than sexual means. AIDS is not just a sickness of gay men or of drug addicts; it is found in all social levels of our culture, and in the heterosexual world as well. We have been seeing more evidence daily about this from medical and cultural studies.

8.   A final thing which sobered us was the role of patriarchy in the shaping of American society. We organized our report with an introductory essay on what it is to study sexuality in America at this time, and followed it with ten specific chapters on problems and issues. In the introductory chapter we noted that patriarchy has molded all of us in society and has been strongly influential in traditional gender roles. Patriarchy, of course, refers to a male dominated society. We see many evidences of this economically and socially in America. When I have talked about this report around the country I find that when I speak of patriarchy, most women present simply nod. They understand what that is and

what it means, and have learned how to adjust to it. Men, by contrast, look a little pained and wish that I would move on to another topic. But this is a critical point. A few examples of patriarchy might include the fact that a patriarchal society tolerates prostitution without any sense of indignation. (We found, by contrast, that prostitution is not simply a social structure for male sexual gratification; it is essentially a matter of the economic exploitation of women). A patriarchal society tolerates without feeling offended a billion dollar pornography industry which lives on graphic depictions of women and children. A patriarchal society tolerates gay-bashing, since the victims are deviants anyway. Most dramatically, a patriarchal society encourages subordinate and sexual views of women. We were surprised to find out that in American society today every month there are more copies of *Playboy* and *Penthouse* magazines sold than there are of *TIME* and *Newsweek* put together. Think of what that means for the depiction of women not only for young men, but also for middle-aged men who continue to read those magazines. We believed that as a church the Presbyterians should stand against patriarchy and the mindsets that it represents.[4]

THE SOLUTION: AN ETHIC TO ENHANCE COMMON DECENCY

What can and should the church do in response to these problems? Why is it that our historic and traditional guidelines for the Christian life have not been helpful for so many people? Have we been more committed to the forms of human relationships than to the substance (or quality) of these relationships? Can the Church offer "a normative vision of sexual integrity that applies to the whole Christian community?" We believe that this is both possible and necessary, and presented a new ethical model which we called "an ethic to enhance common decency." It would have the following characteristics:

(1)   It operates with a single moral standard, with the same implications for men and women, single people and married people.

(2)   It is based on the norm of justice-love (or "right-relatedness"); this means mutual respect and genuine caring as ethical criteria for relationships.

(3)   It recognizes the plurality of types of relationships and intimate needs of persons in the Christian community.

(4)   It stands against abuse, exploitation, and violation of persons in any type of relationship.

(5)   It affirms the goodness of human sexuality, of eros and passion, as a part of the human yearning for connection and communion.

(6)   In all sexual relationships it values mutuality, consent, and the bodily integrity of the other.

(7)   It stresses responsibility for our choices and actions, urging that Christians avoid dependency on alcohol, drugs, or any chemical substance as means of facilitating sexual activity.

(8)   It urges fidelity in our relationships. Fidelity means, among other things, the making and keeping of covenants and promises. Fidelity is a moral category, not a legal one.

The goal of this ethical model, we maintained, is to help Christian people become "more faithful, courageous, and compassionate—full of passion for justice, for joyful and loving touch, and for the goodness of life together." (Report, second printing, p. 23.)

Several comments are in order about this ethical model, since it has been so widely misunderstood or ignored. It does move the ethical emphasis away from legalism to an ethic of the spirit. It does not deny that there is wisdom in traditional moral norms; conventional morality, after all, arises from practical consequences and societal needs as well as from theological convictions. Of course there is wisdom in sexual abstinence for teenagers and young adults, for faithfulness in marriage and bonded relationships, and for personal integrity for single persons of all ages. This model recognizes that the different levels of maturity of age cycles requires special concern for young people; it believes, however, that young people need guidelines, compassionate counsel, clear visions, accurate information, and moral examples, not just exhortations or preachments.

An ethic to enhance common decency appreciates that we make decisions about our sexuality in a "moral grid"—i.e., a contextual web that involves other persons. It reminds us that all of our actions have consequences. It stands against all forms of coercive or abusive sexuality. It recognizes that we all have the capacity for rationalization and self-deception, especially in relationships where our emotions are involved, so it emphasizes commitment, honesty, and integrity for Christian people. Contrary to many allegations, this is a conservative and cautious ethic about sexuality issues. It is *not*, as some critics have alleged, a perspective that boils down to "among consenting adults, anything goes." Our committee felt that this ethical model, taken seriously by Christian people, would enhance the quality of life in the Christian community.

At the heart of this ethic is the Biblical theme of "justice-love." This theme summons us to be other-enriching, faithful, joyous, and socially responsible. It invites us to a higher vision of what sexuality means in the Christian life.

It needs to be pointed out that this ethical model in no way denigrates the life choices of those persons who prefer to live a chaste or celibate life. These are viable and honored ways of being in the world. This ethic is offered primarily for those Christians who are or want to be sexually active, as a guide for a responsible life in a culture that advocates and teases with commercial sexual innuendoes.

POINTS OF CONTROVERSY

On the whole, our three years of research taught us that the issues of human sexuality are more complex than most of us had thought. Of course it is true that the most important sexual issues are the hardest ones to talk about. I want to stress, however, that though we came across interesting statistics, our report was not basically a statistical or social science analysis. It was a reflection on sexuality and people; ourselves, our children, our parents, our friends, our neighbors. Why did our proposal for "an ethic to enhance common decency" evoke such controversy? What issues surfaced in the Presbyterian debate?

1.   Our concerns for single people provoked extensive debate. We discovered that primarily because of the church's commitment to marriage it has historically said little about the sexual needs of single people. On the whole, Protestant churches have regarded single people as "half-selves," wandering in the world to find another "half-self" in order to become whole through marriage. We defended the integrity of the single state as an equally valid way of living the Christian life. It has its problems, just as being married has problems. But single people need ethical guidance from the Church just like married people do. We tried to propose an ethic of sexuality that would be just as helpful to single people as for married people. A responsible Christian sexual ethic, we argued, would be an ethic of the spirit rather than an ethic of the law. The ethic to enhance human dignity that we proposed stressed the values of mutuality, bodily respect, integrity of the partner, consent, the ability to be responsible for our own actions, and a commitment to fidelity in our relationships. Christianity has historically been more interested in the legal form of male-female relationships; it has had less to say about the quality of human relationships, especially among non-married people. We argued, however, that Christianity should affirm loving and caring relationships, whether people are married or not, if the appropriate ethical qualities are present. Each person is to reflect on those values and is to

decide before God about their choices. We noted with sadness that so many marriages have lost these qualities, and encouraged Christian married people to work towards egalitarian relationships modeled on partnership. We recognized three diverse groups of single people: young people who are delaying the age of marriage; middle-aged people who have been divorced and living between marriages but often in a serious and caring relationship; and thirdly, older adults, the post sixty-five generation made up of many widows and widowers who cannot legally or financially afford to get married, but who are still in the need of a nurturing relationship. All three of these groups need special care and compassion. We believe that the church needs to show concern for all such persons, and to emphasize an ethic of love, mutuality, and fidelity.

It is unfortunate that our attempt to say a constructive word for single people was picked up by opponents of the report and was made into an endorsement of fornication and promiscuity. Some people even charged us with being in favor of adultery. These charges are a part of the "naming of the issues" problem I discussed in the Introduction. Nothing like the endorsement of fornication, promiscuity, or adultery are in the report. Whether one be single or married, we believe that fidelity to our relationships is the proper Christian ethical model. Much emotion surrounded all of this discussion, however, and we spent a great deal of time trying to make clear just what we were advocating in the way of compassion and sensitivity for single people.

2.   A second controversial matter revolved around our position on gays and lesbians. The ethic of common decency applies to their relationships as well. We were deeply grieved at the scope of the hatred and animosity which has been fostered in our culture against such persons. There is no doubt that our concern for gays and lesbians triggered the rejection of this report at the General Assembly. We did indicate that homophobia is a controlling ideology in America, and it was sad to recognize that mainline churches are so much a part

of that continuing spread of homophobia.

3.   A third point of controversy was related to our sympathy for feminist theology and our endorsement of the critiques that it has brought against a patriarchal society. That was so strong, in fact, that a number of men argued that our document was a "male-bashing" document. There is some strident language in the report about male attitudes and actions, I admit, but much of that relates to the legitimate anger and frustration that women and minority persons have experienced in our society. We did not intend, however, to be anti-male; we wanted to offer new models of masculinity for caring men, and did in fact include guidelines about that in our chapter on "Men's Issues."[5] A point often made by critics was that feminist liberation theology is "Un-Reformed," i.e., incompatible with the starting points of traditional Reformed theology. I would have more sympathy for that argument if any two reformed theologians could agree on just what the "great Reformed tradition" really is. It is true that it includes John Calvin, Karl Barth, Emil Brunner, and Thomas Torrence. It also includes Reinhold Niebuhr, H. Richard Niebuhr, Charles West, Robert McAfee Brown, Frederick Herzog, Beverly Harrison, and Alan Boesak. Critics of the report seemed to forget the great reformation motto *reformata semper reformanda*, "reformed but always reforming," and members of our committee felt that there is ample elasticity within the Reformed tradition to incorporate liberationist views and methods.

4.   Another controversial area dealt with our understanding of the Bible, and with our interpretation of the Bible as a source for contemporary Christian ethical thinking. I noted in the introduction to this chapter that Presbyterians have a number of literalists in their ranks, such persons objected to the overall method of interpretation which we conveyed in our report. Basically we argued that the differences between the Biblical worlds and our world are so vast that one cannot move simply or easily from the literalism of

Biblical text into the complex quandaries of the modern day. How should we today interpret the ancient texts that regard women as the property of men? That describe menstrual blood and semen as unclean? That endorse polygamy, levirate marriage, concubinage and prostitution? Our report offers the following interpretive guideline:

> Whatever in Scripture, tradition, reason, or experience embodies genuine love and caring.justice, that bears authority for us and commends an ethic to do likewise. Whatever in biblical tradition, church practice and teaching, human experience, and human reason violates God's commandment to do love and justice, that must be rejected as ethical authority.
> ("Keeping Body and Soul Together: Sexuality, Spirituality, and Social Justice," first printing, p. 27).

This guideline, while new to some, is solidly grounded in the newer perspectives on theology today. It is consistent with the criterion for authentic, valid religion that Hans Küng, the distinguished German ecumenical theologian, has proposed in his book *Theology for the Third Millennium*. Struggling to find where and how Christians can compare the truth in their own tradition with truth that might be found in other world faiths, Küng proposes the following guidelines:

> a) Positive criterion: Insofar as a religion serves the virtue of humanity, insofar as its teachings on faith and morals, its rites and institutions support human beings in their human identity, and allows them to gain a meaningful and fruitful existence, it is a true and good religion.
> In other words:
> Whatever manifestly protects, heals, and fulfills human beings in their physical and psychic, individual and social humanness (life, integrity, justice, peace), what, in other words, is humane and truly human, can with reason invoke "the divine."
> b) Negative criterion: Insofar as a religion spreads inhumanity, insofar as its teachings on faith and morals, its rites

and institutions hinder human beings in their human identity, meaningfulness, and valuableness, insofar as it helps to make them fail to achieve a meaningful and fruitful existence, it is a false and bad religion.

In other words:

Whatever manifestly oppresses, injures, and destroys human beings in their physical and psychic, individual and social humanness (life, integrity, freedom, justice, peace), what, in other words, is inhumane, not truly human, cannot with reason invoke "the divine."[6]

The hermeneutic of "justice-love" served as our norm for evaluating all individual Biblical Texts. It is equally valid when applied to religious rituals, customs, and institutions. It is fair to say that more liberal or progressive persons in the church were sympathetic to our viewpoint: the more conservative elements of the church object to it on the grounds that it did not give enough weight to the literal meaning of specific texts. I believe that this issue clarifies the necessity for continuing serious discussions in the Presbyterian Church and other churches on how the Bible should be utilized as a source for contemporary Christian ethics.[7]

INTERNAL DISSENT AND "PARADIGM SHIFTS"

These reflections will convey something of the complex areas in the Presbyterian debate, and what emerged as the most controversial issues. Of course it would have been easier to say nothing about these matters. Churches need to provide some clarification of these issues, however, because to do or to say nothing is to convey that the church has nothing to say about these serious matters of human identity, values, gender roles and lifestyles which impact on us all.

I need to clarify that while the Presbyterian Committee struggled together with all of these issues, in the last analysis there was not unanimity on the theological perspective we should employ to interpret the data, on the type of report we should write (should it be descriptive of issues or be an advocacy document?), or on the matter of the authority of Biblical texts. Eleven members of the Committee endorsed the majority report. The members who dissented for different reasons caucused at the close of our deliberations and decided to have their dissents published together. Collectively this constituted the minority report. It had no real cohesion, however, hence was difficult to read. Two members of the Committee for different reasons decided at the end not to endorse either the majority nor the minority report. It was the majority report which was the major focus of the Presbyterian debate.

I certainly recognize that the Presbyterian report is an imperfect document and has all the limitations of only four years of work on many complex areas. I have said many times that the issues raised in the Presbyterian report are more important than the answers that we gave them. I do think, however, that the report points in the right direction, and that all Christian denominations are trying to come to grips with several "paradigm shifts" that have impacted on sexuality matters in our culture. By the term 'paradigm shift" I mean a major shift in intellectual, social, or political consciousness. Two examples might be: (1) The nature and focus of the Catholic Church prior to, and after, the Second Vatican Council. That Council so changed the priorities and theological interests of the Catholic Church that after Vatican II (1962-65) none of the earlier studies or documents of the Church had the same weight or force. There really was a "new" Catholicism. (2) The shift in the Soviet Union prior to Gorbachev and the emergence of the new Commonwealth of Republics in 1991 under Boris Yeltsin. None of the old "cold war" strategies and assumptions of the west are valid anymore. Things have changed, and we need new strategies and fresh thinking. In the last decade the Christian churches have experienced several such "paradigm shifts." The emergence of feminist, womanist, and black theologies; the awareness of the pluralism of our people and of hitherto voiceless persons; the recognition that old views of the negativity of sexuality are inadequate; the need to reach out to a younger generation that is not finding help in the churches; the need to develop a "journey" theology that has the capacity for growth and evolution—all of these movements call us to new modes of thought and action. We can now see things that previous generations did not see. We may have, as Harry Emerson Fosdick once said, abiding stars, but there are changing astronomies. Much of the continuing debate over sexuality will revolve around how as Christians we cope with these paradigm shifts, and whether they will lead us to new light, or to anger, and defensiveness, and withdrawal.

END NOTES

[1] This turbulent chapter of American Presbyterianism has recently been analyzed by Bradley J. Longfield in his book *The Presbyterian Controversy: Fundamentalists, Modernists, and Moderates* (New York: Oxford, 1991).

[2] For more on this phenomenon see Milton J. Coalter, John M. Mulder, and Louis B. Weeks, eds., *The Mainstream Protestant "Decline": The Presbyterian Pattern* (Louisville: John Knox/Westminster Press, 1990)

[3] For a fuller discussion of these stereotypes and of related social scientific literature, see Linda Garnets and Douglas Kimmel, "Lesbian and Gay Male Dimensions in the Psychological Study of Human Diversity" In J. Goodchlld's, ed., *Psychological Perspectives on Human Diversity In America* (Washington, D.C.: American Psychological Association, 1991).

[4] The Presbyterian Committee, of course, was not the first or the only group to note these trends and problems of sexuality in our culture. See the *Christian Century* symposium, *Sexual Ethics and the Church*, edited by James B. Nelson (Chicago: The Christian Century Foundation, 1989), and the subsequent volume edited by Susan Davies and Eleanor Haney, *Redefining Sexual Ethics* (Pilgrim Press, 1992). Many of our concerns about the use and misuse of the Bible were articulated by Episcopal Bishop John S. Spong in his *Living in Sin?* (Harper and Row, 1988), and his *Rescuing The Bible from Fundamentalism* (Harper Collins. 1989).

[5] This is developed further in Chapter XII.

[6] *Theology for the Third Millennium* (New York: Doubleday, 1988), p. 244.

[7] Two excellent starting points for this discussion are Thomas W. Ogletree's *The Use of the Bible In Christian Ethics* (Fortress Press, 1983) and Bruce C. Birch and Larry L. Rasmussen's *Bible and Ethics in the Christian Life* (Augsburg Press, 1989).

CHAPTER II

THE THEOLOGICAL FOUNDATIONS OF
THE PRESBYTERIAN REPORT

The survey of the findings of the Presbyterian Report is one way of understanding why the Report said what it did. At a deeper level, however, we need to consider the theological and Biblical assumptions which shaped our interpretation of the social and cultural data. In this chapter I will comment on nine guiding principles that were influential in the committee's work, and on four theological convictions that guided those members who supported the majority report. All of these themes deserve fuller elaboration, and I have discussed them at length in various lectures around the country. For our purposes here, however, the following delineation will clarify the theological orientation of the committee.

NINE GUIDING PRINCIPLES

1. *Human sexuality is complex.*

It implicates all dimensions of our lives, including the emotional, the spiritual, the rational, the cultural, and the political. Our understanding of our own sexuality is critical for our identity and is closely intertwined with gender roles, i.e., how we live out our lives as women and men in our society. The study of human sexuality has complex anthropological, sociological, and psychological components, as well as theological and ethical dimensions. Each of us is familiar with the tension between our public lives and our private worlds of sexual imagination and fantasies. (Even Jimmy Carter admitted to "lusting in his heart...".) All pastors and counselors are aware of the deep and often irrational powers of human sexuality. The literature in all these related fields is enormous. The Committee believed that human sexuality needs to be grasped in all of its complexity and cannot be reduced to simplistic formulas or jargonistic phrases. A simplistic approach undercuts credibility and does not serve the Presbyterian Church, or any church. Reinhold Niebuhr once observed that one of the great problems of the Christian churches is to offer simple answers to very complex questions.

2.   *Human sexuality has diverse and subtle expressions.*

Our sexuality shapes our understanding of what it is to be female and male. We now know (through reputable and accepted studies) that all of us embody various masculine and feminine characteristics. We have learned that people have diverse sexual experiences and that bisexuality is not an uncommon phenomenon. We know that human sexuality is experienced in different ways, with different emotions, at different times in the life cycle. Hence, we need to be aware of special issues of sexuality in the youth culture, during the middle years, and during the older years of life. Religious communities need to be careful lest their perspectives are too narrow, or not sensitive enough to the evolving sense of personhood.

3.   *Sexual norms are culturally shaped and serve various purposes.*

Sexuality is understood and expressed differently in various cultures. Contemporary North American middle-class culture has a hard time understanding this, but it might do well to recall some of the religiously sanctioned sexual practices (such as polygamy, wife-purchasing, and giving of daughters to strangers for raping) in ancient Israel. Studies in the history of sexuality show that different patterns, priorities, and values shape the expression of sexuality in various societies and cultures.[1] Sexuality was one thing in primitive societies; another in Greco-Roman cultures; another in 15th century England in the days of courtly love; another in 18th century France; another in the culture of American Puritans; and still another in 20th century America. At various times and for various reasons, even the Christian tradition has exalted celibacy and singleness over the married state. Some African Christian communities still practice polygamy. This awareness, widely recognized by specialists who have studied the history of human sexuality, that sexual norms are socially malleable keeps us from glibly claiming that we know a single Divine norm which governs human sexuality in all times and places. At the least, it should keep us from absolutizing the norms of our own culture without careful reflection and close scrutiny. Most of the Christian discussion about sexuality seems to go on with no reference to the vast historical, sociological, and psychological literature about sexuality.

4.   *Heterosexuality is the dominant sexual norm in American culture today.*

The norm of heterosexuality, which celebrates the coming together of male and female for procreation and the perpetuation of the family, dominates our contemporary understanding of sexuality. Sadly, our Committee learned that despite the inherent goodness of this norm, its contemporary expression is powerfully intertwined with issues of power, dominance, and control. The norm of heterosexuality in American culture today rests on the subordination of women, and out of this has come much pain and exploitation. The sexual abuse of women and children, the economic exploitation of women, pornography and prostitution are all tragic consequences of a society shaped by long patterns of male domination. Alternative sexual life styles (gays and lesbians) have been rejected as "un-Godlike" or deviant, while heterosexual deviance is ignored or indulged. Our traditional marriage pattern is still based on the assumption of male dominance; we found that even the strongest marriages often struggle with these deeply embedded assumptions. We advocate a model for all bonded relationships that is based on equal partnerships.

5.   *The Bible is not primarily concerned about questions of sexuality.*

The Bible is a collection of sixty-six different writings, spanning hundreds of years, which testify to the reality of God, God's presence in the world, God's action in history, and God's transforming power in the lives of women and men. Biblical references to sexuality within these broad contexts are incidental and anecdotal, passing references within a larger theological agenda. Our study of the diversity of Biblical writings reminds us that there is no one clear, uniform viewpoint on sexuality which persists throughout the writings of Scripture. (This viewpoint, widely accepted among progressive Biblical scholars, was a basic point of contention between the majority of the committee and two members who dissented from the majority report.) Readers concerned or interested in this point may wish to consult Victor Furnish's Appendix to this volume.

6.   *The Presbyterian Church has many constituencies with different agendas concerning human sexuality.*

These include single persons; racial-ethnic persons; elderly and disabled persons; abused women and children; teenagers; and clergy in need of professional help. Rapidly changing developments in reproductive technology and family planning complicate our decisions. Feminist concerns require women and men alike to rethink questions of gender roles and identity. The Presbyterian Church needs to understand and speak to all these persons, for all face dilemmas important for the life of the church. While our Committee struggled with and spoke to the issues of gay and lesbian persons, it also saw clearly that gays and lesbians are but one of many constituencies in need of guidance on sexuality issues.

7.   *The impact of the AIDS crisis may be the most significant new issue in any contemporary study of human sexuality.*

Although sexual activity is but one way that AIDS is contracted (drug needles and blood transfusions have also been sources of the spread of this epidemic, particularly into the middle class), it differs from other sexually transmitted diseases in that it has fatal consequences and no cure. Many specialists say that AIDS is the great new social and medical fact of our time. AIDS forces us to face the close intertwining of sexuality and death. Our report has a major chapter on this phenomenon, which has many implications for the teaching and ministry of the church. Most middle-class heterosexuals, however, do not want to hear about this problem, and presume that it does not, and will not, affect them.

8. *Biblical ethics and Christian ethics for the church today are not the same thing.*

Biblical ethics, by which we mean those ethical systems found in and related to the life and concerns of ancient cultures, were molded by assumptions that the modern church does not share: for example, the notion of women as property and ancient ritual taboos of purity. Theories of "Holy wars" and vengeance upon one's enemies—which shaped so much thinking in Old Testament narratives—are difficult to reconcile with Jesus' teachings in the New Testament. In recognition of this, the Committee rejected any approach to Biblical interpretation which allowed for selecting biblical texts out of their historical context and applying them directly into the modern situation. While we as Christians affirm the biblical testimony to God's reality, covenant presence, and grace throughout history, we believe that sound biblical interpretation today has to be shaped by solid exegesis, tested by our human experience, and scrutinized for ideological bias and cultural limitations. It is precisely this thoughtful and critical approach to scripture and tradition that theologian Edward Farley calls "critical modernism; " this is, he argues, the genius of the Presbyterian heritage. This distinguishes the Presbyterian tradition from fundamentalism on one side and from secularism on the other. The historical-critical approach to scripture has been taken for granted in Presbyterian (and ecumenical) seminaries for over forty years,[2] and on this point our committee's assumptions stand squarely within the

Presbyterian mainstream.

9.   *The Presbyterian Church (U.S.A.), like all denominations of the universal church, needs help in the matter of human sexuality.*

The physical and emotional abuse of both women and children takes place within the families of the Presbyterian Church as well as in families outside the Presbyterian Church. Our denomination has more incidents of clergy sexual abuse of women (often growing out of counseling relationships) than we can bear to admit. Indeed, the pervasiveness of sexual abuse in our culture was one of the shocking discoveries of our work as a Committee, and there is much evidence that our clergy have not been helpful in assisting women who face this tragic problem. Sexual harassment still confronts women employed by the church as well as those employed in other sectors of society. Most of our seminarians do not take courses In human sexuality, and hence are not equipped to deal with the nuances and complexities of these problems as they confront them in the parish ministry. Our report addresses all of these issues and has suggestions for the church's response.

FOUR THEOLOGICAL CONVICTIONS

1.   *Human sexuality is intrinsically good.*

We emphasized this because there has been so much negativity about sexuality in the Christian tradition. Some of it has been tied to the antithetical way that the church has interpreted "the body" versus "the soul." Some is tied to the way in which our tradition has affirmed the goodness of the mind (our higher nature) as opposed to the stirrings of our emotions and desires (our lower nature), and has characterized the former as "male" and the latter as "female." The report stresses that the church needs to recover an understanding of personhood that has a legitimate place for the erotic and the affirmation of our bodies. We need an authentic theology of sexuality, and our Report tries to show what that would look like. There are at least four books and countless articles which can point the way for this newer, fresher, and constructive theology. James B. Nelson's book *Embodiment* (Augsburg, 1978) is still regarded as a classic in the field for its openness and theological sensitivity. Carter Heyward's *Touching our Strength: The Erotic as Power and the Love of God* (San Francisco: Harper and Row, 1989) is a powerful book, holding that in eros we find joy, a source of knowledge, an essential ingredient in all relationships, a cosmic force, and a motivation for political action. Nelson's most recent book *Body Theology* (Louisville: John Knox/Westminster Press, 1992) calls for a new "sexual theology," not just a "theology of sexuality," and pays special attention to male issues and medical issues which will be a part of that transition. Alexander Irwin has pointed out in his *Eros Toward the World: Paul Tillich and the Theology of the Erotic* (Minneapolis: Fortress, 1991) that Tillich's theology is a rich resource for a reappraisal of eros, especially as opposed to older neo-orthodox emphases on agape.

Much literature from feminist theologians and ethicists supports this shift of emphasis, and this new paradigm will be essential for a more flexible and healthy Christian community.

2.   *Righteousness and guilt, sin and race, exist in a dialectical relationship.*

Those who have exercised discipline and restraint in their lives, and who have been able to lead lives contained within conventional norms, rightfully feel that they have overcome many temptations and that others should follow their example. Church people need to be very cautious about this, however, lest assumptions of righteousness and postures of judgment alienate others who are desperately seeking help. Why is it that most adult persons struggling with sexual quandaries would not think of turning to the church? Why is it, asked Paul Tillich years ago in a famous sermon, that children turn from their righteous parents, and husbands from their righteous wives, and vice-versa? Why do Christians turn away from their righteous pastors? Why do people turn away from righteous neighborhoods? Why do many turn away from righteous Christianity and from the Jesus it paints and the God it proclaims?[3]

We are all sinners in the church, and we all stand in need of forgiveness. We are each received by God not because of our own merit but by God's grace. This sobering realization should mitigate against any condemnation of those who are struggling, seeking, and needful. Church discussions have been marred by the assumption that it is the other, the outsider, who is sinful. Compassion and not judgment should characterize our concerns about human sexuality; this theme is developed further in Chapter XVI of this book.

3.   *The church is called to be an inclusive community.*

The Christian church has historically justified its separation from Judaism on the grounds that in Christ Jesus, the believing community became more inclusive. The famous text in *Galatians 3:28*, where Paul says, "there is neither Jew nor Greek, there is neither slave nor free, there is neither male nor female; for you are all one in Christ Jesus," (RSV) has been cited countless times to justify the many streams of the human family that form Christendom. In recent years, the Presbyterian Church (U.S.A.) has become increasingly aware of the diversity in its ranks: black and white. Asian and Caucasian, rich and poor, and people from all social strata. The urgent plea of gay and lesbian persons related to the Presbyterian Church is that now this broader vision should also include them. In hearings around the country, our Committee listened to the great pain of gay and lesbian persons, and we are now persuaded that the understanding of gays and lesbians in our country has been shaped by many cruel myths and stereotypes. We addressed those myths in the chapter on "Gay and Lesbian Issues," and feel that the Presbyterian Church (U.S.A.) would be more faithful to the message and ministry of Jesus if its commitment to inclusiveness also included gay and lesbian persons as children of God and as full members of Christ's Church.

4. *The church's commitment to justice must encompass sexual justice as well.*

What does sexual justice mean? We are mindful that in the comfortable world of the majority of Presbyterians, many people are happily married. They like who they are, the choices they have made, and the cultural ethos in which they find themselves. We are also mindful, however, that within our culture and our church, many people have been alienated, exploited, marginalized, and injured in body and soul. Our structures work better for men than for women, are kinder to whites than to racial-ethnic minorities, reward middle-class persons and punish the poor, advance established persons and hinder immigrants, protect the properties and cast out the homeless, embrace heterosexuals, and repudiate gay and lesbian persons. Does the Church have any obligation to hear the voices of those who are marginalized by society? Does it have any obligation to work on their behalf as an instrument for social change and an agent of sexual justice? We believe that both the love of God and the church's prophetic call for justice call us to be a force for a more just society. In that spirit, we have attempted to learn from the voices of feminist theologians, from people who speak for minority cultures, from handicapped persons, abused women, young people and the elderly. Eloquent passages in *The Book of Order* call the Presbyterian Church to a commitment to justice. Indeed:

The Church is called to be Christ's faithful evangelist...

...

(3)   Participating in God's activity in the world through its life for others by

(a)   healing and reconciling and binding up wounds,

(b)   ministering to the needs of the poor, the sick, the lonely, and the powerless,

(c)   engaging ln the struggle to free people from sin,fear, oppression, hunger, and injustice,

(d)   giving itself and its substance to the service of those who suffer,

(e)   sharing with Christ in the establishing of his just, peaceable, and loving rule in the world.

Book of Order, G-3.0300(c)(3).

We hoped that the Presbyterian Church (U.S.A.) might be as good as its eloquent language in *The Book of Order*. The Baltimore General Assembly, however, taught us something else about the Presbyterian Church (U.S.A.), and reminded us that in denominational life theological convictions are tempered by political realities.

It is to that memorable event that we now turn.

END NOTES

[1]See, for example, Mlchael Foucault's three volumes on *The History of Sexuality* (Vol. 1. New York: Pantheon Books, 1978: Vol. 2. Random House, 1985: Vol. 3. Random House, 1983) and John D'Emilio and Estelie Freedman's *Intimate Matters: A History of Sexuality In America* (San Francisco: Harper and Row, 1988). Foucault's work is especially valuable in showing the influence of culture on patterns of sexuality, and the influence of Victorian thinking on our modern mores and attitudes.

[2]See Farley's article, "The Presbyterian Heritage as Modernism: Reaffirming a Forgotten Past in Hard Times," in Milton J. Coalter, John M. Mulder, and Louis B. Weeks, eds., *The Presbyterian Predicament* (Louisville: Westminster/John Knox Press, 1990), pp. 49-68, esp. pp. 52-53.

[3]"To Whom Much is Forgiven" in *The New Being* (New York: Scribner's, 1955), p. 13.

CHAPTER III

THE PRESBYTERIAN GENERAL ASSEMBLY IN BALTIMORE, JUNE 1991

> If the issue before the denomination is primarily one of identity, the prominence of the sexuality issue is not surprising. No other matter touches so deeply on people's understanding of themselves. The very meaning and nature of human community is at stake. The sexuality issue has a parallel in the ecclesiastical issue: What does it mean to be the Church?
>
> John P. Burgess, "Conversation, Conviction, and the Presbyterian Identity Crisis," *The Christian Century*, February 24, 1993, p. 204.

THE ROAD TO BALTIMORE

The media blitz which followed the publication of the Presbyterian report on February 22, 1991, set the stage for an intense meeting of the General Assembly in Baltimore from June 3-13, 1991. The Presbyterian report was prepared as a report for the General Assembly. The committee was authorized by the General Assembly in 1987 and mandated to report back to the General Assembly of 1991. Any sanction or endorsement of the report would have to begin with the General Assembly. In the months preceding the General Assembly various conservative organizations in the Presbyterian church mounted a major campaign to discredit the report. The Reverend Harry Hassel of the Highland Park Presbyterian Church in Dallas was given a leave of absence from his ministerial responsibilities at that church to orchestrate a nationwide campaign against the report. His activities were funded by Presbyterians for Renewal. Groups such as Presbyterians for Renewal, Presbyterians for Religion and Democracy, and Presbyterians for Biblical Sexuality rallied their constituencies by offering alarming interpretations of the report. As Janet Fishburn describes in Chapter IV, the Presbyterian Lay Committee, Inc. which publishes the *Presbyterian Layman,* launched a massive attack on the report long before it was published. The moderator of the church, Price Gwynn, a conservative businessman from Charlotte, North Carolina took it upon himself to urge rejection of the report as he travelled around the country even before he had read the report or before the report was published. In the months from February 22 until June 3, 1991 many presbyteries had special called meetings to consider the report and to pass on some resolution to the General Assembly about what they thought should be done with the report. Presbytery executives in the southeast gathered at Hilton Head Island off the South Carolina coast on March 2 and 3, 1991, to consider how they might assure the rejection of the report. Despite a fair and balanced introduction to the report by Stated Clerk James Andrews, discussions there only confirmed the instincts of the presbytery executives that acceptance of the report would be profoundly disturbing to the peace and unity of the church. One attending executive was subsequently quoted in the *Charlotte Observer* as saying "We are going to kill that sucker." Strategies for contacting other church leaders and presbyteries were agreed upon. Many persons present acknowledged, however, that they had not read the report.

An overwhelming number of the resolutions from presbyteries to the General Assembly urged the rejection of the report: the more disappointing thing is that across the church less than ten per cent of persons present and voting in presbytery meetings had actually read the report. Charges were rampant that this report supported free sex, adultery, and promiscuity, and that it denied fundamental teachings of the Presbyterian heritage. Marge Carpenter, the feisty

Texas journalist who is in charge of the Presbyterian communications office in Louisville, was widely quoted for her observation that "the report spits in the face of scripture," although her qualifications as a Biblical scholar are not clear. The church as a whole seemed preoccupied with the issue of gays and lesbians, and whether or not they should be regarded as eligible for ordination to church office. Newspapers across the country ran stories about the report; virtually all the stories focused on gay and lesbian ordination, and the fact that the report endorsed that possibility. All the major television networks gave coverage to the report either before the Baltimore meeting or during the General Assembly itself. I appeared on CBS *Nightwatch* and *Good Morning America* to discuss the report prior to Baltimore, and on CNN and ABC's *Nightline* during the Assembly. Like my colleagues Marvin Ellison, Sylvia Thorson-Smith, and Janet Fishburn, I spoke at various presbytery meetings and to as many churches as I could find time to visit prior to the General Assembly. My phone rang constantly with interview requests from journalists and with requests to appear on radio shows. It seemed like hysteria was moving through the Presbyterian Church. Lutherans and Methodists laid low and tried to learn from the Presbyterian experience. The central headquarters of the church in Louisville tried to distance itself from the Report and from the committee. Only two church administrative units—the Women's Ministry Unit and the Committee on Justice for Women—unequivocally supported the report from beginning to end. Only after the more balanced and judicious coverage by *The Christian Century* in its May 8, 1991 issue and by *Christianity and Crisis* in its May 27, 1991 issue did this firestorm begin to subside. Karen Lebacqz of the Pacific School of Religion, at that time President of the Society of Christian Ethics, answered the critics of the report as she began her review of it in *Christianity and Crisis*:

AT LAST: a report on sexuality worth reading. AT LAST a report that places sexuality squarely within the framework of concerns for justice in church and society. AT LAST a report that names the realities of sexual violence which permeate our society. AT LAST a report that seeks truth by attending to voices of the marginalized. AT LAST a report that tries to "keep body and soul together" by honoring the joy, the pain, the gift, the struggle of human sexuality. Kudos to the Special Committee on Human Sexuality of the Presbyterian Church, USA!

On Sunday evening, June 2, the 1991 General Assembly convened in the Baltimore Convention Center. On June 3 the June 10, 1991 issue of *U.S. News and World Report* hit the newsstands. Its cover story was entitled "Sex and Religion: Churches, The Bible, and the Furor over Modern Sexuality." The eyes of America—the churched and unchurched alike—looked to Baltimore.

THE STRUCTURE OF THE GENERAL ASSEMBLY

Approximately 600 persons from around the church are elected annually as voting commissioners to the Presbyterian General Assembly. A fresh set of commissioners are elected each year. Each presbytery elects representatives from clergy and lay people. Each presbytery is also authorized to elect a youth advisory delegate (called a "YAD"), and there is another delegation of theological students who form a group called "TSADS" (Theological Student Advisory Delegate). They have the privilege of voting as a block on all issues before the General Assembly before the official commissioners vote. All of them seemed intensely interested in the report, not only in its substance. but also for what it would reveal about the mind of the Church.

In order to handle the business that is before it in the way of resolutions, overtures, and recommendations from ministry units, the General Assembly usually divides itself into ten standing committees of approximately 60 persons each. Each commissioner is assigned to a standing committee by computer analysis. The 1991 General Assembly set up a standing committee on human sexuality to receive the report from the special committee: its task was to make a recommendation to the General Assembly as a whole as to what action the Assembly should take on this report. The 196-page report was referred to this standing committee, and the committee had approximately six days to decide how to respond to the report. The standing committee on human sexuality was chaired by the Reverend Gordon Stewart, pastor of the John Knox Presbyterian Church in Cincinnati, Ohio.

The leadership of the standing committee on sexuality was exemplary and notably gracious to all members of the special committee which produced the report. I was invited to meet with the leadership of the special committee in Baltimore prior to the General Assembly to discuss strategies and procedures. Gordon Stewart was very sensitive about process matters, knowing how emotional many of these issues were and being mindful of the deep concerns expressed throughout the denomination. With permission of the stated clerk and other denomination officials, Stewart invited members of the standing committee on sexuality to come two days early to Baltimore to undergo some process training and to get to know each other better. In the course of the committees' deliberations about the report, every member of the special committee was invited to speak to the standing committee. The standing committee also scheduled a time for an open hearing on the report in the large convention center; at that time any commissioner could speak for or against the report. There were probably over one thousand observers in the Convention Center as over eighty people spoke for and against the report in a three hour block of time. A dramatic and highly orchestrated way of presenting concerns about the report came when those speaking in opposition identified the number of persons in their churches and/or presbyteries, conveying an impression that they spoke on behalf of all persons in their churches or presbyteries. Much of this testimony, like what the special committee heard when it held open hearings around the country, was highly emotional. The hearing, however, was conducted with notable fairness, and pro and con speakers were alternated during the afternoon.

Persons opposed to the majority report had apparently concluded in a pre-General Assembly caucus that the minority report, prepared as it was as a binding together of four very different dissenting opinions, but not clear enough nor substantive enough to stand as an alternative to the majority report. A group of conservative scholars convened in St. Louis in April 1991, and prepared a more comprehensive document which they hoped might be considered by the General Assembly as an alterative to the majority report. Several well-known Presbyterian scholars collaborated in the preparation of this alternative report: Elizabeth Achtemeier, Bruce M. Metzger, and C. Ellis Nelson. This 71-page document "fleshed out" some of the concerns of the original minority report and broadened the scope of the discussion. It became known as the "St. Louis Statement," and was circulated to members of the standing committee. It reflected a general viewpoint that scripture is self-authenticating, that clear answers to contemporary sexual dilemmas are given in scripture, and that God has ordained clear sex roles for men and women. Marriage is God's norm for humankind, rules have developed for our guidance, and single persons should make a renewed commitment to abstinence. The statement is readable and coherent, if one agrees with the theological premises.

There was considerable discussion as to what status the "St. Louis Statement" should have at the General Assembly. It was formally introduced by an overture from a Presbytery. It was occasionally cited in the committee's discussions, and eventually included in a list of various reference documents which Presbyterians were encouraged to consult.

I sat, along with other members of the special committee, through virtually all of the deliberations of the standing committee. Most sessions were covered by television cameras. Baltimore and regional TV stations carried daily updates on the debate. There were times when people made emotional speeches and the normal parliamentary procedures were recessed in order to allow others to comfort or hug a speaker. Sometimes the group adjourned into a non-parliamentary mode to discuss matters informally. Occasionally the committee went into executive session. Almost all the deliberations were shaped by the over-arching question of what the church should do about self-acknowledged and practicing gay and lesbian persons. Concern was expressed to the committee by some conservative young people (of a general Inter-Varsity or Youth for Christ theological persuasion) that the report should be rejected because it did not give absolute admonitions to young people. I recall no open discussions, however, of what our report presented as women's issues, men's issues, sexual needs of handicapped persons, sexual concerns of older adults, reproductive technologies, or of violence and coercive sexuality. Opponents of the report generally felt that it was anti-marriage, non-biblical, unreformed, and did not reference enough the classic confessions of the Reformed tradition. It was interesting for me to realize that in these kind of intense debates, if some things are repeated long enough and loud enough it eventually does not matter what the truth is. People who were persuaded that this report is "unbiblical" would never be persuaded of its legitimacy just because we could read at length to them what the report actually said about the Bible and how it should be interpreted. It was clear that differences over Biblical authority divided the committee.

The standing committee was also well aware of the political overtones of the report. There were ominous allegations made that should this General Assembly give any type of endorsement to the majority report, an untold number (hundreds? thousands?) of congregations would sever their ties with the Presbyterian Church (U.S.A.). The committee that prepared the report had also heard many of these things, but we had finally decided it was our task to prepare a report as faithfully as we could and that we should not be swayed by political threats or innuendos. The report, incidentally, was offered to the General Assembly as a two-year study document. Forty-eight recommendations were attached to the report, most of which were supportive of church programs already being developed in the church. The nine recommendations which would require some changes in church policy were recommended to be deferred for two years and acted upon by the 205th General Assembly meeting in 1993.

As I saw it, the standing committee found itself between a rock and a hard place. On the one hand, even members who disagreed on how the church should respond to sexual issues were aware that there was great pain and confusion in the church about these matters. On the other hand, they had to confront the anger, emotion, and political overtones in the church if they even endorsed the report as a study document. The standing committee did what most church bodies do when faced with similar circumstances: it compromised. Under the leadership of Mr. Stewart the standing committee discussed and eventually approved the following resolution as its report to the General Assembly:

The Committee recommends that the 203rd General Assembly:

1. not adopt the Report of the Special Committee on Human Sexuality, the recommendations that are included in that report, or the Minority Report.

2. dismiss the Special Committee on Human Sexuality with thanks and recognition for their hard work and courage, and express our concern for the personal pain they have endured in undertaking their work.

3. request the Theology and Worship Ministry Unit to assist the church in exploring the significant biblical, theological, and ethical issues raised in the church around human

sexuality during this past year. Their work may be informed by the majority and minority reports, "The St. Louis Statement on Human Sexuality," the 1978 and 1979 reports on homosexuality, the "Witness for Biblical Morality," and other appropriate resources. The Theology and Worship Ministry Unit shall report its proposals and plans to the 204th General Assembly (1992) prior to initiating any churchwide program. The resources that they provide shall include appropriate instruments for feedback and shall:

a.   encourage congregations to undertake serious biblical study of the Issues raised by these reports;

b.   emphasize our concern for the importance of our confessions and preliminary principles;

c.   be inclusive of a variety of interpretive perspectives;

d.   be open ended, encouraging the congregations to discover their own conclusions, rather than directing them to conclusions;

e.   recognize that all study, dialogue, conclusions and any recommendations must grow from this congregational process;

f.   consider, study, and engage in dialogue around these issues that are critical in the life of the congregation.

4.   send a pastoral letter to the congregations which addresses these matters:

a. We affirm the scriptures to be the
    unique and authoritative word of
    God, superior to all other authorities.

b. We affirm the unconditional love of
    God for all persons.

c. We affirm that sexuality is a good
    gift from God.

d. We strongly affirm the sanctity of
    the marital covenant between one
    man and one woman to be a God-
    given relationship to be lived out in
    Christian fidelity.

e. We acknowledge the pain felt by
    many persons of every perspective
    on these sensitive issues and the pain
    engendered on these reports, and we
    urge their participation in the
    dialogue and study.

f. We continue to abide by the position
    of the General Assemblies of 1978
    and 1979 regarding homosexuality.

The intent of the resolution was to (a) mollify the conservative wing of the
church by clearly saying that the report should not be accepted, even as a study
document, and (b) to placate the more progressive wing of the church by
recognizing the importance of the various issues named in the report. There was
considerable debate as to whether or not it was necessary to include point (f),
since that would be the case anyway, but the conservatives wanted it and
Chairman Stewart clearly supported it. The resolution of this political/theological
tension (again, a favorite technique of virtually all church bodies) was to refer the
matter to yet another church ministry unit, the Theology and Worship Ministry
unit, with a request that they prepare materials indicating how congregations

might go about the study of human sexuality.

THE FLOOR DEBATE

When the compromise document was presented to the full General Assembly it precipitated extensive debate. Inasmuch as the proposal legitimated the reprinting and utilization of the majority report, conservatives attempted to forbid its reprinting, but all of their parliamentary maneuvers on the floor failed. The motion to insert in the compromise document a statement that all sexual relations outside of marriage are regarded as sinful by God also failed. From the liberal side, a motion to have the General Assembly repudiate the 1978 and 1979 statements that self-acknowledged and practicing gay and lesbian persons would be ineligible for ordination to church office failed by a percentage of approximately 65 to 35. A motion to keep the sexuality report from being reprinted as a part of the minutes of the General Assembly failed. After several hours of debate, the General Assembly voted to adopt a recommendation of the standing committee by a vote of 534-31, or a percentage vote of about 96 to 4. This was widely interpreted in America's newspapers (including *The Baltimore Sun*, *The Washington Post*, and *The New York Times*) as the Presbyterians "overwhelmingly" repudiating the sexuality report prepared by the special committee. What the overwhelming vote in fact indicated was the approval of a compromise document which placated conservatives but which acknowledged the depth and scope of sexuality issues in our culture and in the Presbyterian (U.S.A.) church. Although the report received no official sanction, the G.A. resolution legitimated its continuing use as a study document for those congregations which might choose to utilize it.

The liberal element in the church was disappointed, because it felt that the action backed away from a prophetic consciousness that the General Assembly might have expressed. With the permission of the newly elected moderator,

Herbert Valentine, members of the Presbyterian Gay and Lesbian Caucus organized a demonstration on the floor of the General Assembly after the final vote had been taken. A number of persons marched the length of the convention center carrying a large wooden cross to make a non-verbal protest over the action of the General Assembly. At the front of the convention center, various persons pounded large nails into the cross as a symbol that once again religious people had nailed Jesus to the cross. On behalf of the PLGC group the moderator invited any persons present who wanted to share in this demonstration to do so. It was moving to watch several hundred people join in this lengthy procession. This included many commissioners who left their seats to join in the demonstration and a number of other visitors to the assembly. The demonstration was entirely silent, except for the singing of the different stanzas of the song "We are a justice loving people, and we are singing, singing for our lives." Another stanza was "We are gay and straight together, and we are singing, singing for our lives." This entire scene was captured on videotape and subsequently included in a special video that the church prepared on the sexuality debate at the 1991 General Assembly.

THE AFTERMATH

Inasmuch as the secular media widely interpreted the action of the General Assembly as a rejection of the sexuality document, the conservative wing of the church felt relieved. It was, in fact, taken by conservatives as a major political and theological victory, as subsequent editorials in *The Presbyterian Layman* indicated. The more progressive wing of the church felt, however, that the General Assembly had capitulated to political pressures and had failed to take a major step forward when the eyes of America were watching the Presbyterians. Generally speaking, progressives felt that it was not a radical or inappropriate step for the church to receive a document on sexuality as a study document. In fact, the repudiation of the report even as a study document was an embarrassment for a church that has historically prided itself on being a highly-educated, reflective, and dialogical Christian community.

In an attempt to interpret its action and to put some salve on the wounds of the church, the 1991 General Assembly authorized the Stated Clerk, the Moderator, and the chair of the Standing Committee on Human Sexuality to send a pastoral letter to all of the congregations in the denomination. This pastoral letter was to be read as soon as possible, and was in fact read in most churches on June 16 or June 23, 1991. It is appropriate that we include a copy of the pastoral letter in this chapter. It reflects both the compassion and the perplexity that the church felt about these matters. People who have attended 20 or more General Assemblies have commented that neither before nor after have they attended a meeting of the Presbyterian Church like the 1991 General Assembly in Baltimore.

THE PASTORAL LETTER

Dear Members and Friends:

We, the commissioners and advisory delegates to the 203rd General Assembly, write you out of pastoral care for our church.

We have acted on a number of important matters. None, however, has drawn more attention than human sexuality. We write to communicate our actions and to offer a pastoral word for our church.

We have not adopted the special committee's Majority Report and recommendations, nor have we adopted its Minority Report. We have dismissed the special committee with thanks for their work, and with regret for the cruelties its members have suffered.

We have reaffirmed in no uncertain terms the authority of the scriptures of the Old and New Testaments. We have strongly reaffirmed the sanctity of the marriage covenant between one man and one woman to be a God-given relationship to be honored by marital fidelity. We continue to abide by the 1978 and 1979 positions of the Presbyterian church on homosexuality.

We are also convinced that the issues raised again by this report will not go away. Though human sexuality is a good gift of God, we and our families are in pain. We are being torn apart by issues of the sexuality and practice of adults: single, married, and divorced; teenage sexuality and practice, sexual violence, clergy sexual misconduct, new reproductive technologies, AIDS, sexually transmitted diseases, and the sexual needs of singles, gay and lesbian persons, the disabled, and older adults.

That pain was felt by us here in Baltimore, expressed by people of very different perspectives. Some of these are issues on which there is considerable theological and ethical disagreement within the church.

We also believe that at the heart of the recent debate lies a painful distrust of the General Assembly by many of our members. Often the General Assembly has been perceived as telling individual members what to think. Let it be said that in Baltimore the 203rd General Assembly (1991) heard the cry of the church for an Assembly that listens to the grass roots. In that spirit, we have instructed the Theology and Worship Ministry Unit of the General Assembly Council to prepare a plan to encourage us as Presbyterians in our theological and ethical decision-making. We reaffirm that the church is healthiest when it honors what we Presbyterians have always believed, as expressed in the "Historic Principles" of 1788: That God alone is Lord of the conscience, and has left it free from the doctrines and commandments of men and women which are in

June 11, 1991
Page -2-

anything contrary to God's Word, or beside it, in matters of faith and worship; and also that there are truths and forms with respect to which people of deep faith may differ (G1.0300). This is an opportunity to learn again what it means to be Presbyterian.

In conclusion, we wish to reaffirm that we are all one as Christ's body and while we are diverse, we are one family of faith because of the unconditional love of God for all persons. We welcome your response to our action as we rejoin you this next Sunday. May the God and Father of our Lord Jesus Christ keep us and bless us in the Spirit of divine grace and love.

Yours in Christ,

Herbert D. Valentin   James E. Andrews   Gordon C. Stewart
Moderator   Stated Clerk   Moderator
203rd General Assembly   General Assembly Committee on
                                                   Human Sexuality

A CALL TO SILENCE OR A CALL TO ACTION?

Many Presbyterians, including church leaders in Louisville, thought that the action of the General Assembly would put the sexuality debate at rest. It could be taken off the agenda, and emotions could be quieted. A number of progressive leaders in the Church feared, however, that the General Assembly action might become an ecclesiastical cop-out, and used as an excuse to do nothing. On September 9, 1992, 72 prominent leaders sent the following open letter to the Rev. George Telford, Director of the Theology and Worship Ministry Unit:

Dear Friends:

The 203rd General Assembly gave you a heavy responsibility when it rejected the report of the Special Committee on Human Sexuality and asked you to develop resources for a continued study of human sexuality to be conducted at the grass root level of the church. We write to support and encourage you in carrying out that responsibility. While some may have regarded the Assembly action as successfully "burying in bureaucracy" the painful issues raised, we urge you to take the Assembly at its word and to proceed promptly to keep those issues alive on the conscience of the church.

While the General Assembly and its pastoral letter doubtless spoke for the majority of Presbyterians, it is our belief that it did not speak for all Presbyterians. Many of the important issues addressed by the Majority Report on Human Sexuality deserve to be addressed by the voice of faith. The Assembly spoke wisely when it noted in its pastoral letter that "the issues raised again by this report will not go away."

The pastoral letter made reference to the pain of the church as it discussed the Sexuality Report. Pain was suffered not only by those who were outraged by the report but also by those who are seeking a more compassionate Presbyterian Church, one which is more loving, more inclusive, and more just to them than our church has yet allowed itself to be. We urge you in the studies you produce to speak to all the pain in the church, all the anger, and all the fear.

We agree with many commissioners that a study of human sexuality should be rooted in scripture. We must recognize, however, that the scriptures historically have lain not only at the heart of our *unity* as Christians, but also at the heart our *disunity*. It is often difficult to discern a single voice in scriptural interpretation. As our Historic Principles of 1788 say, "there are truths and forms with respect to which people of deep faith may differ." Scripture does not speak with a single voice, for instance, on the issue of slavery. The texts advising slaves to be submissive to their masters are still there. Yet we believe it was not a rejection of scripture when the church finally took a decisive stand against slavery. We believe it was an affirmation of the mind of Christ, to which all scripture, despite diversity, points. Scripture does not speak with a single voice on the rights and dignity of women. The texts which treat women as the property of men and deny women full exercise of their gifts in the church are still there. Yet we believe it was not a rejection of scripture when the church finally moved to respect women's rights and dignity and to open the way for the full use of their gifts in the church's ministry. We believe it was an affirmation of the mind of Christ.

Just so, scripture does not speak with a single voice in the issues raised in the Sexuality Report. It is possible that what we have taken to be the single voice of scripture has been the voice of certain powerful and hitherto dominant forces in our culture and that those voices have been so loud that we have been unable to hear the voice of Christ. Engage the church we beg you, in a study of the Bible in all its tension and diversity, opening us up to the possibility of discovering new and deeper truth inspired by the Holy Spirit and help us as much as is humanly possible to hear more clearly the voice of the One who is Lord of Scripture.

Believing that the Holy Spirit, as it has in the past, may now be drawing us closer to the mind of Christ with regard to human sexuality, we look to a future day of God's creating...

When the church may be so open to the Holy Spirit's prompting, and faithful to its leading that it may study human sexual and ethical issues, Biblically, theologically, and ethically, unafraid that the truth can do any other than set free all of us whether we be single, married, homosexual, heterosexual, women, men, or adolescents.

When the church may be so blind to sexual orientation, that the many gay men and lesbian women who are ordained and who now serve in the church faithfully, as well as those who are seeking ordination, may be permitted the grace not to have to hide who they are.

When women's concerns, fidelity, chastity, marriage, sexual expression in single adulthood and adolescence may all be informed by not only the letter of the law of scripture but also by its Holy Spirit.

When we in the church may learn the language of love so well that we may study the scriptures and be guided by them in such a way that we may learn from our differences rather than reject and fear them.

May God bless and guide you in your difficult and important undertaking.

In Christ,

Rev. Jon Walton
Westminster Pres. Church
Wilmington, DE

Rev. Fergus Smith
First Presbyterian Church
Philadelphia, PA

Rev. Thomas P. Stewart
Westminster Pres. Church
Buffalo, NY

Rev. Joanna Adams
North Decatur Presbyterian Church
Decatur, GA

Mrs. Eugene Carson Blake
Stamford, CT

Rev. John Macnab
First Presbyterian Church
New York, NY

Rev. Tiara Mathison-Bowie
Eugene, OR

Rev. Robert Lamar
First Presbyterian Church
Albany, NY

Rev. Stephen Montgomery
Church of the New Covenant
Doraville, GA

Rev. Theodore J. Wardlaw
Central Presbyterian Church
Atlanta, GA

Rev. Norman Pott
First Presbyterian Church
San Rafael, CA

Rev. Patrick Wilson
St. Stephens Presbyterian Church
Ft. Worth, TX

Rev. Sidney Skirvin
Church of the Pilgrims
Washington, DC

Dr. Isabel Rogers
Presbyterian School of Christian Education
Richmond, VA

Rev. Richard Spalding
Presbyterian Church of the Covenant
Boston, MA

Rev. Eugene Bay
Bryn Mawr Presbyterian Church
Bryn Mawr, PA

Rev. Gail Ricciuli
Downtown United Presbyterian Church
Rochester, NY

Rev. T. Guthrie Spears, Jr.
First Presbyterian Church
New Canaan, CT

Rev. William Schram, Emeritus
Westminster Presbyterian Church
Dayton, OH

Rev. John Buchanan
Fourth Presbyterian Church
Chicago, IL

Rev. Dr. Albert Curry Winn,
President Emeritus
Louisville Pres. Theo. Seminary

Rev. Dr. Donald W. Shriver
Union Theological Seminary

Dr. Peggy L. Shriver
New York, NY

Rev. Robert Davidson
West Park Presbyterian Church
New York, NY

Rev. P. C. Enniss, Jr.
Bronxville, NY

Rev. Tom Hewger
Presbyterian Campus Ministry, U. of Oregon
Eugene, OR

Rev. Douglas Huneke
Westminster Presbyterian Church
Tiburon, CA

Rev. Robert Early
Vanderbilt University
Nashville, TN

Rev. John Cairns
Third Presbyterian Church
Rochester, NY

Rev. Cynthia Jarvis
Nassau Presbyterian Church
Princeton, NJ

Rev. Joseph S. Harvard III
First Presbyterian Church
Durham, SC

Rev. Stewart MacColl
Rev. Jane MacColl
Northwoods Presbyterian Church
Houston, TX

Rev. Rosemary C. Mitchell
Downtown United Presbyterian Church
Rochester, NY

Rev. Ms. Robin White
First Presbyterian Church
Dover, DE

Rev. John R. Sisley, Jr.
Utica, NY

Rev. Phil Tom
Indianapolis, IN

Ms. Barbara Wheeler, President
Auburn Theological Seminary
New York, NY

Elder Virginia West Davidson
Rochester, NY

Rev. Dr. Howard Rice
San Francisco Theological Seminary

Rev. Dr. Patrick D. Miller, Jr.
Princeton Theological Seminary
Princeton, NJ

Rev. Dr. David Kelsey
Yale Divinity School
New Haven, CT

Rev. J. Barrie Shepherd
Swarthmore Presbyterian Church
Swarthmore, PA

Rev. James Angell
Madison Avenue Presbyterian Church
New York, NY

Rev. Larrimore Wickett
First Presbyterian Church
Deming, NM

Rev. James Noel
San Francisco Theological Seminary
San Anselmo, CA

Rev. Harrell D. Davis
St. Andrew United Presbyterian Church
Marin City, CA

Rev. Dr. Johanna Bos
Louisville Pres. Theo. Seminary

Rev. Michael Dunfee
Waverly Presbyterian Church
Pittsburgh, PA

Rev. Paul Smith
First Presbyterian Church
Brooklyn, NY

Rev. Charles Amatain
Madison Avenue Presbyterian Church
New York NY

Rev. Timothy Hart-Anderson
Old First Presbyterian Church
San Francisco, CA

Rev. Laura Jarvis
Dir Westside Fed. for Senior Housing
New York, NY

Rev. K. C. Ptomey
Westminster Presbyterian Church
Nashville, TN

Rev. Dr. Robert McAfee Brown
Palo Alto, CA

Rev. Cynthia Campbell
First Prebyterian Church
Salinas, KS

Rev. L. Douglas Throckmorton
First Presbyterian Church
White Bear Lake, MN

Rev. Dr. Herman Waetjen
San Francisco Theological Seminary

Rev. William H. Johnstone
Rev. Deborah Block
Immanuel Presbyterian Church
Milwaukee, WI

Rev. Dr. George Stroup
Columbia Theological Seminary

Rev. Dr. Wallace Alston
Nassau Presbyterian Church
Princeton, NJ

Rev. Jean Richardson
Seventh Avenue Presbyterian Church
San Francisco, CA

Rev. Sheila C. Gustafson
First Presbyterian Church
Wausau, WI

Rev. Gayraud Wilmore
Interdenominational Theological Seminary
Atlanta, GA

Rev. Dr. David Ramage, President
McCormick Theological Seminary
Chicago, IL

Rev. William H. Creevey
First Presbyterian Church
Portland, OR

Rev. R. David Steel
Christ in Terra Linda Presbyterian Church
San Rafael, CA

Rev. Michael Hertz
California Pacific Medical Center
San Francisco, CA

Rev. Linda E. Regan
Clayton Valley Presbyterian Church
Clayton, CA

Rev. Mark Goodman-Morris
Rev. Cheryl Goodman-Morris
Valley Presbyterian Church
Portola Valley, CA

Rev. Andrew Robinson
Montclair Presbyterian Church
Oakland, CA

Rev. Dr. John E. Burkhart
McCormick Theological Seminary

Rev. Dr. Donald Steel
Franciscan School of Theology
Graduate Theological Union
Berkeley, CA

The Theology and Worship Ministry Unit did in fact prepare a report for the 1992 General Assembly as to how interested congregations might pursue the study of human sexuality. It was approved with virtually no dissent. It encourages the utilization of many sources and the use of Bible study. How extensively their proposals will be followed, however, remains to be seen.

THE SHIFTING FOCUS OF THE DEBATE

We have learned in the past two years, however, that none of the sexuality issues will go away. The Presbyterians for Gay and Lesbian Concerns seem even more determined not to let their concerns rest. In the last year the focus on the status of gays and lesbians has shifted to the widely-publicized Janie Spahr case in Rochester, New York. Janie Spahr is a lesbian who was ordained prior to 1978 and who has had a specialized ministry to the gay and lesbian community in San Francisco. She was called by the Downtown Presbyterian Church of Rochester to become an associate pastor on their staff. Her call was supported by the Genesee Valley Presbytery, but appealed by her opponents to the Permanent Judicial Commission of the Synod of the Northeast. That group also upheld the legitimacy of the call, but opponents appealed still again to the Permanent Judicial Commission of the denomination. In the fall of 1992 the Permanent Judicial Commission voted 12-1 that her call to the Downtown Presbyterian Church of Rochester could not be upheld, inasmuch as Janie Spahr is an acknowledged lesbian. Because she was ordained prior to 1978 she was "grandmothered" into legitimate status as a Presbyterian minister. The technical issue was whether that "grandmothering" keeps her limited to the work that she has been doing, or whether she is free to accept another call in spite of the 1978 General Assembly decision. The overwhelming vote of the denomination's permanent judicial committee (only one dissenting voice) does not augur well for those who have hoped for a more flexible or open position in the church on this issue.

This chapter clarifies what the 1991 General Assembly of the Presbyterian Church did and did not do. It reminds us that the deeper issues are still unresolved. We shift now, however, to a different focus.

Janet Fishburn analyzes the role of the media in this debate—an interesting, eye-opening, but basically depressing story.

CHAPTER IV

THE ROLE OF THE MEDIA: CONFUSING THE LANGUAGES OF MORAL DISCOURSE

by

Janet F. Fishburn

The following examination of the language of moral discourse used by the writers of the Presbyterian Sexuality Report and that of their interpreters leads to two conclusions. The first is that media reports about the contents of the Report pre-empted serious discussion of the Report. The second is that interpretations of the Report in two unofficial Presbyterian publications influenced "secular" news articles. Both misrepresented the theological perspective in the Report because the Report writers and their interpreters were speaking two different languages.

In recent studies by sociologists Robert Bellah and Robert Wuthnow, both note an ambiguity in the language of moral reasoning since the 1950's. This is especially pronounced with regard to the meaning of "freedom" and "justice." Although both concepts are part of the biblical heritage of Presbyterians, the use of these terms in the Report mystified its most outspoken critics. Their misunderstanding of a theological use of the biblical concepts of "freedom" and "justice"[1] in the Report substantiates Wuthnow's claim that there is currently no language available in which moral discourse about freedom and justice can be conducted.

Chapter IV

I. TALKING ABOUT RELIGION AND SEX IN PUBLIC

On April 21, 1991, an article in the Sunday edition of *The Washington Post* announced, "Church Shaken by Report Endorsing Joy of Sex." A sub-head told readers, "Presbyterian Panel Attacks Strict Moral Codes, Challenges Importance of Marriage." The article was widely republished across the nation; the Report immediately became a hot topic on radio talk shows. The Report, "Keeping Body and Soul Together: Sexuality, Spirituality and Social Justice," was published by the Presbyterian Office of the General Assembly in February and had no official status until a committee of the General Assembly meeting in June acted on it. Between April and June of 1991, the complex 19 page Report was widely discussed in public media, including the bi-monthly publications of two Presbyterian special interest groups.

The June meeting of the General Assembly was carried as news on all three major television networks. A debate moderated by Ted Koppel was arranged for *Nightline*. Koppel tried to help viewers grasp the different perspectives represented by John J. Carey, the chair of the 17 member Tack Force that had written the report, and critics of the report represented by a former moderator of the General Assembly, Charles A. Hammond. There was little common ground for discussion between the two. Carey spoke about the importance of the church recognizing and responding to sexual injustice and the pain of those who experience it. Hammond had been quoted in the *Post* article saying "...their deification of sexual needs...attempted to turn us into fertility cults." He continued to repeat the most frequently heard objection to the report, that the writers did not respect the authority of Scripture, especially with regard to "the covenant of marriage" and "the sinfulness of homosexuality." Carey explained that, in opening the possibility of legitimate forms of sexual relationship outside of marriage the Task Force did not intend to undermine marriage.

The general public was not aware of work underway in the Task Force appointed in 1987 until the spring of 1991. But recipients of *The Presbyterian Layman*, the publication of one of the denomination's twenty-some approved lobby groups, had read in February 1991, that the Task Force sanctioned adultery, fornication and sodomy.[2] Pastors and members of congregations from coast to coast who received the December 1990 issue of *reNEWS*, the publication of a relatively new lobby group, Presbyterians for Renewal, had also read that "...after some discussion the committee concluded that, indeed, its definition of marital fidelity does not necessarily include marital monogamy. Readers were told that what the Task Force said about marriage "...has struck at the heart of what makes us who we are as Presbyterian Christians: our confidence in the Holy Scriptures of the Old and New Testaments as the final authority in all matters of faith and practice."[3]

Shortly after these articles were published, many pastors and session members (the official board) were invited to hastily called unofficial meetings to organize opposition to the Report, then barely off the presses. Early attempts by church officials at "damage control" were just one part of a well-organized movement that led 86 Presbyteries to send overtures about the Report to the General Assembly committee charged with responding to the Report.[4] That many of the overtures were written before Presbytery members had read the Report, indicates near hysteria in a denomination known to value an educated clergy, careful study of issues and democratic procedures.[5]

In the text of the Report, the Task Force recommended that the document be studied by Presbyteries for two years before any official action was taken. The overwhelmingly negative response before the General Assembly met to consider their recommendation represented a major lobbying effort to make sure that the Report would never become official policy or be studied by Presbyterians. The influential articles in *The Layman* and *reNEWS* were reports about a discussion of the first draft Task Force members had seen of the Report. The writers had not seen the draft under discussion. Only Task Force members had read the draft under discussion.

Most of the articles about the Report were published between April 21, the day of the *Post* article and June 12, the day the General Assembly agreed "not to adopt" the Report by a vote of 534-31. Articles in *Newsweek* and *The New York Times*, written in the same vein as the Post, aroused public interest and Presbyterian anger and anxiety. Although the Task Force had carefully defined words like "sexuality" almost no media writers noted the difference between "sexuality" and "sex." *New York Times* headlines saying "Presbyterians Reject Report on Sex" (June 11, 1991), "Sex Report Fails at Meeting" (June 9, 1991) were typical. Writers for the "secular" media seemed as intent as Presbyterian special interest groups on destroying the credibility of the Report.

The Assembly approved a pastoral letter to be read in every Presbyterian congregation in the country the Sunday after the Assembly adjourned, an unusual action for Presbyterians. In the letter, Presbyterians were told that we (the commissioners and advisory delegates) "...have reaffirmed in no uncertain terms the authority of the scriptures of the Old and New Testaments. We have strongly reaffirmed the sanctity of the marriage covenant between one man and one woman to be a God-given relationship to be honored by marital fidelity. We continue to abide by the 1978 and 1979 positions of the Presbyterian church on homosexuality.''

The letter also said that "...at the heart of the recent debate lies a painful distrust of the General Assembly by many of our members. Often the General Assembly has been perceived as telling individual members what to think. Let it be said that in Baltimore the 203rd General Assembly (1991) heard the cry of the church for an Assembly that listens to the grass roots."[6] While it is true that leaders of the newly reunited northern and southern "streams" of the Presbyterian

Church (USA) had been working hard since 1983 to gain the confidence of both constituencies, this was not just a case of distrust of the General Assembly. It also meant that most Presbyterians were more ready to believe public news media and unofficial Presbyterian publications than they were to read the Report before taking action. Given the nature of what was and was not said in the media, only someone who had read the Report before taking action would have known that the discussion of marriage and "singles" in the Report occupied only 12 of 196 pages. Topics treated included "Honoring the Diversity of Families," "Marriage: Strengthening Mutual Well-Being Over Time," and "Respecting Singles as Sexual-Spiritual Persons."[7]

It is inaccurate to characterize either media attention to the report or the action of the General Assembly as a "debate." The difference between what the Task Force had written and what the public believed they had written was so great that there was no possibility of reasoned disagreement with the Report. A comparison of the text with interpretations of the Report shows major differences in the perspectives of the Task Force and its critics about social analysis, ecclesiology and interpretation of scripture. The differences were not issues that were discussed. Before the media blitz began in April, the topic most discussed among Presbyterians was homosexuality; after the media blitz, the issue was identified as marriage and the authority of scripture. The only line of defense open to Carey and the Task Force was to object that they were continually quoted out of context. Finally, the Task Force and the denomination that appointed it were speaking two different languages and looking at the world from quite different perspectives.

A letter from an "interim general presbyter" to *The Times-Picayune* in New Orleans (May 3, 1991) objecting to the "inflammatory" article reprinted from *The Washington Post* explained that Presbyterians have historically held a very high standard for sexual morality. He pointed out that it is part of the historic Presbyterian tradition to speak on these issues to members of "the Presbyterian family" and also to "our society." He had read the Report and said that, "By opening ourselves to talk to a variety of individuals about their human condition, we are not merely "praising the joys of sex" but attempting to speak to those who are hurting and being hurt."

His description of Presbyterian tradition and practice was historically accurate but it was not descriptive of the behavior of "the Presbyterian family" in 1991. Very few commentators, Presbyterian or otherwise, realized that the Report was written in way that viewed the Presbyterian Church as part of a social context influenced by American culture, yet capable of standing for distinctively Christian values regarding sexuality. The writer apologized "if our conversation on human sexuality is misunderstood or misinterpreted by the public." It is the argument of this paper that there is very little difference between the way representatives of the general public — especially the news media — and the Presbyterian Church (U.S.A.) responded to the work of the Task Force on Human Sexuality. This may be a classic case of talking about religion and sex in public. But it was not "public moral discourse."

II. PRESBYTERIAN UNIONS AND SPECIAL INTEREST GROUPS

Many explanations for the unprecedented amount of media attention to "a conversation in the Presbyterian family" have been offered to date. Some say that the media loves conflicts and creates such events. Others say that the new union was too fragile to handle a subject as controversial as sexuality. Some have observed that the new denomination lacked agreed-upon procedures in policy making. It has been pointed out that the Task Force that described the effects of "patriarchy" on sexual ethics became the victim of the cultural dynamics it described. All of these are partially correct. But none can fully explain anxiety so high that otherwise thoughtful and cautious people would so totally misunderstand and misrepresent the content of a Report. Or why national public media writers were so willing to repeat arguments of writers published in *reNEWS*, an unknown "church" publication in its first year of publication.

The controversy surrounding the Presbyterian Sexuality Report is an example of what James Davison Hunter calls *Culture Wars*. As indicated in his sub-title, a part of the controversy is related to *The Struggle to Define America*.[8] Hunter believes that continuing conflict in church and society grows out of the post-W.W. II collapse of the Judeo-Christian consensus in public culture and the subsequent expansion of pluralism. He argues that an important aspect in this collapse is the waning of denominational loyalties and the proliferation of special agenda para-church groups that coalesce around issues and institutions of public culture — law, government, family and sexuality.

In traditional reformed theology, law, government, family and sexuality are regarded as related issues. In a survey of Presbyterian sexuality reports written before 1987, Dieter Hessel lamented the "Calvinist habit of seeking to involve government in enforcing standards of decency in sexual expression."[9] When Presbyterians engage in theological reflection about sexuality they do relate issues of sexual morality to civil law and government. However, "Keeping Body and Soul Together: Sexuality, Spirituality and Social Justice" broke new ground among Presbyterians with a social analysis of cultural values in the related areas of sexuality, family, civil law and church policy. In a time when there is widespread disagreement about each one of these issues, the Task Force addressed four issues regarded as essential to social and economic well-being by both the Presbyterian Church and society. Their opposition came from a coalition of well-organized Presbyterian special interest groups.

> Hunter argues that "The impasse in articulating positions dispassionately has been intensified by the technology of public discourse — direct mail, paid political advertisements, a "sound

bite" on the evening news, talk shows, etc." (He) maintains that the rhetoric required by the new communication technologies trivializes the nature of public debate, eclipses the middle ground position of millions of Americans, and only aggravates the hostility between cultural conservatives and cultural progressives.[10]

A curious feature of the Presbyterian non-debate is that there was no organized liberal support for the Report. Liberal voices were almost entirely silent. In part, this reflects a thirty year period during which conservative Presbyterians had learned to organize opposition to a denomination they regarded as too liberal. The northern "stream" regarded as more liberal in the North-South union of 1983 included former members of The United Presbyterian Church of North America. This smaller, more conservative denomination located primarily in Pennsylvania, Ohio and the midwest, had merged with the larger, more liberal, northern Presbyterian Church in 1958. After that union, conservative Presbyterians in the north acquired considerable skill in public advocacy of their then minority position on the church and social policy.

The Presbyterian Lay Committee, Inc., publisher of *The Presbyterian Layman*, was founded in 1965 to fight the proposed Confession of 1967 on grounds that the Confession humanized the Bible. They took out ads in newspapers to arouse public opinion against the confession. "It was difficult...to separate resistance motivated by purely theological questions from hostility animated by the prophetic style of social advocacy that C-67 represented. J. Howard Pew, one of the founders of the Presbyterian Lay Committee, epitomized the linkage by his consistent attacks on church leaders who "meddled" in political matters."[11] Pew, an accomplished politician in the so-called "public" realm, had been a leader of opposition to "New Deal" politics that led to the founding of the National Association of Manufacturers. In 1939, he had urged the business community to fight back with "a campaign of education in the meaning, the significance, the value of our American system of free enterprise."[12] The southern "stream" also brought lobbying skills to their 1983 union with the "northern" stream. The southern church was also smaller and more theologically conservative than the northern church. But beginning in the early 1940's, a coalition of seminary and college professors had made a popular denominational weekly, *Presbyterians in the South* (later renamed *The Presbyterian Outlook*) an effective instrument for more liberal views on Scripture. Their influence fostered a new biblical theology which moved away from Old School affirmations of a static conception of revelation to the view that the scriptures were a dynamic record of "the mighty acts of God." In time, this understanding of scripture was incorporated in "A Brief Statement of Faith" adopted by the 1962 General Assembly. The Brief Statement included an implicit rejection of the doctrine of "the spirituality of the church", an ecclesiology used originally to defend the southern Presbyterian stance on slavery. In 1861, they had agreed that "no ecclesiastical body possessed the right to address matters pertaining to the secular sphere," for the church and the civil order were "as planets moving in different orbits."[13] The Brief Statement quietly laid this principle aside, saying that

> The range of Christian responsibility is as wide as human life...Christians as individuals and as groups have the right and duty to examine in the light of the Word of God the effects on human personality of social institutions and practices.[14]

In 1973, eleven years after "The Brief Statement" was adopted, the Presbyterian Church in America was formed. Most of the congregations in the new denomination had left the southern Presbyterian Church to defend scriptural inerrancy and Old School theology. Dick Nutt argues that a group called The Continuing Church Movement used the *Southern Presbyterian Journal* to carry on a running debate with the more liberal *Presbyterian Outlook*. *The Southern Presbyterian Journal* acquainted people with the issues, developed a network of

conservatives and told its constituents who the key players were.[15]   When the
southern Presbyterian Church united with the northern church only ten years
later, its members brought a recent history of theological conflict, a capacity to
organize communications networks and a fear of schism with them.

The northern church recognized theological diversity by requiring special
interest groups to report annually to the General Assembly.   This "...procedure
carried over into the re-united church....by 1988, these groups numbered twenty."
Most were single issue groups with objectives as diverse as anti-abortion, support
for gay-lesbian concerns, the eradication of oppression in all human institutions
and the free enterprise system.[16]

Presbyterians For Renewal (PFR) was organized in 1988 saying they
wanted to be an umbrella group that would not be divisive as single issue groups
in both the north and south had been before the union.   Leaders are committed
to providing "information on issues flowing back and forth across the
country...and advocacy of renewal concerns within the PC (USA)."   "Regional
Renewal Advocates work closely with both the national board members by region
and the five separate regional boards/groups."   As the Task Force on Human
Sexuality neared the release of its Report in February, 1991, they joined forces
with the even broader National Evangelical Network.[17]

Hunter asserts that public media are responsible for aggravating the
hostility between liberals and conservatives.   In this case a segment of the new
Presbyterian constituency used prior experience with lobbying and public relations
to orchestrate conservative opposition to the Task Force Report.   Presbyterians
tend to think of public media as "secular" and journals like *reNEWS* as
"religious."   An analysis of the content and chronology of public media articles
attacking the Report indicates that the so-called "secular" media did aggravate
"hostility" to the Report: but most of their script came from *reNEWS*, the PFR
publication.   Articles published in *The Washington Post*, *Newsweek* magazine and

The New York Times in April and May (1991) show direct influence from articles published in *reNEWS* in December (1990) and March (1991).

Members of Presbyterian congregations had received conflicting reports about their denomination from publications like *The Presbyterian Layman* and *reNEWS* for over 40 years. This was not a new technique. But by 1990-91 only denominational leaders and officially appointed groups like the Task Force were still concerned that news be released through "official" denominational channels and publications.

By the late 1980's it was no longer clear to many Presbyterians which were or were not official publications of their denomination. But it did make a difference when they read the same things about the Task Force Report in both unofficial Presbyterian and national news publications.

It was not difficult to create near hysteria among members of a denomination with two strained unions in thirty years (1958 and 1983), a recent schism (1973) and an ingrained distrust aimed at "the bureaucracy." For a denomination trying to find a stable identity in a time of "culture wars," it mattered very little to anyone that what was published about the Task Force Report was selective misrepresentation of the text as a whole. In this atmosphere, Task Force reports to the press and the General Assembly about the work of the Task Force were of very little interest to anyone, with the possible exception of officials in denominational headquarters in Louisville who still believed that official publications are important.

For this reason, a collection of papers written by Task Force members as a part of their study and decision-making process was published in the December, 1989 issue of *Church and Society*, an official journal of the church. There readers could learn that the two most difficult issues under discussion were "biblical perspectives that shaped earlier studies" and "how to transpose concerns for sexuality into recommendations about public policy for the larger society."[18]

One year later, readers of *reNEWS* were told that the Task Force was "...striking at the heart of what makes us Presbyterian Christian: our confidence in the Holy Scriptures of the Old and New Testaments as the final authority of faith and practice."[19] It was implied that the "justice hermeneutic" being used by the group leads to an inevitable discrediting of the importance of "marital monogamy." There was no hint that there had ever been acknowledged differences between conservative and liberal Presbyterians about what it means to say that the scriptures are "the final authority of faith and practice."

The same people who accused the Task Force of being "monolithic" were themselves one-sided in their presentation of the Task Force Report. The following analysis of what they did and did not tell their readers about the contents of the Report will argue that this highly publicized event in the world of religious news was not even a case of two parties talking past each other. There is no evidence that the opposition ever engaged the issues raised in the Report. That an event in the life of a denomination with an unstable internal identity would be so important to both "the Presbyterian family" and the American public suggests that the Task Force violated social and moral norms of great importance.

III. PRESBYTERIAN COVENANT THEOLOGY, A JUSTICE HERMENEUTIC AND "THE PRESS"

When the 1991 General Assembly sent a pastoral letter to all Presbyterian congregations saying that they had reaffirmed "...in no uncertain terms the authority of the Old and New Testaments" and "the sanctity of the marriage covenant to be honored by marital fidelity" they were telling Presbyterians what they expected to hear. All media reported that the Task Force had "challenged" or "rejected" traditional beliefs about marriage and biblical authority, but only church-related media cared about the absence of the language of covenant theology. Earlier Presbyterian sexuality studies had carefully incorporated the familiar language of covenant theology into their texts. Even so, a "northern" General Assembly received but did not adopt a 1970 report containing a broadened position on sexuality. Like the 1991 General Assembly, the 1970 Assembly went on record as affirming traditional sexual norms regarded as "...the moral law of God as revealed in the Old and New Testaments...."[20]

After the 1991 General Assembly, James M. Wall observed that religious liberals are not represented in public debate about changing sexual mores because they are trapped between inflexible moralists and freedom worshipping secularists and have no moral base from which to enter the debate. Wall went on to say that

> ..the Presbyterian Church (USA) tried to correct this institutional paralysis...when it considered a study document designed to confront the inadequacy of both an empty moralism and an arrogant secularity...The inherent ambiguity within such an enterprise was beyond the capacity of the media to comprehend, and as a result the document was pilloried by religious moralists and by secularists, both of whom assume that religion is supposed to condemn and control, not guide and sustain.[21]

Wall was correct that the document was pilloried by religious moralists and secularists alike. *Christianity and Crisis*, the only religious journal to publish appreciative reviews of the Report, also cited a criticism that the Task Force had failed to defend "the justice-love concept over against the Covenant concept." The same critic accused the group of "political incompetence for not taking the family seriously.[22] Yet, it was only in *Christianity and Crisis* that anyone defended the Task Force against charges of cultural accommodation.

Language and Themes in reNEWS and "The Press"

Two articles published in *reNEWS* provided the outline subsequently found in most "public" media coverage of the Report. Their tone was apocalyptic; they said that the way the church responded to the Report was a life and death matter. If marriage was no longer considered normative by Presbyterians, it would mean the death of The Presbyterian Church (USA). Both articles made it clear that the Task Force had "deserted biblical authority," that the Report was "anything but Reformed" and that "committee" members were not representative of Presbyterians.[23] The writers, Betty Moore and Elizabeth Achtemeier, wanted readers to understand that neither the Task Force or the Report they had written were representative of Presbyterians or Presbyterian theology.

The Presbyterian Layman also carried articles designed to convince readers that the Task Force was not representative. Put it was the themes and quotations from the Report discussed in the December, 1990 and March, 1991 issues of *reNEWS* that appeared in various forms in national news publications in April and May, 1991.

When Kenneth L. Woodward and Alden Cohen published "Roll Over John Calvin" in the May 6 issue of *Newsweek*, two of the three quotations featured in an insert were almost identical with two of the four quotations offset in the Achtemeier article published two months earlier in *reNEWS*. In *Newsweek*, the quotes were used — as they had been in the two *reNEWS* articles — to make only the point that "the proposed Presbyterian guide to sexual relations would constitute a distinct break from past practices." Like the March article in *reNEWS*, the *Newsweek* article also implied that the future of the church was at stake. The point of view was changed from the "we" language of the Presbyterian publication to the "they" language expected in news coverage; but the point was the same. The *Newsweek* article concluded by saying that the issue at stake was "how far any Christian denomination can go in comforting people without losing the integrity that makes the church the church."[24]

reNEWS and *Newsweek* offset the following quote to indicate that the ethics in the Report constituted an attack on marriage. "A Christian ethic of sexuality is needed that honors but does not restrict sexual activity to marriage." Both writers failed to indicate that they had quoted only the first half of the sentence. Both omitted the second half which explained why the Task Force questioned the wisdom of the traditional ethic in which "the only legitimate options for moral propriety" are marriage and celibacy. The Task Force did question the morality of absolute claims about heterosexual marriage, saying that a preoccupation with marriage as form can be construed as approval of any sexual behavior that occurs within marriage. But monogamy was not the subject of the much quoted half-sentence. The full sentence in the Report reads as follows:

> A Christian ethic of sexuality is needed that honors but does not restrict sexual activity to marriage alone, nor blesses all sexual activity within marriage as morally acceptable.[25]

An analysis of articles published in *The Washington Post, Newsweek* and *The New York Times* indicates that the Achtemeier article which included page citations with quotes from the Report helped religion news writers locate quotable material to extract from a complex, nuanced discussion of Christian sexual ethics intended to address the sexuality of all persons, married and single, heterosexual and homosexual. The following quote from the Report was included in *The Washington Post* article of April 21, 1990. It is found immediately after a sentence quoted in the Achtemeier article.

> Rather than inquiring whether sexual activity is premarital, marital or post-marital, we should be asking whether the relation is responsible, the dynamics genuinely mutual and the loving full of joyful caring.[26]

Post readers were told that the Report recommended that the church no longer regard "sex outside marriage" as a "sin" because the church is seen as irrelevant to "most people's lifestyles." "Lifestyle," cultural code language for gay-lesbian relationships, is not used in the Report. The Task Force never suggested that the Presbyterian church should consider a different approach to sexual relationships because the church is regarded as irrelevant. The reason for a proposal of a more inclusive sexual ethic was evidence from experience that the traditional ethic did not address the sexual issues of large numbers of people. The Report said that instead of the church acting as "moral police" and "naysayer," it would be more credible for the denomination to "start encouraging responsible, loving and justice-bearing sexual relations wherever they occur."[27]

While Laura Sessions Stepp of the *Post* quoted a sentence that illustrated her headline saying that the report endorsed "the joy of sex," Achtemeier had quoted the sentence before it. Achtemeier's choice was meant to convince readers that the Task Force had written a Report that had nothing to do with biblical ethics since their ideas "obviously" contradicted what the Bible says about marriage and homosexuality. The Task Force understood justice-love to be the primary criteria for an inclusive sexual ethic. She construed the following quote about "justice-love" as an argument against marriage.

> Where there is justice-love, sexual expression has ethical integrity. That moral principle applies to single, as well as to married persons, to gay, lesbian and bisexual persons, as well as to heterosexual persons. The moral norm for Christians ought not be marriage, but rather justice-love.[29]

Articles in *reNEWS* and in national news media cover the same limited choice of topic, marriage and scripture. Critics never told readers that the Report contained discussions of "authority, sources and norms," "the centrality of Scripture" and "criteria for selection of theological discernment."

Articles in *reNEWS* and "the press" used similar language, some of it biblical. As critics pointed out, the Task Force Report was not written in the language of covenant theology. In addition, traditional references to sexual "sins" like "adultery, fornication and sodomy" appeared only when interpreting biblical passages using that kind of language. It was pointed out in the text that the biblical use of the word "sodomite" has been misunderstood.[29]

As was the case with points made and quotations cited, Achtemeier had written at length concerning biblical injunctions against these "sins." She wrote that "...fornication or sexual practice before marriage is forbidden in both Testaments, as are seduction, rape, sodomy, bestiality, incest and prostitution. Such acts are often grouped together in the New Testament under the heading of "immorality." This is the heart of her argument that "an ethic of justice-love, defined by the committee, has been substituted for the authority of the Bible."[30]

"Fornication" is not language used in news media except when someone appeals to a nineteenth century fornication law in a court case. Yet, in "Roll Over John Calvin," Newsweek writers titled one of the quotes from the Task Force Report, "On Fornication." The quote saying that "the moral norm of Christians ought not to be marriage but "justice-love " was offset as an example of Task Force approval of "fornication" in both *reNEWS* and *Newsweek.*

Whether religion columnists for national news media were directly influenced by articles published in *The Presbyterian Layman* and *reNEWS* or not, they all used similar language. Their language and thought categories were not those used in "Keeping Body and Soul Together." None of the five articles under consideration ever mentioned two major themes of the Report, what Task Force members had learned about the pain of oppressed sexual minorities in the church and the amount of sexual disorder and violence experienced in both church and society because of distorted power relations. Topics as well-known as clergy misuse of sexual power, rape in and out of marriage, violence against gay men and lesbians were never mentioned as the "pain" that prompted the Task Force to look for a biblical theme other than the "covenant" to address the misuse of sexual power in both church and society.

Both the church-related and the national news media missed the purpose of a social analysis that implicated church and society in a privileged use of power to perpetuate an ethic that legitimates violence against women, children and gay men and lesbians.[31] Achtemeier dismissed this as "the ideological feminist view that the Scriptures are totally patriarchal, sanctioning the rule of men over women." She missed the point of the social analysis, i.e., the social consequences of beliefs legitimated by social and religious norms, and responded as if the social analysis was a criticism of Scripture. "Surely it is time for the church to put to rest, once and for all, the charge that the Scriptures sanction the inequality of the sexes and the rule of male over female."[32]

The absence of reference in *reNEWS*, *The Presbyterian Layman*, *Newsweek*, *The Washington Post* and *The New York Times* to the amount of injustice documented in the report is striking when compared with two *Christianity and Crisis* articles in which Vivian Lindermayer and Karen Lebasque discussed the importance of these issues to the Report. They recognized that when the word "patriarchy" was used, the subject was the social sources of disorder and violence in sexual relationships as that affects Presbyterians and the society they live in.

Opponents were unable to see that "patriarchy" referred to a culturally shared set of norms and was not just a "grim portrait" functioning as a "single, simple reason" to explain a "massive, deep-seated crisis of sexuality." "Patriarchy" was used to connote the way social arrangements and ideas about sexuality negatively impact the church, the society and individuals in their personal relationships.

Lindermayer recognized that the "justice hermeneutic" used in the Report referred to a quality of God's relationship to human beings that should be embodied in relationships between individuals and in the church as the covenant community. Because she grasped the connection between social arrangements and individual experience, she saw positive value — rather than alarming amorality — in the substantive sexual ethic contained in the Report.

> Central to the committee's conclusions is the notion that sexuality is a gift...in need of integration into the whole of a person's life. The committee adds that integration by developing a set of guidelines and a context for realizing substantive biblical imperatives in our life together. For example, "Rather than inquiring whether sexual activity is premarital, marital, or post-marital, we should be asking whether the relation is responsible, the dynamics genuinely mutual, and the loving full of joyful caring.[33]

National news media made much of the fact that the Report was an immediate "best-seller." *reNEWS* and *The Presbyterian Layman* countered the possibility that the report might influence anyone with their campaign to destroy the credibility of committee members and its Report. Presbyterians For Renewal (PFR), the source of *reNEWS*, was part of a network of approved church lobby groups that carried out a variety of strategies to convince Presbyterian people that nothing said by the Task Force majority should be taken seriously. Another such group, Presbyterians for Biblical Morality, supplied commentary to pastors for use in congregational newsletters and in a letter writing campaign to Task Force members. They also collected 2,140 resolutions from sessions who signed a "covenant" called "Witness to Biblical Morality." The resolutions were presented to the General Assembly as evidence of the importance of the "covenant of marriage" to Presbyterians. PFR and other members of the National Evangelical Network successfully lobbied Presbyterian pastors, their sessions, denominational officials and the General Assembly. They were taken so seriously by public media that both *The New York Times* and *Newsweek* repeated (without citation) their prediction that chances of the Report being accepted were exceedingly slim.

IV. THE SOCIAL FUNCTION OF
PRESBYTERIAN COVENANT THEOLOGY

It would be an understatement to say that the Presbyterian Sexuality Report "touched a nerve." Why were Presbyterian special interest groups, with help from "the press," able to evoke massive anxiety among Presbyterians as well as segments of the non-Presbyterian public? Both church-related and "public" or "secular" media used the same kind of language; both failed to grasp the theological perspective reflected in the language of the Report.

The Presbyterian Church as Moral Guardian of a Democratic State

A recent report about a research project designed to help Protestants link faith and daily life described the major life issue of participants as "stress-filled lives." When they talked about this, they could identify problems they faced as institutional and structural, yet believed that the only possible response was individual action. Participants had no language for social analysis; they resisted discussions of structural relationships and social confrontation. This reaction suggests that a typical group of Protestant laity were far less interested in the prophetic and justice dimensions of ministry than in help with the way institutions affect them as individuals.[34]

Presbyterian failure to grasp the role of the social analysis in the Task Force Report suggests that they, too, have no language for social analysis. Although the northern "stream" of the Presbyterian Church adopted a Confession oriented toward justice in 1967, when the Task Force developed the implications of justice as a biblical theme guiding theological reflection about sexual ethics the phrase "justice-love" was treated with disbelief and derision. The fact that "justice-love" was defined as "right-relatedness" and the terms used interchangeably throughout the Report made no difference. Justice does not seem to exist in the Presbyterian theological vocabulary.

That does not explain why Peter Steinfels of *The New York Times* ridiculed the language of the Report, saying it "begins at first to cloy, then to stick like molasses." Steinfels claimed that "The manner in which "Body and Soul" argues its case...may...go a long way to explaining why this product of three years work will be virtually dead on arrival when...Presbyterians gather...for the General Assembly." Taking his cues from opposition leader Charles A. Hammond who suggested that the Report had a fundamentalist cast to it, Steinfels told readers that the Report was written in what, "by its own terms, is a patriarchal style. Its ideological framework totally controls the terms of the discussion."[35] It is one thing for a member of the press to present two sides to the internal conflict of a religious group; it is another to join one side against the other.

Perhaps the reason why some of the news media appeared to be rooting for the opposition is that, like Presbyterians, they believe that if "the church" is not the guardian of moral standards, it will negatively impact social order. They do not have to agree with Presbyterian theology, or even claim that the ideas are biblical, to agree that were marriage no longer regarded as the normative form for sexual relationships, social chaos might prevail. Put another way, they may believe that social stability depends on — as Woodward said — "the church being the church." That writers in a national news magazine would defend a particular role of "the church" in society suggests that this particular understanding is of great importance to them.

Presbyterians in "America" believe that the democratic form of government is patterned after the Presbyterian form of government. In that sense, they regard themselves as almost prototypical Americans and as guardians of the representative process. Many Presbyterians still harbor a hope that "America" is a Christian nation which, if "renewed," will return to the prosperity of the post W.W. II years. The 1950's and early 1960's were a time when their self-image as guardians of morality in a democratic society was reinforced by the public visibility of Presbyterians John Foster Dulles and Robert McNamara. At that time the northern "stream" opened a Washington office as a communication network between the Presbyterian Church, its constituents and the federal government. It was also a time of church growth.

David B. Watermulder, retiring President of the Board of Princeton Seminary reminisced recently about the early 1960's. "JFK was President and there was a new feeling in America...as if we were going to change the world. The churches were booming. The Presbyterian Church was increasing in membership and we were making money and spending it for missions around the world. It was a great time."[36]

This is not just the attitude of an older generation. Watermulder's son, Paul, a founder of Presbyterians For Renewal hopes to rebuild the confidence of members in the denomination. PFR is committed to "a covenant of renewal" through evangelism and "making disciples among all peoples...." To achieve this, other founders say they must "overcome distrust of the denomination," "come together around a common vision and implement it," and "renew our commitment to the Scriptures as God s infallible word...."[37]

The group articulates belief that the Presbyterian Church is or should be a positive influence in society. Their emphasis on membership growth implies that the formative power of the Presbyterian Church in American culture depends to some extent on how many Americans are also Presbyterians. Their candidate for moderator of the 1991 General Assembly said he was "thrilled" with the Book of Confessions, which brings into "proper holistic balance the relationship between a spiritual, evangelistic message and the social implications of that message. Moreover, since many of the key leaders of our society are a part of our Presbyterian Church, we can make much greater impact on our society than our numbers might suggest — if we get the nerve to move forward in strong positive ways."[38]

Like laity who understand their own life issues as institutional but regard the solution to be individual action, PFR leaders believe that Presbyterians influence society as individuals. The response of their writers to the Task Force Report and their extensive lobbying indicates that they see the Presbyterian Church as a guardian of a particular kind of sexual morality without which American society would fall into disorder and chaos. When they say that defeating the Report is a life and death matter for Presbyterians, this is not hyperbole. Presbyterian identity is linked to society in a way that recalls historian Sidney Mead's observation that America is a nation with the soul of a church. For many Presbyterians, this means that "the state" takes care of the material realm and "the church" takes care of the spiritual realm. From this stance, when half of this partnership flourishes, so does the other but the reverse is also true. if one degenerates, so does the other.

Less than three months after the 1991 General Assembly, the Stated Clerk filed an amicus brief in the Supreme Court of Kentucky on behalf of The Presbyterian Church. He was implementing official policy which says that the Presbyterian Church will work to eliminate "laws which criminalize private sexual acts between consenting adults." The church is on record as opposing civil law regarding adultery, fornication and sodomy as an infringement of civil rights. At the same time that official policy says this should not be civil law, the same acts between consenting Presbyterians are considered "sinful." That many Presbyterians do not distinguish civil law from church law was born out by the anguished but predictable response to the clerk's action.

A letter from a Texas pastor to *The News of the Presbyterian Church (USA)* said, "...here again we are witnessing human reasoning and intellectual deliberation that, as usual, have a way of going against the revealed will of God.

How can God bless our national church when so much that is decided and acted on is against His will?"[39]

While not all Presbyterians would agree with articles published in *The Presbyterian Layman* about the moral deterioration of American culture, approximately 13% of 2.9 million members receive the publication. After the General Assembly, the publisher sent out 400,000 questionnaires saying (in advance) that the results would tell the leaders of the Presbyterian Church how Presbyterians really feel about homosexuality. The same issue featured an article titled "Making Virtue Respectable Again." The article was originally a speech given to executives of the Sunstrand Corporation.

The last sentence of the speech summarizes a perspective on democracy with which many people, including Presbyterians, would be comfortable. "A free society is totally dependent upon people who voluntarily live by codes of moral conduct. That will not come by government fiat, but from the self-disciplined behavior of a people whose faith in God has been restored. Only then can virtue be made respectable again."[40] Among the threats to "the virtues of the American Republic now under siege," he included attacks on patriotism and on the family. Although Presbyterians For Renewal present themselves as moderates and want to distance themselves from a publication like *The Presbyterian Layman*, this line of reasoning about "a free society" is similar to their understanding of the relationship of church and state. It is also a theme found in early national documents concerning the role of religion in a democracy.

"The Covenant" as a Theological, Social and Political Norm

During the last twenty years there have been only two areas of Presbyterian policy in which proposals for change have been consistently rejected by General Assemblies. They are sexuality and proposals that "encourage

conscientious objection."[41]   The Task Force Report was published during the
enormous burst of patriotism surrounding The Gulf War. Given the importance
of patriotism and "the" traditional moral code to the Presbyterian understanding
of the role of "the church" in American society, when the Task Force violated a
theological norm, it also violated a social and political norm.

To question marriage as the exclusive sexual relationship among
Presbyterians is to challenge the authority of Scripture and the viability of the
American democracy. PFR members are conservative to moderate Presbyterians
who may not follow absolutist principles on every theological issue. But their
response to the Task Force Report indicates that there are no possible alternatives
to marriage as the one, unchanging biblical standard for heterosexual morality.
However, if the belief that the health and prosperity of society is directly linked
to this standard of sexual morality, then their understanding of the way the world
works stands or falls on this issue. It is not possible for them to imagine any
alternatives to what they regard as moral absolutes that are declared so by the
"authority" of scripture. From this point of view, an ethic that questions any of
the givens in "the" moral code is, by definition secular, humanistic, relativistic
or situational. Every theology has at least one absolute, non-negotiable principle:
The Presbyterian principle defended by the successful opposition movement was
heterosexual marriage.

Presbyterians in America have reduced a historic covenant theology to a
set of moral absolutes which they often refer to only as "the marriage covenant."
References to the church as "a covenant community' can imply that since the
church is part of God's eternal order it is not also located in a culture which
inevitably influences its structures and ideas. The coalition of pressure groups
opposing the Task Force Report evoked a response from Presbyterians who do
not seem to regard their church as a social institution. This implicit affirmation
of the old southern principle of a church whose power is exclusively "spiritual"

precludes the possibility of recognizing that the social context or life experience of people who are the church does influence their interpretation of scripture.

From an absolutist point of view, if the church sanctions one exception to "God's moral law," it may as well sanction all exceptions. Since 1970, the Presbyterian Church has not sanctioned any exceptions to "the moral law of God as revealed in the Old and New Testaments". However, in 1978, the denomination added to "the moral law of God" as found in scripture when the General Assembly voted to refuse to ordain "practicing" homosexuals. This action — in effect — wrote civil law on sodomy into church law.[42]   Many Presbyterians now believe that homosexual acts are both a "sin" and a crime.

Anthropology and Ecclesiology in Covenant Theology

The conservative perspective on sexual ethics depends on believing that individuals choose their behavior, that free will is essential to salvation. Freedom of choice and freedom of religion in the American democracy are essential to an anthropology which depends on exercising will power. Thus, if people choose to commit "sins," they should suffer the consequences. At the level of the role of the church in society, this implies that the God of the covenant will punish a society that violates "the moral laws of God." The belief system of this modern covenant theology legitimates the connection between God's blessing and "the" code of biblical morality, economic expansion, and a growing church.

The 1991 Report on sexuality was influenced by the Presbyterian sexuality reports of 1970, 1974 and 1980 in which more attention was given to human experience — the social and behavioral sciences had been incorporated into theological reflection. More emphasis than ever before was given to theological reflection in dialogue with human experience in the 1991 Report. Yet, this was also the first sexuality report to use a feminist/liberation rather than some version of neo-orthodox theology.[43]   In making this choice, the Task Force distanced themselves theologically from both conservatives who had never been comfortable with the social issue stance of neo-orthodoxy and from neo-orthodox liberals who were not comfortable with a social analysis of culture.

The covenant theology of the 1970 sexuality report written by liberals had a Barthian flavor. A high doctrine of the church prevailed even though critics said there was no distinction between "the covenant community" and non-Christians because the writers had introduced prevailing sexual mores into Christian ethics. Conservative opponents of sexuality reports since 1970 have regarded any proposed change or expansion of what they take to be "the moral law of God" as cultural accommodation. However, liberals and conservatives did not disagree about the ecclesiology of the 1970 report which included an analysis of a changing society but not a social analysis of culture. In other words, it was not suggested that the church was deeply influenced in its sexual ethics by the values of its culture. The Presbyterian self-image of playing an essential role as the moral guardian of society was not challenged.

The covenant theology of the 1970 report had a Niebuhrian flavor since the focus of discussion remained the sexual behavior of individuals in a model of traditional Protestant virtue. Although Niebuhr was preoccupied with social issues, his anthropology depends on individual choice expressed as personal morality in sexual and family relations. This combination of a Barthian ecclesiology with a Niebuhrian concern for social issues allowed Presbyterian liberals to express convictions about the social role of the church while theologically affirming the "otherness" of the church. At this point, conservative and liberal Presbyterians had an anthropology in common: both relied on the free will of individuals in a free society. They differed primarily about the use of scripture in theological reflection, sexual ethics and the role of the church in society.

Although a feminist analysis of patriarchy was used in a study paper on pornography adopted for study (without protest) by the 1988 General Assembly, the analysis did not charge the church with complicity in a patriarchal society. Instead it described "the shalom of the covenant community" called to "witness to God's intention for the whole created order."[45] Though there was much discussion of sexual exploitation, violence and "victims of a patriarchal, alienated society," the writer always suggested that it was the task of the Christian community "to change the systems that debase and distort the life of persons and communities."

Neo-orthodoxy remained intact. The idea that the church itself might be in collusion with the social systems that alienate and debase, while implicit, was not developed. It was not suggested that the church was a sinful social institution.

It was the consistent use of a liberation social analysis that was new to conservative and liberal Presbyterians in 1991. In usual Presbyterian fashion, the report began with a description of the present situation and saw a "crisis." Citing the social and economic analysis found in the pornography report of 1988, the writer went on to make another typical observation, that "The Presbyterian Church stands in a crucial position." This was followed by a major departure from all spiritualized notions of the church as "other."

> ...the church must own up to and repent of its own historical involvement in the perpetuation of patriarchal structures now being exposed and shaken everywhere....We face a moral choice. On the one hand, the Presbyterian church can retreat into silence, or, worse yet, participate in a reactionary effort to buttress traditional patterns of oppression and sexual exclusion. On the other hand, the church can work diligently to dismantle this dehumanizing edifice. With courage and intelligence, the church can extend to people struggling with questions of sexuality the church's long-standing commitment to human liberation and justice.[44]

Having said this, the text continues by affirming belief that the church can be different if it will renew a Christian understanding of personhood and community, reorder the internal life of the church and offer resources and energy for dismantling the effects of patriarchy in other social institutions.

The overwhelmingly negative response to the Report confirms suspicions long expressed by historians that American Protestants can scarcely distinguish the values of their religious tradition from those of American culture.[47] Apparently, in matters pertaining to church and society, most Presbyterians share some key assumptions about the relationship between the two with national news columnists who were comfortable with the ideas and language of the Presbyterian opposition. Why else would *Newsweek* feature writers express concern that the Presbyterian church, referred to simply as "the church," maintain a particular kind of moral standard unless they shared an assumption that "the church" is an essential moral guarantor in the American democracy?

V. RELIGIOUS LEGITIMATION OF AMERICAN CORE VALUES

The possibility of a theological commitment to human liberation and justice was unfamiliar to most Presbyterians in 1991. A few influential Presbyterian leaders had pursued a social justice agenda with considerable energy since the 1960's but most Presbyterians appear to have a commitment to justice and freedom as core values of the American democracy. In a survey conducted in the 1970's, Presbyterian clergy gave top priority to having America serve as an example of justice and liberty to all nations.[48]

The strong opposition to the Sexuality Report suggests that many Presbyterians think of justice and freedom in ways that do not differentiate religious from national connotations of these core values. That is, they believe that "God created all men(sic) equal" and that a good society provides "freedom and justice for all." And they believe it with emotional intensity because it is a part of Presbyterian identity to support these values in American society.

However, "justice" as a cultural value functions in a way that does not require "the church" to exemplify what it would mean to seek justice for all people. On the other hand, "freedom" generally means "freedom of choice" in the language of Presbyterian theology and that of cultural values.

This substantiates Robert Wuthnow's claim that "The moral imperative defined by the value of freedom is to make a choice."[49] Conservative and liberal Presbyterian theology is predicated on free will and freedom of choice. In saying that all human behavior is not freely chosen, the writers of the Sexuality Report challenged a cultural core value. If they are correct that freedom of choice is not available to everyone, then the Presbyterian understanding of both salvation and the role of "the church" as the moral guarantor of a democratic society is called into question.

A "...cultural conflict is about power — a struggle to achieve or maintain the power to define reality."[50] The absence of discussion about the social analysis of culture in the Sexuality Report suggests that Presbyterian identity does function to legitimate national ideals. This suggests that those who so strenuously objected to the Task Force Report have identified Presbyterian theology with cultural core values in a way that is reminiscent of nineteenth century attitudes when Protestant values were a dominant influence in defining the "American" reality.

Although conservative Presbyterians deplore the moral decay in contemporary society, they continue to believe that religious "renewal" will restore a moral America, and by implication, Presbyterian cultural hegemony. They have wanted to believe that when people experience injustice, it is their own fault. They have tended to deny that cultural dynamics that generate sexual violence and injustice effect everyone. It is possible that the graphic first person narratives of Presbyterians who suffer sexual injustice found in the text of the Report violated a deep desire to believe that freedom does guarantee personal safety and economic security to "moral" people.

Two Vocabularies of Moral Discourse

The authors of *Habits of the Heart* describe three sources for ideals held in common by Americans. They do so in terms of figures whose vocabulary and concepts are representative of three typically "American" forms of moral reasoning — biblical, republican and utilitarian-expressive. For example, they associate the "expressive" tradition with Walt Whitman "...luxuriating in the sensual as well as the intellectual...." They associate the utilitarian with thinkers influenced by Ben Franklin, noting that their "...focus was so exclusively on individual self-improvement that the larger social context scarcely came into view."[51]

An analysis of the difference between language use and thought categories used by the Task Force and that of their critics suggests that the Report described biblical themes in expressive language which their critics interpreted in republican-utilitarian terms. To their critics, and the press who took their cues from the Presbyterian opposition movement, the Report seemed to regard individual sexual rights as civil rights that should be honored. Repeated accusations that the Task Force was accommodated to the sexual practices of the culture came from writers like Elizabeth Achtemeier who discussed the question, "Is Sexual Intercourse a Right?" at some length. She translated "moral rights" language about "sexuality" in general to mean that every individual has a right to experience "sex." She took the following sentence from the text of the Report to be a demand by the Task Force that the Presbyterian Church "approve every lifestyle."[52]

> All persons have a moral right...to be sexual persons...to explore our own sexuality.[53]

The Sexuality Report was written in a style greatly valued by Task Force members as a passionate expression of non-dualistic biblical values. Public, press and Presbyterians all objected that the presentation of eros as a positive value sounded like "...a sermon on Eros prepared in the heat of politically correct passion."[54] The subject of the Report was sexuality defined as "the nature of human experience that is our way of being in the world as embodied selves, male and female." Most detractors had impressions about the subject of the Report similar to that of the *Newsweek* writers.

> Fundamental to the committee's argument is the assumption that sexual gratification is a human need and a right that ought not be limited to heterosexual spouses or bound by 'conventional morality.'[55]

It was believed that the Task Force identified individual civil rights with sexual "rights": this led critics to say that the Task Force was promoting "adultery, fornication and sodomy." This suggests that the language of the opposition movement comes from a combination of biblical, republican and utilitarian values.

By "moral right" the Task Force meant that since all human beings, as created by God, are essentially social and sexual, persons can only know themselves as sexual-social beings in relation with others. This is not a statement about sex, intercourse, or individual rights. A "moral right" is biblical-expressive language for a "spiritual-sexual right" to be the whole, embodied person God intended in relation with others. But from a republican-utilitarian point of view "moral right" suggests that everyone has an "inalienable right" to sex.

Primary writer Marvin Ellison stated that the intention of the Task Force was to offer ethical "values and commitments" not found in the perspectives of either "sexual traditionalists" or "libertarians and liberals." He wrote that "For Christians freedom is never mere liberty or license to do as one wishes, but rather freedom to be with and for one another in community." Traditionalists persisted in believing the Report was itself libertarian.[56] The corporate dimension of the ethics advocated in the Report was invisible to the republican-utilitarian values of Presbyterians who believe that individual choice is a necessary condition of both salvation and the social good.

There was no possibility that proponents of an individualist anthropology could dialogue with an ethic that considers the social-communal dimension of human life essential to well-being. The belief that everyone needs to be able to express affection in relationship with others is not necessarily dependent on any particular social order, economic system or type of government. Given the social analysis of church and culture, the Task Force concluded that only a church that repented of its complicity in sexual injustice would be capable of guaranteeing the freedom for "self-discovery in community" needed by everyone, but especially those persons robbed of that opportunity by a patriarchal and heterosexist culture. That is why civil and ecclesiastical law limiting the freedom of choice and self-expression of gay and lesbian persons was said to be cruel and unjust. In the Report, this observation was made with reference to the social relationships regarded as integral to salvation by the Task Force.

Wuthnow has described ambiguity in theological reasoning about moral values since the late 1950's when the relationship between religion and culture was seen as that of values to behavior. Although there were differences as to whether a good society was more dependent on proper motivation or on good behavior, there was agreement that the role of religion in a democratic society was to "insure good behavior."[57] The concern expressed in the Sexuality Report was not good behavior or even primarily a good society. The justice hermeneutic used to ground theological reflection about moral values led to an expressed desire to "dismantle sexism and heterosexism" in order to "enhance the weil-being of persons...." This objective was described as faithfulness to "a way of being that is glimpsed most clearly and powerfully in the person and ministry of Jesus

Christ."[58]

Wuthnow also points out that the Judeo-Christian tradition had never placed complete emphasis on individual freedom. "Always there was constraint."[59] Since Presbyterians usually describe "constraint" in terms of "self-restraint" it was not typical of Presbyterian moral reasoning to define limits to freedom in terms of constraint of social arrangements, vested interests and power distribution. In "Keeping Body and Soul Together," the purpose of human freedom was discussed in theological terms as "humanizing" because it

> ...is the freedom to act fittingly in relation to others. Freedom is a gift of empowerment to love, to be loved, and to seek justice or right-relatedness. For Christians, the exercise of freedom is always for the purpose of enhancing the well-being of self and others and for strengthening communal ties.[60]

The response to the Report supports Wuthnow's argument that there is no cultural language available in which moral discourse about either freedom or justice can be conducted. Freedom is valued as a cherished ideal, but an ideal without stated purpose. He points out that because "freedom" is a self-legitimating American ideal it is difficult to demonstrate the absence of freedom.[61] Instead it is valued for its instrumentality to achieve other ends...like economic growth, church growth or even, spiritual growth. Here is another instance where the republican-instrumental language and thought categories of Sexuality Report critics made it impossible for them to grasp the substantive connotations of freedom in the Report. In addition to freedom from unjust power distribution, Ellison described freedom as a spiritual characteristic of a church that will "...witness to the inbreaking of a radically new order, the basileia or commonwealth of God."[62] As the Task Force understood it, it is in so doing that the church becomes the body of Christ.[63]

Robert Bellah points out that contemporary moral traditions provide resources for thinking about procedural justice but say relatively little about distributive or substantive justice. The recent Presbyterian experience suggests that in a reformed theological tradition in which respect for the biblical witness is repeatedly affirmed, a theology in which both the substance and distribution of justice is described in biblical terms is unrecognizable.

"Keeping Body and Soul Together: Sexuality, Spirituality and Social Justice" laid bare the extent to which modern covenant theology has conformed to cultural norms regarding the meaning of freedom and justice. The social analysis of culture in the Report challenged both covenant theology and "American" patriotism in claiming that many people "do not enjoy freely chosen behavior." Its writers came dangerously close to saying that the Presbyterian Church (USA) is in apostasy if it continues to legitimate the warped values of an unjust society.

"The Church " "The State," and "The Press" in the American Democracy

The publicity surrounding the work of the Presbyterian Task Force on Human Sexuality for the three years of its life, especially media attention between April and June of 1991, means that for a brief time religion was national news in 1991. It was a time when the public learned something about the inner workings of the Presbyterian Church (U.S.A.), including the fact that an officially appointed study group had written an outrageous Report that rapidly became a best-seller. It was a time when the Presbyterian segment of the public was alarmed, confused, or embarrassed by membership in a church receiving national media exposure under such circumstances. Still, public media attention to a denominational event, especially when presented by writers who join the opposition forces, hardly constitutes moral discourse, or even a public conversation about religion.

There was no public dialogue about the issues raised in the published

Report. Differences between the Task Force and its opposition did not surface as two sides to moral discourse even in the public debate format of *Nightline*. There are two reasons for total failure to join the issues. The first is that when one party to a disagreement is defending a standard of morality regarded as a moral absolute (what the church has always believed), dialogue is ruled out by definition. The second is that the Task Force presented its convictions in language and concepts unfamiliar or unacceptable to both liberal and conservative Presbyterians.

There are deeper cultural reasons why the Report's critics could only attack the Report as "weird" and "immoral" while defending their own position instead of engaging the issues raised in the Report. It is not accidental that references to the committed relationships of gay and lesbian people in the Report were treated only as negations of "the marriage covenant." For reasons supported by republican, biblical, and utilitarian traditions in moral reasoning, homosexuality is considered a threat to social order, moral decency and heterosexual marriage. It is regarded as a violation of civil law and biblical authority. This suggests that Presbyterians want to believe that homosexual relations are a violation of civil law as much as the public wants to believe that the Bible says homosexuality is a "sin."

As the Report challenged the reality of freedom in American culture, the writers also questioned the belief that homosexual acts are always freely chosen and, therefore, sinful. The Presbyterian policy that forbids the ordination of "practicing" homosexuals depends on believing that homosexual "acts" are freely chosen "sins" against God. Covenant theology depends finally on what it means to say that all human behavior — both heterosexual and homosexual — is a freely chosen response to God.

That the reaction of the press and some of the public to what was said about the Report was so similar to that of Presbyterian critics indicates a widely shared belief that religion is essential to the well-being of the nation. The emotional intensity of the response is an expression of deep anxiety that a changing cultural consensus regarding sexual morality — especially the belief that homosexual relationships are abnormal — could lead to social disorder or chaos. This suggests that the continuing presence of churches on the landscape functions to convince Americans that freedom and justice and moral order do exist, but perhaps only for as long as religious leaders continue to uphold the value of heterosexual marriage.

Given the power of these beliefs about the relationship of marriage and homosexuality to social order, the fact that the primary topic in the Report discussed by Presbyterians and national news media was marriage suggests that support for "the institution of marriage" was a way to silently condemn homosexuality. There was little discussion, in print, of the obviously controversial recommendation of the Task Force that the church consider honoring monogamous homosexual relationships with commitment ceremonies.

Many, if not most, Presbyterians did not understand that the General Assembly "amicus brief" supporting civil rights for homosexual persons represents a distinction (typical of traditional reformed theology) between what is good for society and the moral standards required of Presbyterians. Americans, in general, do not ask if civil law prohibiting sexual relations between consenting adults in private is an infringement of civil rights. Most would not know that civil law prohibiting adultery and fornication is unique to the United States.[65] Yet, if "the state" has the power to oversee sexual relations in private between consenting adults, why is this not regarded as interfering with the freedom of choice otherwise held in such high regard?

An equally vexing question about the reality of freedom and the democratic process so highly valued by Presbyterians relates to the work of the Task Force. What does freedom of religion mean when a denomination is subjected to intense public scrutiny about what might be construed as theological dialogue internal to the business of that institution? What does it mean when "the press" engages in advocacy journalism when a denomination re-examines its stance on moral issues? and what does it mean when a denomination forbids private (meaning not in public) discussion by a group appointed to study so intensely personal a subject as human sexuality? What do the categories "private" and "public" mean when a social institution can not conduct its business in private?[66]

At the very least, all of this suggests that in this time of cultural conflict over who has enough power to name reality, the boundaries between the role of "the church," and the role of "the state," and the role of "the press" in American culture are definitely shifting.

ENDNOTES

[1]These themes are developed in some detail in Robert N. Bellah, *Habits of the Heart* (New York: Harper and Row, 1985) and Robert Wuthnow, *The restructuring of American Religion* (Princeton, New Jersey: Princeton University Press, 1988). As sociologists, both are concerned with the content and social function of ideas.

[2]"G. A. Task Force Revises Sex: Ethic: Approves of Homosexual, Premarital, and Extramarital Sexual Relations," *The Presbyterian Layman* (Vol. 74, No. 1), Jan/Feb, 1991, p. 1.

[3]"Alert," *reNEWS*, A Publication of Presbyterians For Renewal (vol. 1, No. 3), December 1990. The section titled "Alert" is a center pull-out that was not numbered as a part of the issue. The "Alert" section, titled "Storm Clouds Gathering Over Coming Report of the Task Force on Human Sexuality," could have been reprinted and mailed separately from the issue of *reNEWS*.

[4]At the time of the "Angela Davis Affair" 17 overtures were received by the 1972 General Assembly. This marked the beginning of grass roots opposition to decisions made by the denominational "bureaucracy." Milton J. Coalter, John M. Mulder, Louis B. Weeks, eds., *The Confessional Mosaic: Presbyterians and Twentieth-Century Theology* (Louisville: Westminster/John Knox, 1990), p. 308.

[5]Jim Gittings, "A Bonfire in Baltimore," *Christianity and Crisis* (May 7, 1991), pp. 172-174.

[6]Letter from Herbert D. Valentine, Moderator, 203rd General Assembly, James E. Andrews, Stated Clerk and Gordon C. Stewart, Moderator, General Assembly Committee on Human Sexuality to all Presbyterian Church (USA) congregations, June 11, 1991. The G. A. Committee on Human Sexuality was charged with drafting a response to the Report from The Task Force on Human Sexuality.

[7]"Keeping Body and Soul Together: Sexuality, Spirituality and Social Justice," A Document Prepared for the 203rd General Assembly (1991) by The General Assembly Special Committee on Human Sexuality, Presbyterian Church U.S.A., pp. 49-58.

98   Chapter IV

[8]James Davison Hunter, *Culture Wars: The Struggle To Define America* (U.S.A., Basic Books, 1991).

[9]Dieter T. Hessel, "The General Assembly on Sexuality: Major Emphases," *Church and Society* (Vol. LXXX, No. 2), Nov./Dec., 198, p. 89.

[10]"The Struggle To Win the Soul of America," *Values and Visions* (Vol. 2, No. 8), 1991, pp. 17-18.

[11]James H. Moorhead, "Redefining Confessionalism: American Presbyterians in the Twentieth Century," in *The Confessional Mosaic*, op. cit., p. 77.

[12]S. Alexander Rippa, *Education in a Free Society*, sixth ed., (N.Y., Longman, 1988), p. 263.

[13]*The Confessional Mosaic*, op. cit., p. 70.

[14]Ibid., p. 73.

[15]Rick Nutt, "The Tie That No Longer Binds: The Origins of the Presbyterian Church in America," Ibid., p. 238.

[16]Ibid., pp. 79-80.

[17]"National Evangelical Network Responds to Issues," *reNEWS*, op. cit., p. 8.

[18]John J. Carey, "The Presbyterian Church and Sexuality: Why This? Why Now?," *Church and Society*, op cit., p. 2.

[19]*reNEWS* "Alert," op. cit.

[20]Donald K. McKim, "Biblical Interpretation in Presbyterian Statements on Sexuality," *Church and Society*, op. cit., p. 98.

[21]*The Christian Century*, (Dec. 4, 1991), p. 1124.

[22]*Christianity and Crisis*, op. cit., p. 176.

[23]Betty Moore, *reNEWS*, op. cit. and Elizabeth Achtemeier, "A Critique of the Report of the Special Committee on Human Sexuality," *reNEWS*, (Vol. 2, No. 1), March 1991, pp. 1, 8-12.

[24]Kenneth L. Woodward and Alden Cohen in New York, "Roll Over John Calvin," *Newsweek*, (May 6, 1991), p. 59.

[25]"Keeping Body and Soul Together," op. cit., p. 30 (lines 1442-1443).

[26]Ibid., p. 56 (lines 2125-2127).

[27]Ibid., (lines 2112-2128).

[28]Achtemeier, op. cit., p. 1.

[29]"Keeping Body and Soul Together," op. cit., p. 102 (lines 3993-3944). The word "sodomy" is from the language of civil law. There are several references to "Sodomites" in the Bible.

[30]Achtemeier, op. cit., p. 8.

[31]"Keeping Body and Soul Together," op. cit., p. 39.

[32]Achtemeier, op. cit., p. 10.

[33]Vivian Lindermayer, "Presbyterian Bravery Under Fire," *Christianity and Crisis*, op. cit., p. 163.

[34] Elizabeth Bounds, "Linking Faith and Daily Life: A First Report," *The Auburn News* (Spring 1991).

[35]Peter Steinfels, "Beliefs," *The New York Times NATIONAL* (Saturday, May 25, 1991), L+ 11.

[36]Barbara Chaapel, "A Time To Remember," *PTS Alumni/ae News* (Fall 1991), p. 10.

[37]"Physiology of a Renewal Organization," *reNEWS* (vol. 1, No. 30), Dec. 1990, p. 3.

[38]"Meet John Huffman," *reNEWS* (Vol. 2, No. 1), March 1991, p. 15.

[39]"Against His Will?", *The News of the Presbyterian Church* (U.S.A.) (vol. 4, No. 7), Aug./Sept. 1991, p. 2.

[40]John A. Howard, "Making virtue Respectable Again," *The Presbyterian Layman* Vol. 4, No. 5), Sept./Oct. 1991, p. 7.

[41]Benton Johnson, "From Old to New Agendas: Presbyterians and Social Issues in the Twentieth Century," *The Confessional Mosaic*, op. cit., p. 230.

[42]Sodomy, defined as "copulation against the order of nature" and a crime at common law was declared a felony in England early in the 16th century. Under Anglo-Saxon codes, sodomy has continued to carry severe penalties. In 1975, a Federal District Court upheld the constitutionality of the Virginia sodomy laws. Since then, state legislatures have begun to remove or decrease criminal penalties for sodomy. From *Grolier's Academic American Encyclopedia* (Rose Library Oak System, Drew University, Madison, N.J).

[43]Mckim, op. cit., pp. 95-101.

[44]Ibid., p. 96.

[45]*Pornography: Far From the Song of Songs*, A Study Paper Adopted by The 200th General Assembly, (Presbyterian Church U.S.A., 1988), p. 8.

[46]"Keeping Body and Soul Together," op. cit., p. 29.

[47]Robert T. Handy, *A Christian America: Protestant Hopes and Historical Realities* (New York: Oxford University Press, 1971), pp. 14-1.

[48]Robert Wuthnow, *The Restructuring of American Religion* (Princeton, NJ: Princeton University Press. 1988) p. 252.

[49]Ibid., p. 280.

[50]Hunter, op. cit., p. 52.

[51]Robert N. Bellah et al., *Habits of the Heart* (N.Y.: Harper and Row, 1985), pp. 33-34.

[52]Achtemeier, op. cit., p. 11.

[53]"Keeping Body and Soul Together," op. cit., p. 46 (lines 1743-1748). The full sentence in the text reads: "All persons, whether heterosexual or homosexual, whether single or partnered, have a moral right to experience justice-love in their lives and to be sexual persons. Being sexual includes the right and responsibility

to explore our own sexuality tenderly, to enjoy our capacity to give and receive loving touch, and to honor our commitment to deepen self-respect in relation to others. The church must actively promote and protect this right for all persons, without distinction." This is the introduction to a section titled, "Enhancing and Protecting Intimacy and Right-Relatedness."

[54]Kenneth L. Woodward, op. cit.

[55]Ibid.

[56]"Keeping Body and Soul Together," op. cit., p. 9 (lines 337-341).

[57]Wuthnow, op. cit., p. 62.

[58]"Keeping Body and Soul Together," op. cit., p. 32 (line 1220), p. 11 (line 396), and p. 17 (lines 616-617).

[59]Wuthnow, op. cit., p. 63.

[60]"Keeping Body and Soul Together," op. cit., p. 30 (lines 1114-1117).

[61]Wuthnow, op. cit., p. 280.

[62]"Keeping Body and Soul Together," op. cit., p. 37 (lines 1408-1415).

[63]Ibid., p. 17 (lines 631-632).

[64]Bellah, op. cit., p. 26.

[65]A statute declaring adultery a criminal offense in New Jersey was added to the civil code some time before 1838. During the May term of the New Jersey Supreme Court, J. W. Miller argued that the crime had not yet been defined. He distinguished the social nature of adultery as a crime from the ecclesiastical (moral) law of some and argued that a crime had been committed only if a child was born of an illicit union between a married man and a married woman. His reasoning was that if there was issue a crime had been committed against the husband of the woman involved and she was, therefore, liable to criminal proceedings. The concern of Miller, who won the case, was purity of blood line. (New Jersey Supreme Court, May Term, 1838, pp. 380-391). Laws on adultery and fornication vary from state to state.

[66]Hunter, op. cit., pp. 55-56.

CHAPTER V
SEXUALITY AS A JUSTICE ISSUE
by
Marvin M. Ellison

A recent study by the World Council of Churches begins by saying that "The fact that the churches are so greatly exercised on the subject [of sex and sexuality] suggests that God is calling us to rethink" these matters.[1] There's no doubt about the conflict and agitation. What is less certain is whether there is any groundswell in the churches to rethink sexuality, intimacy, gender politics, and family. Instead, what I find in privileged white Protestant churches is fear and avoidance along with well financed, highly organized resistance to any challenges to conventional Christian teaching and practice about sex. Given the deep-seated crisis of sexuality, this is not very surprising.

Joseph Burnside of Long Island City, New York certainly had no trouble expressing his unhappiness with the Presbyterian sexuality study, "Keeping Body and Soul Together." In his letter to me, Mr. Burnside complained that since I helped produce that study, I must belong to a "bunch of ultra liberal educators." He wrote, "It is with a good deal of gratification to me that this report has been rejected.... It's about time that the Presbyterian Church stands up and acts like a church ...." "I'm rather inclined to think," Mr. Burnside continued, "that if Christ were around today, you and your report would be kicked out of the Temple as the money changers were. If Calvin were around, you would indeed suffer a worse fate."

Mr. Burnside and I concur about one thing at least: it *is* about time the Presbyterian Church among other religious communities — stands up and acts like a church when it comes to matters of sexuality, spirituality, and social justice. Our disagreement lies in what that requires. And, of course, this is far from a personal conflict alone. As James Davison Hunter observes, this society is in the midst of intense culture wars. None rages more intensely than the battles over sex and family.

It is important to recognize that the religious sex debates are taking place within a more comprehensive and multifaceted cultural crisis, an historically complex global process of reorganizing social relations at every level — politically, economically, and culturally, including religious practice. We are experiencing social and cultural dislocations as turbulent and historically significant as those of the 16th and 17th centuries. As a transnational global economy extends and solidifies its reach, we see signs of this global crisis as nation-states crumble and reappear in unexpected forms. The contours of this structural crisis are also experienced closer to home within families and intimacy relations.

The contemporary crisis of sexuality is best viewed within the context of this broader cultural crisis, a sexuality crisis embedded in and affected by all the changes happening at other levels. This crisis of sexuality shows itself in distorted, negative attitudes and practices about sex, the body, women, and other marginalized peoples, but we are confronted with much more than bad attitudes or even serious misunderstandings. At the heart of the crisis is social conflict over unjust power dynamics between men and women, as well as entrenched patterns of male violence against women, children, and marginalized men. Of great moral significance, then, is the historic re-emergence of a feminist movement and the call for gender and sexual justice in the family and throughout the social order, including the church. The church owes an enormous debt to the moral wisdom of the feminist and gay liberation movements. They rightly insist that the church can gain moral credibility on these matters only insofar as it addresses issues of power and control in our intimacy relations. The church must address, with much more candor and insight than it has managed to date, how sex and intimacy are distorted by violence and injustice — by sexism, racism, heterosexism and homophobia, by ageism, economic exploitation, and so on — and how to reverse these patterns in our personal lives and social relations.

As I see it, a major contribution of the Presbyterian study is its clear naming of sexuality as a justice issue. The moral challenge before the church is how to reframe sexuality —theologically, ethically, pastorally — through a justice lens and how to help people make connections between their personal pain and larger social dynamics. We will not be able to talk sensibly about sexuality apart from cogent analysis of the dominant social order which shapes and, to a great extent, misshapes our lives as sexual persons.

Fresh moral insight does not come from intellectual activity per se, but emerges from within social justice movements and from the communal effort to reconstruct religious traditions. In order to move beyond the conventionality, moralisms, and stale rhetoric about sex and sexuality so rampant in white Protestant churches, above all else we need to move into real-life solidarity with women, with gay men, lesbians, and bisexuals of all colors, with victims and survivors of sexual violence, and with those whose bodies and spirits are routinely violated in this culture, especially the poor and the elderly.

Here's the rub for many in our churches: about sex and sexuality, we are often at our worst, caught in a paralyzing grip of fear and fixation about the erotic, about women's power and moral agency, about the body, about passion. Many religious people fear difference and avoid flesh-and-blood contact with those "not like them." Because of ill-fated attempts to build community by exclusion rather than by practicing inclusive justice, white-skinned privileged

Protestants often lack the kind of real-life connectedness, in the small and large places of our lives, that would enable us to appreciate how our own lives are diminished by gender and sexual injustice, as well as by racism and class oppression. Out of touch with our own pain, we tend not to pay attention or know how to respond to the pain of others.

Constructive work on sexuality and sexual ethics cannot be done without appreciation for the voices and contributions of those struggling, in Mary Hunt's wonderful phrase, with "fierce tenderness," to survive and even thrive on the underside of history and theology. Feminists, gay persons, and our allies are pressing the church to come of age about sex and confront how the church's sexual code legitimates male control of women's bodies and women's lives. The conventional Christian sexual ideology is more than inadequate. It is dangerous to life and limb.

The moral challenge before the church is this: the Presbyterian Church, but not the Presbyterian Church alone, must choose whether, on the one hand, to perpetuate a patriarchal ethic of sexual control and gender oppression or, on the other hand, commit to an ethic of gender justice, of mutuality between women and men, and of respect for sexual diversity. To meet this crisis, the churches must be willing to examine their own involvement in the patriarchal construction of sexuality, ask why Christians have such an alienated history about sexuality and spirituality, and commit to explore what must be done to reverse this legacy.

If there is no other change in the immediate future, I dearly hope that our churches will at least stop framing the moral debate as if the problem of sexuality is somehow "homosexuality" or non--marital sex. The moral crisis, and there is one, is the distortion of human intimacy and relationality by patterns of exploitation and abuse and by sexism, heterosexism, and other dynamics of injustice. Moral complicity in injustice results in spiritual fatigue and inertia in the face of evil. A people fearful of the body, of passion, and without hunger for justice will not likely make a very joyful noise. The spiritual crisis in our churches comes from compliance with injustice — and from the refusal to break with patriarchy's central norm of compulsory heterosexuality. To be candid, the contemporary crisis of sexuality is fundamentally a crisis in heterosexuality, in the sexist ordering of social relations legitimating male gender supremacy. More truthfully, this is primarily a crisis in male sexuality. A contribution the church can make is to help us name names accurately.

What is shaking the foundations is the open, passionate, and courageous call for a non-sexist, non-racist, non-abusive moral order in family, society, and church. The reason many fear Christian feminism and gay liberation is that these social justice movements no longer grant moral authority to the patriarchal order of things. Their aim is to topple not the family, but rather the patriarchal family and likewise the patriarchal church and, I dare say, the patriarchal academy.

Church and academy serve people's well-being by teaching and modelling how to resist injustice. The educational task is to equip persons to embody sexual justice in our institutions and in our intimacy relations. There may be no deeper spiritual yearning among us than learning how to *eroticize equality* to celebrate mutual respect and care among persons and groups and to embrace right relations as erotically powerful.

The spiritual quest, as I see it, is a quest for a genuinely ethical eroticism — an eroticism powerful to the senses and also ethically principled. That won't come easily in this culture or in most of the churches. One small vignette illustrates this difficulty. At an open hearing about the Presbyterian sexuality study, a woman in anger and distress berated the task force for invoking justice-love as the appropriate moral norm for sexual and social relations. "What's all this about justice-love?," she asked. "That's something you are making up. There's nothing in the Bible about justice."

For myself, the pathway toward spiritual and political renewal is by way of doing justice together. This requires becoming a contrast-community and devoting ourselves passionately to righting wrongs, including sexual wrongs. It is only by making common cause with the marginalized and rejected, especially with gay men, lesbians, and bisexuals, that we stand a chance of reclaiming counter-cultural wisdom and power, and perhaps a measure of truth, as well. As Flannery O'Connor has said, "You will know the truth, and the truth will make you — odd."

ENDNOTES

[1]Robin Smith, *Living in Covenant with God and One Another* (Geneva: World Council of Churches, 1989), p. 3.

CHAPTER VI

ALL OF THE CRITICS ARE NOT CONSERVATIVES:
A REPLY TO CAMILLE PAGLIA

Camille Paglia's article "The Joy of Presbyterian Sex" in the December 2, 1991 issue of *The New Republic* was the most convoluted and confused response to the Presbyterian Sexuality Report that I have read in the year following its publication. Paglia's article tells us far more about herself than it tells about the Presbyterian report. She gives readers no information about the origin or structure of the report; conveys no awareness of the broad themes of the report or positive response to the report by leading Christian ethicists; and is inaccurate in her interpretation of what happened to the report at the General Assembly meeting in Baltimore in June of 1991. While attempting to be critical of a report by Presbyterians for Presbyterians she identifies herself as "a lapsed Catholic of wavering sexual persuasion" who affirms the pagan world, and as one who from her girlhood in Syracuse, New York was in rebellion against Protestant culture. The majority report of the Presbyterian committee was nearly 200 pages long and dealt with many complex issues. That makes it all the more irresponsible of Paglia not to set her quotes in context. Her specific references to the report are consequently highly selective, distorted, and misleading. If one did not know what this report is about before reading Paglia's article, you would never gain any idea about it from what she says. She uses the Presbyterian report as a launching pad for her strident anti-feminist agenda, and for her intrigue with the decadent forces of culture. It is not at all clear, in fact, where Paglia fits into this dialogue. By what authority does she speak? She is not a Presbyterian, a Christian, or even a specialist in human sexuality.

For one who is a professor, Paglia utilizes a dramatically unacademic methodology in her attack on the Presbyterian report. At a document that is multifaceted and nuanced she swings a literal meat axe to discredit and mock the report. She describes the report as "banal," simplistic, naive," and "sentimental." She says that it is filled with "contemporary platitudes and ignorance of world history and culture." She alleges that it is rooted in an "arrogant, condescending welfare agency model of life" and that the report "reduces love to a Hallmark card." She takes pride in her anti-feminist posture, and lambastes the Presbyterian report because it does not address all of the dark, complex expressions of sexuality in the secular culture, e.g., pederasts, prostitutes, strippers, pornographers, sadomasochists, and transvestites.

It is true that there are a number of dimensions of sexuality in the broad culture that this report did not address. I described some of those in my article in the August 15, 1991 issue of *Christianity and Crisis* entitled "Sexuality: What We Couldn't Say." The point that Paglia misses, however, is that this committee was not appointed to review all of the complex components of sexuality in modern culture. (We don't say anything about bestiality, either). The report was written to be a guide to Presbyterians as to (a) how we might better understand the Judeo-Christian heritage about sexuality; (b) how we might better understand the social conditioning of all patterns of human sexuality; (c) how we might better understand the communities of people in the Presbyterian Church who are bearing great pain under the assumptions of the current majority culture; and (d) how we might better understand the needs and problems of special constituencies within the Presbyterian Church, such as adolescents, older adults, persons with disabilities, gay and lesbian persons, persons with AIDS, and single people. The goal was to help Presbyterians come to a more positive sense of human sexuality, and to assist them in integrating sexuality with their commitment to lead a Christian life.

Paglia mocks the report because she says it paints a "grotesque picture of America." She chides us for reporting that "wife battering is rampant and almost 40% of rapes happen inside heterosexual marriages." Is that an incidental or irrelevant statistic? She condemns us for our concern about sexual harassment and violence, which the report acknowledges can take such diverse forms as "cat calls, cartoons, and snide asides." She passes over these matters by saying women should be more appreciative of humor, irony, and bawdiness. She might think that issues such as wife battering and sexual violence are incidental features of our culture, but our committee finished its three years of work by thinking that sexual violence and coercive sexuality are perhaps the most critical sexual issues in American culture, and they are found inside and outside the churches.

Paglia attacks the report because in her view it has an inadequate understanding of evil and guilt. It may be that in our theological assessment of the present situation we did not deal adequately with the hardness of the human heart, but we did describe the blindness that comes with majority privilege and the propensities toward Pharisaism which lurk in all who consider themselves righteous. These are the special sins of established groups. Sin comes in many forms and distorts us all. There is no naïveté in our report about that.

Paglia says that the report "tries to paper over with words the raw elemental experience and conflicts of our mortality." *Eros*, she says, is defined as "a zest for life"; she adds, "is this a soap commercial?" In fact the glossary of the report says the following about *eros*: "*Eros*, literally a Greek word for love. In English and contemporary usage particularly *eros* has come to mean passionate sexual love. As we use *eros* in this report, it refers to a passion for relatedness that comes to us first from God and may be experienced in all different kinds of human relationships as a zest for life and joyful response to life's goodness." This is but one example among many of the inaccurate and superficial ways that Paglia treats the Presbyterian report. Unlike most knowledgeable people who write in the area of human sexuality, Paglia does not think that patriarchy and homophobia are matters of serious concern.

She says, "our problem is not patriarchy but, in the urban industrialized world, collapsing manhood." It is not clear just what *uncollapsed* manhood is. One suspects that she is thinking of John Wayne, Clint Eastwood, the Marlboro Man, or maybe even Mike Tyson.

Since the report was published I have traveled all over the country speaking to congregations, Presbyteries, seminaries, colleges, and universities about the report. I have acknowledged that this report is not perfect. It reflects the limitations of what seventeen professional people were able to do in the time that we had. We have learned much in the debate about the report, and clearly there are matters which could be fine-tuned in the text. I have said repeatedly that the issues raised in this report are more important than the answers that we gave them, and we have urged Presbyterians and other Christians to grow in their understanding of the complexities of these issues. We have found that issues of sexuality are not easily talked about, and that on the whole our various Christian traditions have not encouraged us in the understanding of the complexity and power of human sexuality. To those critics who charged the committee with creating controversy in the Presbyterian Church by bringing up such issues, I have always replied that we did not create these issues, we simply named them. On the whole, our Committee would like to see more compassion in the Presbyterian Church (U.S.A.) and in all churches.

If Paglia's attack on the Presbyterian Sexuality Report had been circulated in mimeographed form by some strange counter-culture group, it could be dismissed as one other strange, uninformed, and bizarre piece of writing. To have her article published in *The New Republic*, however, mandates that it be responded to publicly. For anyone who wonders who Camille Paglia is, she was featured in the profile section of the January 13, 1992 issue of *TIME* Magazine. The article describes her as "the *Bete noire* of feminism" and begins with a quotation from her 1990 book *Sexual Personae: Art and Decadence from Nefertiti to Emily Dickinson* (Yale University Press). Paglia says "There is something in my book to offend absolutely everybody. I am pro-abortion, pro-the legal use of drugs, pro-pornography, child pornography, snuff films and I am going after these things until Gloria Steinem screams." We read that when she speaks she usually shows up with two massive body guards togged out in black leather jackets. She was dismissed from the faculty of Bennington College in 1979 after a long history of fights and tiffs. Her personal vendetta against feminism colors all of her talking and writing. She has become a media event herself, and apparently thrives on that notoriety. Since the press often loves an anti-hero, she appeared on the cover of *New York* and *Harpers* in the same month.

Paglia, of course, can write what she wants. The question is why any reputable journal should give publication space to her bombastic, vitriolic, and distorted writing. The real losers in the credibility issue, it seems to me, are the editors of *The New Republic*, who in publishing a piece like Paglia's give public acknowledgment to the fact that they themselves have never read the Presbyterian Sexuality Report.

Let us hope for more editorial insight and discretion from the editors of *The New Republic* in the future. For our purposes in this book, however, let us now turn to the struggles and debates of four other denominations. The American sexuality debate has many wider circles.

PART TWO:

ECUMENICAL EXPERIENCES AND REFLECTIONS

✝ HUMAN SEXUALITY AND THE CHRISTIAN FAITH

A study for the church's
reflection and deliberation

The Committee to Study Homosexuality
Offers the Church...

Its Report,
Its Conclusions,
Its Recommendations

CHAPTER VII

THE UNITED CHURCH OF CANADA: CRISIS AND CREATIVITY

by

Thomas C. Bandy

In August, 1992, the General Council of the United Church of Canada met in Fredericton, New Brunswick. Past General Councils had been marked by controversy, particularly around sexuality issues. Delegates gathered by Conference to march in procession to the place of meeting in a dramatic gesture of church unity.. The 1988 decision of a previous General Council affirming that sexual orientation would not be a barrier to ordination had resolved a policy question, but had not resolved the stress which had continued to divide the church. This meeting of the General Council was expected to move forward toward a new spirit of church unity and enthusiasm. As the procession of Conferences began its course, they turned a corner to meet a silent gathering of men, women, and children holding a large banner of protest. It read: "They have taken away our Lord, and we do not know where they have laid him." The impact of the criticism was visible on the faces of the commissioners. Nevertheless, the commissioners gathered in what has been widely described as the most united and enthusiastic General Council in over a decade.

This vignette is a helpful introduction towards an understanding of the sexuality crisis for the United Church of Canada. It was the first North American church to address the issue of sexual orientation and ordination directly, and the impact of its policy decision has been in many respects unique among North American churches. It leads me to say at the very outset that:

1) Stress around this issue is by no means over;
2) There is a large gap between policy resolution and the consensus of the people;
3) The church of 1988 and the church of 1993 are not quite the same church;
4) The 1988 resolution has allowed both the context of church life, and the theology of church life, to evolve in perhaps surprising and unexpected ways.

The present stress of the United Church arises not because the church is at an impasse from which there is no safe escape, but because the church now moves through a transition which is sometimes exciting, sometimes alarming, and certainly mysterious. This means that there can be no single voice in the denomination that can authoritatively claim either to understand, or to control, what is happening within the denomination. All that I can offer as a national staff person whose portfolio is Congregational Mission and Evangelism, is an informed perspective.

THE CHANGING CONTEXT OF CHURCH LIFE

The United Church of Canada is organized into overlapping judicatories designed to maximize congregational autonomy for program and ministry on the one hand, and national vision for personnel and policy on the other hand. It is a "curious blend" of Methodist, Presbyterian, Congregational, and (today) Aboriginal structures for ministry. Aside from the local congregation, the Presbytery is the key unit of the church for mission strategy, oversight of pastoral relations, and program resource. The Conference enables regional coordination and additional program resource, and monitors initiation into the Order of

Ministry. The General Council sets overall policy, resolves foundational theological questions, and generally provides a national vision for the church.

The tension in every judicatory is that leadership is expected to be simultaneously prophetic and concordant. That is to say, leadership is expected both to unsettle and challenge the church on the one hand, and represent and unite the church on the other. This has been increasingly difficult to accomplish, and it is in the context of this dilemma that the sexuality crisis of the church needs to be understood. Leadership is generally perceived today as being prophetic and **discordant.**

The struggle over sexuality issues has revealed that the real crisis of our church is not about sexuality, but about leadership. The strong social conscience of our church has encouraged a prophetic leadership style that is driven by individuals or by standing committees, but not by congregations. Yet it is the congregation and the Presbytery which have the real mandate to "do ministry" in behalf of the church. Whatever the policies set by the General Council, and despite the resources offered by the Conference, it is the local congregation and Presbytery which must implement the policies and use the resources. More than this, it is the local congregation and Presbytery to which is given the ultimate "ownership" of church policy. The perception today, however, is that, while leadership may challenge the church, it does not give voice to the concord of the church.

This explains why the key issue leading to the 1988 General Council debate over sexual orientation and ordination was whether commissioners voted as representatives of their constituencies, or according to their own conscience. Urgent appeals for a church-wide referendum were refused by the Executive of the General Council, which argued that the denomination was a **conciliar** church in which elected delegates voted by conscience. Unfortunately, while such a ruling was judicially correct, it missed the point of the leadership crisis. The church as a whole did not want conciliation, but concordance. In foundational matters of faith and values, leadership was expected to facilitate, not the compromises of a Council, but the "concord," the "harmonious agreement," of the whole church.

The impact of the 1988 General Council decision, and of the sexuality crisis in general, has been to drive a deeper wedge between prophetic and concordant leadership.

First, trust for the entire electoral process has been weakened, and is only gradually being restored. There has been enormous political pressure on all church structures. Most Conference and national Divisions, and many Presbyteries, are undergoing anguished "re-structuring" programs. The process of decision making is being "flattened" to be less hierarchical; the style of decision making is becoming ever more intentionally concordant; and the people who do decision making are being selected with painstaking scrutiny. Conference and National staff positions have undergone tremendous changes both in personnel and job description. As many as one third to one half of the volunteers in many committees and divisions have been replaced. Accountability everywhere is being tightened. Even the smallest decisions are made slowly, and with unexpected intensity.

Second, the regionalization of the denomination has been accelerated. It is an expression of congregationalism in which local units desire a larger connection to do ministry, but are wary of losing "grassroots" or "sidewalk" control of church policy. It is not, as some believe, an abandonment of prophetic consciousness, but a trend to locate prophetic consciousness away from individuals and committees, toward the congregation itself. The local congregation wants to be in control of the denominational agenda.

Bearing all this in mind, let me describe seven specific directions in which the sexuality crisis is influencing change within the United Church of Canada today.

1)   **Authority and Interpretation of Scripture:**

The study documents prior to 1988 regarding the discussion of sexual orientation and ordination, and homosexuality in general, intensified a growing interest in the authority and interpretation of Scripture. The very next national study initiative has been in this area, and still continues. In part, this is a matter of educating the church about the higher critical method which emphasized the limited cultural context of Biblical passages regarding sexuality, marriage and divorce.   More significantly, however, this is a matter of interpreting the place of Scripture in the Wesleyan Quadrilateral which was lifted to greater lay awareness during the "Confessing Our Faith" curriculum resource of the early 1980's.   With or without the sexuality crisis, this study would have been necessary.   First, the growing tension between prophetic and concordant leadership style had been raising questions about the identity of the church which could only be resolved through a renewal of Biblical literacy and a broader understanding of the mission of the church.   Second, the emphasis on contextual theology upon which discussion about sexuality relies, provoked deeper anxiety about the foundational authorities of faith.

2)   **Same Gender Covenants:**

Within two years of the 1988 decision not to regard sexual orientation as a factor for ordination, advocacy for the development of national liturgical resources for same gender covenants became vocal.   Already the "official" language of the church had begun avoiding the terminology of "husbands" and "wives," in favor of the terminology of "partners."   However, a proposal to authorize national liturgical resources for same gender covenants made to the 1992 General Council was defeated, and the Division of Mission in Canada was directed only to provide study resources for the local congregation. This was, in fact, quite consistent with the decision regarding sexual orientation and ordination, which made clear the continuing commitment of the church to the integrity of marriage, and which reaffirmed the authority of the local church for worship and liturgy. By referring the development of same gender covenant liturgical resources to the local church, the General Council neither encouraged, nor discouraged, such a course of action, and located responsibility within the congregational mission of the local context.

The same General Council instructed the Division of Mission in Canada to provide resources that enabled congregations to become more open to gay men and lesbians. Significantly, however, the Council insisted that such resources only be provided upon request by the congregation. It is this latter signal which has had the most telling impact on church life, for it is generally seen as a move to shift responsibility for prophetic mission away from initiative by individuals or standing committees, toward the congregation itself. It is now at the congregational or Presbytery levels that further work in this area is deliberately being chosen or not chosen.

3)   **Sexual Harassment Guidelines:**

The debate over sexual orientation and ordination has fueled an even larger debate over sexual abuse and harassment. This was because the debate in the United Church never artificially separated orientation from behavior, and the general public tended (mistakenly) to associate homosexual behavior with sexual abuse or harassment. If the sexual orientation and ordination debate did nothing else, it made very clear the reality that sexual abuse and harassment were not tied to sexual orientation. Feminist and child advocacy voices which had at first been frustrated by the public attention on sexual orientation, were in the end enabled to pursue the even larger issues of abuse and harassment. This lead to the adoption of the most rigorous Sexual Harassment Guidelines currently in place among Protestant denominations in North America by the General Council in 1992. Although the process of clarification continues, and further effort is required to offer Order of Ministry personnel protection from malicious litigation, it does appear that unhelpful distinctions between heterosexual and homosexual behavior which had undermined efforts to enforce normative standards of moral behavior for all, are being replaced by more careful distinctions for healthy and unhealthy relationships in general.

4)   **Changing Influence of Community Advocacy Groups:**

A key question emerging from the sexual orientation and ordination debate needed to be addressed: "To what extent will the church allow outside community groups, who do not necessarily share the faith or mission of the church, to control the agenda, leadership energy, and financial resources of the church?" The prophetic identity of the church appeared not only limited in its understanding of the total mission of the church, but it had been perceived as driven by individuals and standing committees who are responding to advocacy goals within the secular community. Anxiety over this question more recently has made the church less sympathetic with demands for National or Conference staff time and budget to address special needs. There are limits to the influence of secular advocacy groups on the church agenda, and there is greater recognition that the church must more clearly identify and advocate its own mission.

5)   **Denominational Membership and Mission Giving:**

The United Church of Canada is the largest Protestant denomination in Canada, with an estimated 3.8 million adherents. The sexuality crisis has so far cost the church an estimated 25,000 members, some Order of Ministry resignations, and some split congregations. According to a 1993 Angus Reid poll, 33% of those regularly attending church believe it has become too liberal in its teachings. This suggests that 67% of the present adherents are in varying degrees comfortable with United Church teaching. Such a split means that controversy will continue over sexuality issues. Similarly, although some congregations have stopped forwarding funds to the denominational Mission and

Service Fund, the fund itself has re-stabilized and experienced about a 1%
increase in givings.

It is significant that anxiety regarding membership and financial
support is tied less to decisions around sexual orientation, and more to distrust of
denominational leadership. Indeed, for many the real concern is not whether the
teaching of the church is too liberal, but to what extent the people themselves
shape the teaching of the church. It is this issue which has lead to a small
movement of "Covenanting Churches" within the denomination who advocate
specific theological perspectives. While the formal "Covenanting Church"
movement does not seem to be gathering momentum, many congregations share
their anxiety. The key issue does not appear to be merely related to the sexuality
crisis, but to the overall tension between prophetic and concordant styles of
leadership. In other words, it is about who takes the real "ownership" of the
mission of the church.

The following vignette from a church in central Ontario offers a
glimpse into the reality of church life:

> A large, ageing, urban United Church in central ontario was
> approached by a small Metropolitan (Gay/Lesbian) Church seeking
> to rent space for worship on Sunday afternoons. The Minister and
> Session engaged in consultation and study over a period of two
> months with the group, and the majority of the Session voted to
> approve the request. The Official Board, however, was wary of
> controversy, and placed the decision before a Congregational
> Meeting. Prior to the meeting, a telephone campaign undertaken
> by several members who had not been involved in the church for
> years was initiated to lobby against approval. Approval was
> denied by a narrow margin. As a result, the Session feels they no
> longer enjoy the trust of the congregation, and there is a crisis of
> lay leadership. The Youth Group is disillusioned with the
> institutional church, and the leadership of their elders. Several
> newcomers withdrew from the congregation. The church, which
> had been gathering momentum for renewal, has been returned to
> stalemate.

Although there are also many examples of congregations who have been able to achieve a creative unity regarding sexuality, there are many more clearly still searching for consensus.

6)   **Changing Role of the United Church and Community Ministerial Associations:**

Perhaps the most painful impact of the sexuality crisis for the United Church has been their loss of leadership in the arena of community Ministerial Associations. Indeed, since United Church congregations were often the backbone of local ecumenical associations, the whole fabric of local, ecumenical cooperation seems to have been weakened in many communities. The following example from Alberta is perhaps typical:

> A local Ministerial was approached to support a "Focus on the Family" style event, the publicity for which tended to be prejudicial against gay and lesbian people, and exclusive of single parent or mixed families. The United Church Order of Ministry representatives referred support to the Official Boards of their congregations. Four out of five Official Boards voted not to participate in the Ministerial project. As a result, issues around family life, which were important to all, became lost in the breakdown of good feeling in the Ministerial. Evangelical Protestant partners felt inclined to start a competitive association. The local press, for whom sexuality issues still have a high profile, made the whole Ministerial look ineffective as an instrument for community action.

It is significant to note how intentional each United Church congregation was, given the media and public image risks involved.

Local ecumenical associations which could not find common ground in doctrine, had depended upon unity in "good works" to provide a context for cooperation and further conversation. Unfortunately, the sexuality crisis (orientation, marriage, divorce, child custody, abortion, etc.) is fragmenting Ministerial Associations. There is no longer a consensus about what the "good works" should be. Since the United Church congregations tended to subordinate doctrine to good works, they had become key mediators for local ecumenical action. As it became apparent that the good works advocated by the United Church were in fact laden with deeper theological assumptions, local church partners have distanced themselves from the local Ministerial. The pain is felt by the laity whose friendships cross ecclesiastical boundaries, and the blame is often laid upon church leadership whose aggressive advocacy policies seem to force community division.

7)   **The Struggle of New Church Development and Evangelism Committees:**

As the church addresses secular society, controversy of any kind has a negative effect for church development. Newcomers who are primarily concerned with the rediscovery of religious meaning in their lives tend to avoid controversial political associations with heavy ideological goals. It is not the sexuality crisis alone which has been damaging to church development and evangelism, but the larger context of tension between prophetic and concordant leadership. People involved in Church Development ministries tend to have little investment in the larger denomination (and little understanding of the larger organization). Their sense of mission is congregational both in its initiation and final goal, and it tends to be controlled explicitly by the congregation rather than by individuals or standing committees. They will be prophetic only if the message is affirmed by the whole congregation. Denominational leadership (whether in politically conservative or liberal manifestations) is generally considered to be meddlesome rather than facilitative.

Witness by "word and deed" in the United Church has always tended to emphasize deeds, rather than words. However, the "deeds" of Christian witness have increasingly been understood to be political actions conceived by "experts", performed by specially trained individuals, and charged with ideological content. The sexuality crisis has encouraged the conflation of evangelism and social outreach **in the minds of church leadership,** but it has encouraged the separate articulation and renewal of evangelism **in the minds of the congregations.** The laity in general are more interested than ever before in the "words" which justify, shape, and interpret the "deeds". They distrust "experts" in the formulation of mission; they want to do mission as a congregation rather than as a committee; and they want greater ideological diversity and more theological unity, rather than the reverse.

THE CHANGING THEOLOGY OF CHURCH LIFE

Some interpreters of the North American Church have argued that the renewal of congregational ownership for policy, mission, and ministry is a negative reaction to the sexuality crisis of the Church. In the United Church of Canada, however, I sense that the renewal of congregational ownership has in fact been positively empowered by the 1988 General Council decision separating sexual orientation and ordination. It has helped the church move beyond the limited theological polarization that shaped early debate, to explore a different theological context in which to struggle with sexuality issues in the future.

United Church theology, and Canadian Protestantism in general, has been dominated by neo-orthodox thought for several decades. This includes the assumption that Agape and Eros are fundamentally antagonistic principles. Any step toward reconciliation or reunion with God could only be accomplished by the divine, and never by the human. There was a radical separation between the human being and human culture, and the divine, such that no human yearning could overcome the gap, and no cultural or creative structure could bridge the gap. Insofar as Eros can be identified with all such forms of self-affirmation, it was seen as at best futile, and at worst arrogant and demonic. Self-sacrifice, self-denial, and the penitent response of absolute obedience to divine will was the only way of salvation.

Such theological assumptions have supported both "right" and "left" wing United Church perspectives in the sexuality crisis. Definitions of obedience might follow conservative doctrine and ideology, or liberal doctrine and ideology, but the separation of Eros and Agape remained. Self-fulfillment was either "sinful" or "middle class", while self-sacrifice was either "holy" or "politically correct". On both sides of the polarity, the fundamental spiritual attitude of the believer was one of apology; the spiritual response was obedience to a specified agenda; the context of meaning was an abstraction of doctrine and denominational policy; the whole mission of the church was to issue the prophetic call to repent; and the model of discipleship was one of self-denial and sacrifice.

Meanwhile, the church declined in influence and numbers, even as culture itself was devalued either as spiritually empty or as a contaminating evil. Aspects of self-affirmation (artistic expression and perception of beauty, personal spiritualities and inter-faith conversation, sexual identity and relationship, invention and technology) were considered irrelevant to the core of faith and belonging. That version of the church which was ideologically "right" fashioned a "fortress" church around confessional dogma; that version which was ideologically "left" fashioned a "minority consciousness" around sociopolitical policy. Either way, the assumed antagonism between Agape and Eros placed the church in only an adversarial relationship with culture. It's role was always to criticize, never to appreciate; always to teach, never to learn: always to lament, never to celebrate. As a result, it became increasingly impotent for cultural change and irrelevant in the universal quest for reunion with the divine which was the primary goal of the larger public. The church became the club of the opinionated, rather than the community of the humble.

Although much controversy in the United Church continues to unfold in the old polarization, my sense is that since 1988 the church is being awakened to a new theological option that reunites Agape and Eros. Suddenly the passionate desire for reunion with God is not only possible, but legitimate. It might be personal, as Spirit awakens infinite passion of God; or it might be corporate, as Spirit awakens the mystical quality of community and inter-personal relationship. Culture itself can become a vehicle for meaning, rather than a roadblock to meaning. Self-affirmation and self-fulfillment are no longer ignoble goals, but gain new value in the arena of responsible community.

The reunion of Eros and Agape changes the fundamental assumptions of religion. Ironically, United Church people have come to see this more clearly and quickly than its own former "liberal" or "conservative" leadership. The fundamental spiritual attitude is becoming one of yearning, and not of apology. The spiritual response is becoming one of searching, and not of obedience to either a dogmatic or an ideological agenda. The context of meaning is no longer a mix of dogma and denominational policy, but the world itself permeated by God. The mission of the church is ceasing to be the prophetic call to repentance, but the proclamation of a vision of unity and an inherent meaningfulness to life that cannot be described by any one symbol. Finally, the model of discipleship is becoming one of self-actualization, rather than self-sacrifice.

One might say that since 1988, the United Church is becoming less adversarial, and more conversational. In previous debate over sexuality issues, each side assumed the radical separation of human and divine; that religious experience hinged on the correct ideological interpretation of a revealed Truth; and that this Truth was essentially fixed. Since 1988, however, more and more congregations are finding new life in a theological context of self-discovery which is surprisingly tolerant. Religious experience for them hinges on a reunion with God in which they are co-participants, and in which Truth can be complex, personal, and evolving.

One might even say that the church is beginning to take itself less seriously. In the 1980's the church saw itself as a competitor with culture, and at heart a religion of criticism. In the 1990's, the church is beginning to see itself in dialogue with culture, and at heart a religion of joy. Such joy is "erotic" because it is not merely self-sacrificial, but self-affirming. Individuals and congregations allow themselves to be touched and transformed by Spirit. The United Church of the past tended to be very conscientious, often intolerant, always worried, and never ecstatically happy. The United Church that is evolving into the future tends to be very caring, often humorous, always curious, and never dull.

Wherever the old polarities remain dominant, either "conservative" or "liberal," the local church tends to decline. Yet wherever the new theological perspective which reunites self-fulfillment and self-sacrifice is dominant (Eros and Agape) is dominant, the local church tends to be growing. Both sides of the old polarity tend to slander such growth as doctrinally shallow or ideologically impure. The truth is that the church is increasingly interested in personal relationship with God, rather than dogmatic unity about God; and ideological tolerance, rather than political uniformity. The old polarities continue to believe that the church is surrounded by a secular society. The growing church has realized what Canadian public opinion polls have recently begun to verify, namely, that the church now exists in a post-secular society alive with the yearning for the divine.

In my view, what has changed is that Agape and Eros are being reunited in the theological framework of the United Church of Canada. The church is beginning to discover that there are theological options other than the past polarizations which have proven so destructive to the church.

CONCLUSIONS

The metaphor which best explains the experience of the United Church of

Canada in the sexuality crisis so far, is that of a storm created by an emerging new weather pattern. The storm broke in 1988, specifically around the issue of sexual orientation and ordination, but precipitated more generally by broader anxieties about leadership and the future of the church. The storm has been confusing, in that it is not always clear today which way the wind is blowing. However, the storm has also been cleansing. It has awakened the church to exciting new options in church life and theology, and it has freed the church from the frustration of old polarizations. Perhaps most importantly, debate over sexuality has allowed the church to ponder theology in a far less rational, and far more experiential way. The most singular impact of the storm, however, is that the climate of church life has changed.

In a sense, the church as a whole has left its own leadership behind. Both "liberal" and "conservative" voices which had been so influential in the debate before 1988, find themselves at a loss to understand or influence the debate after 1988. Fewer people are listening. More congregations are finding their own way. Advocacy is no longer the key expectation of leadership. Vision and the ability to build unity are the new expectations of leadership. At the same time that congregations are claiming for themselves the prophetic consciousness that once was the specialty of their leadership, they are also demanding that leadership spend more time building and voicing the concord of the church, rather than criticizing and challenging the church .

The sexuality crisis will continue to be intense in the future, but I sense an evolution taking place in the perspectives of both conservative and liberal camps that reflects the changing context of church life. Conservative concerns are moving away from policy making, toward foundational theology and faith development. At the same time, the pastoral preoccupation of the conservative voice is moving away from sexual orientation, to concern for the family and covenants of relationship. Liberal concerns are also shifting. Their emphasis is also moving away from sexual orientation, toward issues of sexual abuse, and indeed, the abuse of creation. The pastoral preoccupation is likewise shifting away from individual persons, toward the quality of personal relationships. This evolution of perspective from both sides helps explain the success of the 1992 General Council as a time of new unity and enthusiasm. Everyone shares a common agenda to pursue foundational theological concerns which help define the parameters of "healthy" human relationships, and promote the quality of life.

Finally, the changing context of church theology is leading to a change in the "major metaphor" for the church by which the denomination understands itself. For years the "major metaphor" of the church has been **The Prophet.** The church saw itself in a confrontational relationship with society, advocating unpopular socio-political agendas in behalf of oppressed minorities, from a community base that was essentially rural. We were a grim people, a serious people, troubled by the secular "wilderness" that surrounded us. We were a people of deeds, rather than words, preoccupied with a "journey" toward a "promised land."

The new "major metaphor" for the church is not entirely clear, but I suggest that it is now **The Sentinel.** It is the "Watchman" in Habakkuk's tower proclaiming a vision that awaits the right time. The church has begun to see itself in a conversational relationship with society, sharing a content of faith and meaning, in a post-secular culture in which true majorities no longer exist, from a community base which has been radically urbanized. We are no longer in a wilderness, but in a city. Long aware of the sacredness of time, the sacredness of space is beginning to dawn upon us. We are becoming a more flexible people, a more tolerant people, a more humorous people. We are more open to ecstasies, in addition to knowledge. We are more aware of the ways personal, spiritual transformation changes society, in addition to the ways social transformation changes persons. We are no longer preoccupied with journeys toward a politically correct "promised land", but with the discovery of meaning in an ambiguous, urbanized oasis.

This, too, helps explain the success of the recent General Council as a time of unity and enthusiasm. The church is certainly not abandoning its long history of social activism, but it is re-discovering a whole new mission to articulate faith and interpret meaning for life. In the past the church offered individual leadership for corporate change; in the future it will offer corporate leadership for individual change.

CHAPTER VIII

THE EPISCOPAL CHURCH

(A) THE RESOLUTION ON HUMAN SEXUALITY PHOENIX, ARIZONA JULY 1991

RESOLVED, that this 70th General Convention affirms that the teaching of the Episcopal Church is that physical, sexual expression is appropriate only within the life-long, monogamous "union of husband and wife in heart, body, and mind intended by God for their mutual joy; for the help and comfort given one another in prosperity and adversity and, when it is God's will, for the procreation of children and their nurture in the knowledge and love of the Lord" as stated in the Book of Common Prayer; and be it further

RESOLVED, that this Church continue to work to reconcile the discontinuity between this teaching and the experience of many members of this body; and be it further

RESOLVED, that this General Convention confesses our failure to lead and to resolve this discontinuity through legislative efforts based upon resolutions directed at singular and various aspects of these issues; and be It further

RESOLVED, that this General Convention commissions the bishops and members of each diocesan deputation to initiate a means for all congregations in their jurisdiction to enter into dialogue and deepen their understanding of these complex issues; and further this General Convention directs the President of each province to appoint one bishop, one lay deputy, and one clerical deputy in that province to facilitate the process, to receive reports from the dioceses at each

meeting of their Provincial Synod and report to the 71st General Convention: and
be it further

RESOLVED, that this General Convention directs the House of Bishops
to prepare a Pastoral Teaching prior to the 71st General Convention using the
learnings from the diocesan and provincial processes and calling upon such insight
as is necessary from theologians, theological ethicists, social scientists, and gay
and lesbian persons; and that three lay persons and three members of the clergy
from the House of deputies, appointed by the President of the House of Deputies,
be included in the preparation of this Pastoral Teaching.

(B) AN APPRAISAL: WAITING ON THE SPIRIT: EPISCOPALIANS AND HOMOSEXUALITY

by

Ephraim Radner and George Sumner, Jr.

The Episcopal Church at its General Convention in July reached a compromise on homosexuality that buys the church time and maintains its fragile unity for three years. The church's Standing Commission on Human Affairs had recommended that individual dioceses might at their own discretion ordain actively gay people to the priesthood. (Another proposal, subsequently rejected, urged that experimental liturgies for same-sex unions be devised.) In response, an opposing resolution recommended that the ordination of anyone engaging in genital relations outside of marriage be forbidden under canon law. Neither of these resolutions passed. Instead, the convention adopted a substitute resolution that vaguely addressed the issue in terms of sexual norms for all people, lay and ordained, and called for a period of study on the topic.

In compromise, the church has managed to avoid a deeper truth. It has hit a theological wall built of its own historical self-understanding. Episcopalians have reached what they dislike most, a moment of reckoning. The bid to approve of gay sex challenges the church's very doctrine. Under what conditions could the church affirm sexual behavior that it has publicly condemned for centuries? The answer it will give to this question will determine what kind of church it will be, under what kind of authority and led by what kind of Spirit.

The "grand compromise" sought to accommodate the various camps in the debate. The church did affirm that "physical sexual expression is appropriate only within the lifelong, monogamous relationship of marriage," understood heterosexuality — a teaching grounded in the Book of Common Prayer and Scripture. But the convention's resolution qualified this affirmation by proposing that the church seek to "reconcile" the "discontinuity" between the traditional teaching and the experience of a number of its members. It does not say how, but at least it implies that Episcopalians ought not to muddle through with their present confusion indefinitely. And while the convention also "confessed" its "failure to lead and to resolve this discontinuity through legislative efforts based on resolutions directed at singular and various aspects of these issues" (e.g., ordination?), it is unclear from what sources it can draw conclusions other than canonical legislation. It seems that the convention will have to say something definite, somehow, in an authoritative fashion.

The resolution mandates more specific actions for the three years prior to the convention's next meeting. It calls for "dialogue" at all levels of the church in pursuit of a "deeper understanding, " and, it is hoped, consensus . In addition, the bishops are to produce a pastoral teaching based on both the reports of the local dialogues and the advice of "ethicists and social scientists."

The compromise resolution papers over deep contradictions, as one might expect. The talk of dialogue, emerging consensus and the latest social-scientific information assumes an evolutionary, progressive understanding of major doctrinal change. This assumption, however, is alien to the traditional affirmation of the exclusive and normative status of heterosexual marriage, with which the resolution opens. What can it mean for the church to affirm a basic teaching and in the same breath devise a temporal process by which potentially to alter it?

When the different camps use the same terms — for example, "spirit of

Anglicanism" and "the Spirit's leading" — they have different meanings. Thus, an advocate of the traditional teaching, Bishop William Frey, said at the debate that "the solution to our dilemma will have to be the action of the Holy Spirit." But Bruce Garner, president of Integrity, the church's organization of gays and lesbians, also said that the compromise "shows the Holy Spirit is beginning to work among us." All agree that the next three years are to be a period of spiritual discernment. But the question is more than what the Spirit will say; it is how and perhaps whether the Spirit will speak at all. The competing claims to heeding the Spirit are less examples of factional self-justification or even of fond hopefulness; they bespeak a general confusion about how the Episcopal Church can speak authoritatively about doctrinal concerns.

Past experience has surely encouraged this confusion. Less than two decades ago the Episcopal Church approved the innovation of women's ordination. Why shouldn't we expect the Spirit to speak in a similar way about gay sex?

In terms of ordination the two issues seem parallel. But in the case of women's ordination the question centered on the proper ordering of the church's particular life and ministry. St. Paul, for instance, never suggests that women have a different salvific status before God or constitute, as a sex, a special moral condition; he affirmed that "there is neither male nor female...in Christ Jesus" (Gal. 3:28). The controversy actually centered on church order — who would do what as a minister. There are tensions within Scripture on this subject that required sorting out.

But on the issue of gay sex, matters of internal church order, like ordination canons and marriage liturgies, are not the real problem. If active homosexuality is morally appropriate behavior for Christians, whether ordained or not, then a permission in canon law or liturgy is superfluous. Ordination of sexually active gay people has therefore quite rightly been seen as an indicator of the church's more general acceptance of gay sex among the non ordained. Unlike the case of women's ordination, then, the crucial point is how applicable scriptural teaching on sexuality and sexual practice might be to all church people. Everyone agrees that homosexuals are "fellow children of God," as a recent General Convention affirmed; and all agree that every church member is a sinner needing forgiveness. But the controverted point still remains: given the scriptural witness, is gay sex morally acceptable?

Advocates of accepting gay sex deal with its biblical condemnations in either of two ways. First, some say that the Bible's strictures really addressed cultic ritual or pederasty rather than sex between consenting adults of the same sex. This might be called a "revisionist" tack. A second approach agrees that the Bible condemns gay sex, but contends that the Spirit is leading the church to new insights on the issue. We call this a "pneumatic" point of view. The revisionist argument has failed to convince many who consider New Testament condemnations of gay sex, such as that in Romans 1, so broad as to make revisionist restrictions implausible. The pneumatic argument has proved more powerful in recent debate.

The real issue is gay sex itself, and if the most compelling argument is the pneumatic one, why is the debate turning on the narrow issue of ordination canons and alternative liturgies? Why doesn't it focus on the major theological problem of Scripture's authority in cases of doctrinal innovation? Why this three-year delay, brought on by a resolution ridden with contradictions and ambiguities?

The obvious answer is expedience. But perhaps a more significant influence is Anglicanism's inherent incapacity for reshaping doctrine. In the case of the Episcopal Church, turning to liturgy and canon law to respond to a contemporary doctrinal challenge is less a matter of expedience than an attempt to circumvent its tradition's doctrinal authorities.

Delving into the murky origins of Anglicanism's self-understanding is necessary here, because from the outset of the Reformation, Anglicans put canon law and the Prayer Book's public liturgies in a realm quite separate from the arena in which doctrinal matters touching Scripture were to be adjudicated. This perspective distinguishes Anglicans both from Roman Catholics and other Protestants.

Like many of their Continental colleagues, English reformers sought to repristinate their church according to what they believed were the faith and order of the first centuries. But, pressured by the conflicting interests that pull at a national church, the Anglicans quickly adopted a decidedly minimalist view of just what constituted this primitive Christian doctrine. They acknowledged some basics that met a scriptural test, but hesitated to go beyond those.

Unlike most other reforming churches of the time, the Church of England refused to adopt a full statement of the faith, a "confession," that might provide its members a coherent outline of Anglicanism's doctrinal commitments. For various reasons the Thirty-nine Articles of Religion (1571) could never fulfill such a role and were not designed to do so. And lacking anything comparable to the Roman church's papal *magisterium*, the Anglican church has never had a clear authority for doctrine, apart from the simple reading of Scripture itself.

Like all Christian bodies, and especially those gathered in the Reformation, Anglicans appeal to Scripture as the only fundamental authority for any matter touching salvation, including moral conduct (e.g., sexual conduct) and theological formulations of the apostolic faith. The question is, as it was at the time of the Reformation: on what basis should Scripture be interpreted? From the 16th century on the church has insisted that only the universal church as a whole, guided by the Holy Spirit, can authoritatively interpret the Bible on major matters of faith and morals.

Further, the only channels by which the universal church might so act were "general" or "ecumenical" councils, officially sanctioned gatherings of representatives from all local and national churches. These councils' authority rested on the subsequent ratification by the universal membership of the church, tested according to Scripture and displayed, perhaps only gradually, over time. Early Anglicans recognized as truly ecumenical, and thus legitimate, only the first four councils, from Nicea to Chalcedon. The decisions of these four councils — regarding the nature of the Trinity and of Christ, their formulation of the creeds and the like — were accepted as authoritative doctrinal statements insofar as the church universal had proven their foundation in Scripture.

In subsequent years, only the Anglicans and not other Reformation churches held firmly to the authority of legitimate ecumenical decisions while carefully refraining from drafting comprehensive statements of faith. Paradoxically, the Anglicans were committed to the primacy of Scripture in **doctrine and** morals, **and** to the refusal to pass authoritative judgments on controversial matters of scriptural interpretation until a general council of all the separated churches might convene. Scripture is a fundamental authority, they claimed, but we can't yet adjudicate its disputed meanings.

Practically speaking, the Anglican church could maintain this paradoxical position only partially. The Church of England did, through a variety of organs, articulate what it understood to be minimal and foundational doctrinal and moral commitments — e.g., doctrines embodied in the creeds, doctrines about Scripture and grace, and doctrines concerning the sacraments. Further, it held to what it considered clear scriptural teaching concerning moral conduct, using the New Testament as its supreme authority. It placed these affirmations above subsequent alteration. At the same time, Anglicans also made non-doctrinal and non-moral issues, such as "rites," "ceremonies" and, to a degree, the shape of the ordained ministry, open and subject to the necessary ordering of the local national church. In Richard Hooker's succinct 16th-century summary, "Law touching matters of order are changeable by the power of the church; Articles concerning doctrine not so." So while permitting private reflection and even debate on Scripture, the church rejected public innovation in this area.

One major historical result of this profound caution before the Bible is that for almost 400 years, the Anglican church has kept Scripture relatively sound from the interpretive turmoil of various modernisms. Despite factional controversies of one kind or another, Anglicanism has not known, until recently, the destructive questioning of Scripture's doctrinal relevance. This was because, for lack of a truly ecumenical council, the church deemed the minimal apostolic interpretation of Scripture the limit for official dogmatic formulation. Anglicanism has freely developed new forms of liturgical expression and order, including the ordination of women, on a multicultural basis, but has also always guarded scriptural and doctrinal tradition.

This doctrinal stasis resulted not from intellectual or spiritual stagnation, as some have asserted. Rather, it has sprung, if only implicitly, from a profound sense of waiting hopefully for the restored unity of a fully catholic church that will decide matters of faith that rest on Scripture in a divinely inspired fashion. Only recently has the notion of the Anglican (and thus Episcopal) church as a progressive force in the unfolding of the kingdom of God been articulated. This last idea contrasts sharply to the almost penitentially discreet stance that Anglicanism has taken until now, with respect to authoritative pronouncements and innovation.

This historical character of Anglicanism explains in part why the modern Episcopal Church authoritatively insinuates doctrinal teaching only through the channels of its non-doctrinal ordering; that is, through its canon law and liturgy. Therefore the Episcopal Church may (tenuously) address the moral appropriateness of homosexual activity only in terms of the ordination canons or in terms of liturgical blessings of same-sex unions. It simply does not have the structures of authority by which to adjudicate scriptural issues of faith and morals in new ways.

The issue of the moral rightness of homosexual sex, however, is a matter of "Articles concerning faith" in Anglicanism, because it touches scriptural teaching. One could argue that to ignore or dispense with such teaching may well be truer to God's will in this era. But such an argument would surely repudiate the entire history of Anglicanism's ecumenically minded structures of dogmatic caution. Even a general council would not have the authority to declare Scripture's teaching void on this point, although it might declare that teaching unclear in some way and offer the church an interpretive refocus in a revisionist fashion.

At the least, as Richard Hooker reminds us, we should recognize that "the mixture of those things by speech which by nature are divided, is the mother of all errors; the matters of discipline are different from the matters of faith and salvation." To confuse the two, as the church is now doing in addressing homosexuality, is a less than forthright discernment of God's will in this matter.

Given its structures of authority and its traditional commitment to "guarding" Scripture for the scrutiny of a general council yet to come, is Anglicanism (the Episcopal Church in particular) able to address homosexuality at all? Were such a council, including Roman Catholics, Orthodox, Evangelicals, Pentecostals and Protestants from around the world, held tomorrow, it most probably would not affirm that the Holy Spirit was moving the greater church to a moral acceptance of gay sex. Still, advocates of such a moral acceptance of gay sex might argue that their views represented the vanguard of the Spirit's movement, independent of universal Christian consensus and the traditional moorings of scriptural authority. This would be the "pneumatic" argument.

As the Episcopal Church waits on the Spirit over the next three years, it faces a far deeper matter for discernment: what kind of church will it become, and in what continuity with its own Anglican past? Only two alternatives appear plausible. Either it will reaffirm Anglicanism's refusal to change doctrine in matters of faith and morals as they touch Scripture until such a time as the church universal shall meet: or it will consciously reconstitute itself as a pneumatic and prophetic church moving at the frontline of other denominations.

These two alternative churches will experience different kinds of waiting on the Spirit. One will wait in hopeful humility and penitence for the unity of a church that simply cannot move forward in the Spirit until the church universal is united. The other will wait in active and perhaps lonely expectation of the Spirit's evolving and progressive movement through history. Advocates of reform can claim that standing on the Anglican past amounts to a "stifling of the Spirit." And the traditionalists will wonder how such a Spirit, cut loose from Scripture, will in time be distinguished from the various spirits within us. Still, cases can and will be made for both of these alternatives. What cannot be disputed is that they are fundamentally divergent.

So, by all means, let us wait upon the Spirit in prayer and study for the next three years. But the sought-after Spirit in these alternative ecclesiologies are not one and the same. This is what we must recognize in the end: two churches, two kinds of waiting, two Spirits. The deeper matter of discernment will be about which of the two we take up, and which of the two we will reject.

CHAPTER IX

THE POLITICS OF SEX AND POWER IN THE CHURCHES[1]

by

Karen L. Bloomquist

THE BATTLEFIELD OF SEXUALITY

Sexuality has in the 1990s become a major battlefield in American society — the arena in which struggles to define social reality, meaning, and purpose increasingly are centered. As James Davison Hunter describes in his book, *Culture Wars*[2], America is in the midst of a culture war that has and will continue to have reverberations not only within public policy but within the lives of ordinary Americans everywhere. At stake is how we will order our lives together, or what constitutes the good society. This war is being fought especially over issues of sexuality.

What is at stake are different systems of moral authority and understanding. These are rooted in basic commitments and beliefs, and even more profoundly, in who we are in our identity as sexual beings. It is because sexuality goes to the core of who we are, that there often is such passion and ultimacy connected with these conflicts. The conflict typically is framed in rhetoric that is absolute, comprehensive, and ultimate, i.e., "religious," even among those who do not consider themselves religious. Scientific evidence or persuasive arguments can do nothing to change the mind of those who are so committed. What has become "sacred" to those in one moral community is viewed as "desecration" to those in the opposing camp.

Occasionally this is extended into apocalyptic language. The struggle is seen as one with a clear dichotomy between what is right and what is wrong, the forces of God vs. the forces of Satan or the Antichrist. We are told, "Satan is ever at work to change God's marriage plan." Those who raise even mild questions about the this order are accused of being "agents of the Devil." As Paul Hetrick, of Focus on the Family (the Dobson organization that has heavily influenced members of many denominations), put it:

> We're talking about a battle of ideas...a third World War between those who defend and respect family and traditional values and those who reject them. We don't believe those two can coexist, and those who win will control the hearts and minds of our children.[3]

As a theologian/ethicist serving as staff director for one church body's deliberations on sexuality,[4] standing at times at the center of the arrows that cross back and forth across this battlefield, at times I find myself grudgingly agreeing with Philip Turner, who has stated, "In America today, sexual ethics serves as an arena for political struggle rather than for moral debate."[5] People engage in "wars" when they have given up on moral discussion, deliberation or debate. Threats (to leave the church or withhold money), caricatures, and refusal to dialogue are the tactics that are resorted to instead — by both sides.

What's at stake psychologically, ethically, spiritually that makes considerations of sexuality such a minefield? I will explore five themes that seem especially crucial for understanding what is going on, before suggesting the shift needed if we are to move beyond sexuality being the battlefield that it is today.

1. FEAR AND POWER ASSOCIATED WITH SEXUALITY

The pervasive fears that continue to be associated with sexuality in our society cannot be overestimated. This includes the fear of our sexuality, of the power of the erotic, and of those who have been seen as sexually "deviant" in our society. These anxieties and fears are probably the single factor that has most affected the sexuality politics in our churches. This is usually not named, much less dealt with. A conference of all-male church leaders can spend five days hearing and talking about sexuality issues, but without ever focussing on their own experience as sexual beings. Although today there is greater openness to talking about sexuality, the overwhelming tendency is to focus or even become fixated on the sexuality of those the dominant group considers to be "other" from themselves: men focussing on women, heterosexuals focusing on gays and lesbians. It is no accident that a mostly heterosexual church becomes so obsessed with talking about homosexuality: keep the problem "out there" so that we do not have to face our own fears connected with the most intimate aspects of our own lives as sexual beings.

Admittedly, some of the fears are connected with the enormous changes in sexual understandings and expectations over recent decades, related especially to the rise of feminism and the growing awareness of sexual abuse and boundary violations. New awareness as well as confusion regarding what is appropriate and inappropriate has stirred up real anxiety in many persons, as well as in society as a whole. Although it is a bit surprising how quickly people have been to denounce the abusive use of power as it occurs in sexual abuse (which was hardly an issue 10 years ago), many can skim quickly across the surface of that issue and then insist on punitively controlling the sexual expression of those who are gay, lesbian, or unmarried heterosexual, without any awareness that too may be experienced as abusive. Those who feel they are losing much of the traditional power they have had, or have aspired to have, particularly white heterosexual males, may be most susceptible to appeals to control the sexuality of others.

For many, bringing up the topic of sexuality also opens up the fear of being judged for being too sexually active or not active enough, of being "found out," of being victimized once again, of being rejected, in a society in which social and economic factors continue to marginalize, reject, and make many feel insecure and alone, without a sense of rootedness or belonging.

2. CHURCH AS "PARENT," CONTROLLER OF SEXUAL BEHAVIOR

It is remarkable how interested the wider society, and especially the media, are in church discussions and position-taking regarding sexuality, in contrast to what churches have said and done on other important social issues. Why is the church's approval or disapproval of certain sexual practices or relationships of such importance? The most obvious reason is that in our rather secularized society the church continues to serve as "parent" when it comes to sexuality. Even for those whose relationship to the church is minimal, or who do not even consider themselves "Christian," the church continues to serve as at least a distant "parent," whose approval or disapproval of sexual behavior continues to serve as an important point of reference.

In the popular imagination, sexuality still is seen as the focus of "sin," no matter how archaic that religious category may seem in the rest of people's lives. In a changing social and economic order, where families are often highly mobile, distant, and/or broken, and where relationships that truly affirm persons are few, many individuals continue to be haunted with the question, "Does God approve or disapprove of what I am doing sexually?" One may have left one's parental church but not one's parental notion of an approving or disapproving God, and the social order which "he" upholds.

Some of the gender politics I as staff director and we as a task force have been subjected to are not unrelated to the reality that despite whatever credentials we might have, many of us are not white males, that is, we simply do not look or sound like those who in the past have defined how the church will control sexuality.

Behind many of the responses I have read is the expectation that the church as parent will tell people what they can or cannot do, so that they can (a) remain obedient children (assured of the parent's favor), (b) rebel against the church's authority (especially with threatened or actual departure from the church?, or (c) accept the inevitability of a gap between the ideal that the church continues to teach and the actual realities of one's relationships. In the latter case, there is often an expressed desire for the church to maintain its traditional positions on sexual matters, set forth as ethical ideals toward which we should aspire, but with the realization that lots of practical adjustment of those ideals will be necessary in light of the actual realities people experience. In this way the ethical and the pastoral tasks are kept distinct, and ethics is compartmentalized from people's actual experience, in which they continue to fall far short of what God or the church expect.

When the church continues to be viewed as a parent expected to control sexual practices, the relevant questions are limited to what God or the church condemn, approve, permit, condone, or allow. The focus is on discreet acts rather than on complex relationships. As one respondent put it, "If the ELCA approves of sexual activity outside of marriage and people do it and get AIDS...then the ELCA is responsible for those people's decisions."

A colleague has reminded me that there only two sentences of a social statement that most people will really be interested in: 1) is sexual intercourse permissible only within marriage? and 2) is homosexual activity sin? Fuller ethical discussions that presume greater moral complexity and maturity are considered by many to be beside the point, or are viewed as high-fallutin' attempts of elites to "liberalize" the church's positions. Give us the prohibitions or permissions — preferably, straight from the Bible — not any convoluted discussions or rationalizations .

3. MORAL ABSOLUTES VS. MORAL RELATIVISM

There is a significant chasm between what are understood as unchanging God-given moral absolutes and human ethical decisions and choices that vary with circumstances, and therefore, are "relative" or "situational." For some, moral relativism on even one sexuality matter is immediately interpreted as "an anything goes" stance on any sexuality matter. Those of such a perspective accused our study of condoning promiscuity and infidelity, which it explicitly rejects. "If there is no absolute, no unchangeable order upon which we can build, there is NO foundation to what we are doing...? "If morality is relative, I will leave the Lutheran church." These are the kinds of responses we have heard in response to our study's suggestion that structures, including those that order our sexual life. are historically conditioned and subject to change.

The very idea of raising questions and inviting people to think about these matters is considered anathema by those for whom the absolutes are God-given, thereby ruling out any questioning or further discussion. "We must question our motives when we start to question God's wisdom." It is not only that such reflection is seen as unnecessary and thus an "immoral" waste of time and money, but to pursue further ethical discourse about these matters is considered a breach of faith. "God's will is clear — our only choice is to obey or disobey the law God has laid down for us to follow." The issue is one of the human will, and how it is distorted by sin. There is no need to use the human mind for further ethical discernment and deliberation. God's all-knowing mind is all-sufficient. "Don't raise questions that Holy Scripture has already settled." The very suggestion that morality may change "borders on apostasy."

What is striking is how these moral absolutes become operationally equivalent to God Himself (sic). To question them is to question not only God's Law but the very being of God as eternally unchanging. "God doesn't change God's mind" we have been told repeatedly.

Now to be fair to members and pastors of the ELCA, most do not fall into the extremes of either moral absolutism or moral relativism, including on matters of sexuality. The responses I have and will be citing are not necessarily typical of where most people in our denomination stand, as more scientific surveys have indicated.? But what has been startling to note is how many of the mainstream members and leaders of our churches seem incapable or unwilling to counter either such absolutist or relativist charges, and the inaccurate generalizations which such charges fuel.

Last year, Michael Kinnamon was narrowly defeated in the election for general minister and president of the Christian Church (Disciples of Christ), a defeat precipitated particularly by his position on the single issue of homosexuality. He reflected:

> Assumptions inherited from the Enlightenment about our capacity
> to discern universally valid norms for evaluating truth claims are
> fast eroding..., which can lead to fragmentation and anxiety, the
> sense that we have lost a secure place on which to stand or an
> overarching purpose or meaning. Two extreme reactions to this
> anxiety are widespread...relativism and its twin, absolutism....Both
> extremes contribute to our politicization and undermine the
> possibility of genuine leadership. Those who believe they have a
> firm grasp on God's will look for leaders who will parrot their
> convictions, and those who have deep doubts that we can ever
> know God's will with any confidence look for leaders who will
> parrot their political agenda. Both groups subvert genuine
> leadership marked by openness to the will of God.[7]

4. HERESY VS. IDOLATRY

Many of us have contended that sexuality is not a matter of basic faith, not a church dividing issue. Or so those of us in the middle of this warfare have been trying to reassure ourselves and others! But perhaps that has not been a valid assumption. Perhaps it is deeply theological, basic faith matters that are at stake, different understandings of biblical faith, which must first be faced if we are to move beyond the present stand-off over sexuality, and open up the possibility for ethical discourse and deliberation.

"Heresy"

At the heart of the "conservative" or "orthodox" lament against those with whom they disagree are charges of **heresy**. The charge is that others have questioned or deviated from the traditional, officially-accepted teachings of the church about sexual practice. In the case of Lutherans and other Protestants for whom there is no canon law and for whom the church's tradition and teaching on ethical issues does not have the same status as it does for Roman Catholics, the standard of orthodoxy is *sola Scriptura* as the rule and norm for faith and life. Those who approach this standard from out of a desire for moral absolutes turn to the Bible seeking clear moral absolutes regarding sexuality. To raise questions about what God has commanded or prohibited is, because the commands or prohibitions are in the Bible, to be heretical (furthermore, social chaos will result). Attempts to bring historical, critical questions to the biblical material, even if for the sake at getting at what truly is authoritative for us today, are rejected out of hand.

The common sense meaning of the text, appropriated directly by the believer, is what matters, with no further interpretation required. If Leviticus says, "you shall not lie with a male as with a woman; it is abomination [to God]" — that settles it; no further discussion needed: homosexuality is clearly condemned by God. To suggest anything else is to be guilty of "heresy" according to those for whom the uninterpreted Bible provides unambiguous rules as to what is right and wrong. To suggest that a text is irrelevant for situations as understood today is seen as the equivalent of declaring God or Scripture irrelevant, i.e., this too is heresy.

I am not implying that all or most of those who are opposed to homosexuality are of this mind-set. The many who are not, yet do hold to the primacy of biblical authority for their faith and life, don't quite know what to do with these charges when they are made. Mainline churches have for the most part not done a very effective job of teaching their members how to interpret Scripture in ways that move between the poles of an a-historical absolutism and a normless relativism (or between fundamentalism and modernism), or how to do ethics in a way that is not primarily focused on what the rules are. To try to do that now, around the heated issues of sexuality, becomes especially difficult.

"Idolatry"

On the other hand, at the heart of the "liberal" or "progressive" lament against those with whom they disagree are charges of **idolatry,** namely, making absolute that which is relative or historical, in other words, mistaking the created for the Creator. Our ELCA study, for example, questions the way in which Lutheran understandings of "orders of creation" have been used in unchanging ways that justify oppression. It goes on to state:

> ...the church proclaims the continual end of the old and the coming of the new creation. That is why Christians view all structures, including those that order our sexual life, as historically conditioned and subject to change. Structures are necessary and helpful, but they cannot become absolutes. We trust not in unchanging structures but in God's unchanging faithfulness. God makes all things new and is not bound by what already exists.[8]

This directly counters the world view discussed above, and has been strongly protested by such persons.

A sense of secure, dependable order or structure is important for human meaning and wellbeing, but when a given order itself becomes the focus of our ultimate trust or faith it can become our god. When we mistake what is created for God, the situation is one of idolatry.

> The idol becomes a veil of illusion, preventing us from seeing alternative ways of being or living. In that sense, it closes off historicity...Whenever anyone of things becomes god for us, it becomes an unquestioned absolute and reigns over us regardless of the human or historical consequences. This is idolatry.[9]

William Countryman describes how the Bible enables us to recognize this idolatrizing.[10] It is the alienness of the Bible — including its teachings and practices re. sexuality (e.g., in terms of purity and property) — that relatives our present. In this sense, it keeps us from absolutizing what is familiar, taken for granted, assumed to be eternal. The absolutistic claims of the present, when subordinated to God's reign, are relativized. Specifically, God's already/not yet reign relatives some of the absolutistic claims that are made regarding heterosexuality.

5. THE "NORMATIVITY" AND "NATURALNESS" OF HETEROSEXUALITY VS. HOMOSEXUALITY

Faith in the "normativity" of heterosexuality has, I contend, become the most difficult matter at the core of current sexuality debates. The only thing that matters to many is how normatively heterosexual marriage is set forth as the only place for sexual intercourse, and how clearly all homosexual activity is condemned as sin. "This study did not clearly reject homosexuality as sin, therefore we reject this study in its entirety" has become a frequent response.

Why is this what alone matters? Why is it that questioning the absoluteness of heterosexual marriage as the exclusive arena for sexual activity is labelled as "heresy" by some, if what is being called into question is not the very god upon which people's sense of order and identity depends?

In a changing social order, in which more and more groups have been striving for justice and human rights, heterosexism has become for many the last bastion issue. Faith in heterosexuality, and in a god who is instrumental to such an ordering of sexuality becomes a matter of basic faith. God authorizes an unchanging moral order, and it is heterosexual. Any "alternatives" to this are unacceptable, period. From such a perspective, the point of the biblical witness when it comes to sexuality is to uphold heterosexuality. Patricia Beattie Jung and Ralph Smith, in their forthcoming book, are particularly insightful in this regard: By reducing sexuality to male/female dichotomies, heterosexism creates an idolatrous focus on one part of the whole. Idolatry occurs when anyone or anything is invested with more significance than is fitting. As an interpretive framework, heterosexism is itself idolatry. Perhaps more than anything else the New Testament witness reveals that Jesus' life, death and resurrection were a confrontation with idolatry.[10]

The basic tendency among many Christians has been to use natural law assumptions for talking about God's law. What agrees with natural law is seen as obligatory, commanded by God. What is natural, given in creation, knowable by all, becomes what is "normative" — what ought to be, what is God ordained through divine ordinances or orders of creation. What is, because it is given by God, is what ought to be. What falls outside of this "norm" is seen as "unnatural" and thus immoral, sinful, or in modern medical terms, "abnormal."

When consensus breaks down, so that certain requirements are no longer commonly assumed to be natural, what is "natural" or God-ordained must then be imposed through the use of dominating authority. As Stanley Hauerwas has pointed out, by attempting to give Christian sexual ethics a "natural law" basis apart from theology, the result is an ethic that appears to many as arbitrary and irrational, and thus requires authoritarian imposition. Ethics based on natural law tempt us to coerce those who disagree with us since its presuppositions lead us to believe we always occupy the high ground. In other words, such an ethical approach tends to cut off discussion, presuming that the church needs no further deliberation about these matters.

In our day, what has been assumed to be "natural" and thus God's unchanging law, is increasingly being called into question by scientists and historians. For example, the historian Thomas Laqueur[12] contends that what we think of as most "natural" in relation to human beings, namely, biology, is not what has defined the sexes historically. The unchanging "natural" body that seems to lie at the basis of modern notions of sexual differentiation between males and females is the product of history. No particular understanding of sexual differentiation has necessarily followed from what are commonly assumed to be undisputed facts about bodies.

For thousands of years it was thought, based on Galen of the second century AD, that the genital organs of females were only internalized versions of males' genital organs, i.e., that there basically was one sexual structure in human beings, with the females' being an inverted, inferior, less perfect version of the males'. Gendered cultural assumptions, with the implied hierarchy of superior and inferior is what defined and structured the social reality that we today refer to as sexuality. The cultural category of gender was primary, not biological sex. What was important in social reality was not whether persons were male or female, but their relative social power, status, and roles. We see this, for example, in the ancient Romans, for whom the relevant sexual distinction was active vs. passive, not male vs. female. The sex of the sexual partner was less important ethically than the social power one had vis-a-vis the other.

It wasn't until modernity that there was felt to be a need for a consistent biological foundation of what was considered "masculine" and "feminine." Sometime in the 18th century the genital organs began to become foundational for incommensurable differences between males and females.[13] Women's bodily differences from men's began to bear an enormous new weight of meaning. The physiological differences between the two sexes were becoming foundational for gender and thus for the wider social reality. All the complex ways in which similarities among bodies confirmed a hierarchic world order were reduced to the single plane of nature, and what in the 18th century began to be assumed as "natural" differences. The battleground of gender roles shifted to nature, to biological sex. Anatomical differences between the sexes became foundational for a moral order in which "opposites attract," i.e., foundational for an essentially heterosexual social order.

Much of 19th and early 20th century thought seemed obsessed with establishing ontological differences between males and females. In a similar way, our society today is caught up in whether or not there are genetic, hormonal or physiological differences between homosexual and heterosexual men, with a flurry of studies attempting to establish that they are constitutionally and thus "by nature" different.

In the contemporary debate over the causes of homosexuality, the distinction is often made between social constructionists and essentialists. It is, however, a debate that cannot simply be reduced to one of nature vs. nurture. No one who believes sexual orientation is biologically based would deny that there are not also social factors operating, and no one believes sexuality can be socially constructed apart from the obvious biological factors. These are two contrasting, sometimes competing, but not necessarily contradictory interpretations of sexual orientation. Whichever theory one operates out of, one can reach a point where sexual orientation becomes a given in a person's life, regardless of whatever combination of biological and social factors may lie behind such. It becomes a "natural" orientation for some persons.

What are the implications of observations such as these for how we today interpret biblical texts? They raise the difficulty involved in talking about the "naturalness" of sexuality, much less building an ethic on the basis of what is assumed to be "natural." In light of these insights, it becomes anachronistic to read back into or impose upon these texts post-18th century assumptions regarding the ontology of sexual differences, assuming these are "natural." In doing so, it may be that we are not being honest to the intention of the texts themselves. We are tempted to make them say what is compatible with our own ideological framework of heterosexuality today.

How might this affect our reading of, e.g., the Genesis texts? The pivotal Genesis 1:27 text clearly indicates that humankind is created in the image of God as male and female. This is descriptive of the human reality God has created. From the beginning humankind exists as two creatures. They are given the blessing to be procreative and care for the rest of creation. But the word used for humankind — ha 'adam — indicates that male and female are not opposite but harmonious sexes with equal power.[14] The Priestly writer seems to be saying, yes, sexual difference is intrinsic in God's creation but don't over-accentuate or absolutize the significance of the differences.

In contrast, the creation of humankind in the Genesis 2 account begins not with two but with one ha-adam, the earth creature, created at first without sexual differentiation. God then sets forth to create "a companion corresponding to the earth creature." (Trible) It is out of this divine intention that the second earth creature is created — for the purpose primarily of companionship. Only with the creation of a second earth creature — who is mostly alike the first earth creation ("bone of my bone...flesh of my flesh") - does the reality of sexual attraction and differentiation first enter the story. Sexuality is the recognition not of division but of the oneness that is wholeness, bone of bone and flesh of flesh.[15]

"And they become one flesh" (Gen. 2:4). The "one flesh" reality becomes normative in sexuality, but many today are asked whether that can only occur in the coming together of male and female. To put it bluntly, is it the penis in the vagina that is constitutive of "one flesh"? Or does this fall into the trap of biological reductionism of what from a Christian perspective is a much wider, spiritual reality in a sexual relationship? What are the ethical qualities of such a "one-flesh" relationship?

I am not suggesting that these texts can or ought be contrived to suggest they provide explicit sanction for same-sex relationships. They assume the male-female sexual relationship to be natural or God-given. But they are not intended for the purpose of ostracizing or pronouncing moral judgment against those who are not heterosexual and married. Their primary intent was not to argue for heterosexuality over and against homosexuality, which is the fighting way in which they frequently are used as ammunition in contemporary debates.

What is considered "natural" or self-evident regarding sexuality in a given era, culture, or by a group of people is never unaffected by human activity, ideology, and historicity. Sexuality is a realm where nature and culture poignantly come together in all their theological ambiguity. To approach sexuality as if it were a natural phenomenon apart from human society and meaning is to fall into a biological reductionism that is theologically untenable.

The ways people categorize sexuality within any cultural context tend to function normatively. In the cultures surrounding the early church, the operating sexual ethic was based on distinctions of domination and subordination. The church, in part, began to challenge that and move toward an ethic of mutuality, although there were lots of quite different moves subsequently. At the time of the Reformation, the operating sexual ethic in the church raised up the ethic of clerical celibacy. Churches of the Reformation challenged that and moved toward an ethic focused on marriage. In American society at the end of the 20th century, the operative sexual ethic seems to have become obsessed with the distinction of heterosexuality versus homosexuality. The question facing the church today is whether this controlling distinction between human beings is adequate and consistent with both human realities and central theological insights of the faith we confess.

Moving beyond...

Much of the politics of sex and power in the churches today is permeated with the above dynamics: fears regarding sexuality, the church as controlling parent over sexuality, moral absolutism vs. relativism, charges of heresy vs. idolatry, and questions regarding the normativeness and naturalness of heterosexuality as the ordering principle for sexuality. Biblical, theological, and ethical arguments are developed, set forth, and argued in ways that typically do not shed a lot of light on the disagreements at stake but perpetuate the polarities and thus the "warfare." Unfortunately, the most persuasive, well-developed arguments can do little to change the hearts of those whose convictions about sexuality are rooted in what is much deeper than rational argument.

Some lament that so much time and energy is being spent on sexuality issues, and diverted from other central tasks or missions we need to be about as a society and as church bodies. I would suggest instead that the present impasse or battlefield on which we stand challenges us to probe for new understandings and ways of being the church, not in ways that replicate or reinforce the above dynamics, but in ways that might witness to and transform these dynamics as they operate in the wider society. The sexuality discussions presently going on — and at time wrenching our churches — provoke new understandings and embodiments of what it means to be the church in this society, new glimpses of what it means to be in ministry with another, new insights into the heart of what the biblical theological vision is all about. What's important is not just the positions we arrive at as churches, but how we deal with another along the way as a community of sexual beings.

I propose the need for a paradigm shift from at least two different directions:

1.   We need to move from a stance of macho fighting to one of bridging or making connections with one another, in the midst of our vulnerabilities. Fighting over sexuality contradicts what is at the heart of God's intention for human sexuality, namely, that it is a means by which we express and deepen our relationships with one another, and not a means by which we exploit, dominate, abuse, or break relationships with one another.

There is an urgent need for communities of faith to be safe places, havens from the continual wounding of judgment. Life-destroying words and actions, spaces where we need not worry about being shamed, battered, abused once again. The church needs to be a healing, i.e., a salvific place of grace, forgiveness, new life, a place where we are truly able to share our pains, struggles, short-fallings, and to do so assured of adequate protections against the harm than can occur in opening up these vulnerabilities. We have much to confess, much that remains broken, and much that speaks of God's presence in our lives.

The African-American theologian Toinette Eugene has put it this way:

> To those who so fear the body that they have an inordinate anxiety about all sexuality issues, there is the Word made flesh, God's stamp of approval upon the body as a medium of divine love. Those who find threatening a society wherein sex roles are challenged and becoming more build, to those who find strength primarily is [macho] force and physical power and who take refuge in unquestioned ecclesial and household authority, there is One who strangely inverts our understandings of power and who invites us out of the bondage of patriarchy into the new human reality.

> To those whose insecurity regarding sexuality is so painful that

they must find scapegoats on whom to lay blame for all anxieties and evils, to those who must prove that they are more Christian or American than others, there is that One who demonstrates the triumph of grace announcing that all are free to live as persons who are unconditionally accepted as full members of the Family of God.[16]

2.   We also need to shift from equating the gospel with liberal tolerance/acceptance to a gospel-formed community of faith that is able honestly to face and grapple with ethical dilemmas as people actually face them in their lives as sexual beings. We need to become communities that have enough trust to challenge, offer guidance, and mutual correction to one another.

God gave us the Law (Torah) out of recognition of the human need for dependable boundaries within which relationships of righteousness and compassion can flourish. Jesus knew well the law and the sexual boundaries of his tradition, but he interpreted them in a more profound way, focussing on internal desires as well as external acts (Mt. 5:27-28). Although structures, laws, and boundaries are necessary for life in society — to show us God's intention and to protect the neighbor from harm — they cannot become more important than the qualities of mutual love, trust, and justice that our sexual relationships, grounded in God's relationship with us, are to embody. Jesus repeatedly challenged the common social boundaries of his day in order to reach out and relate to those who were oppressed by the law, and did so in the name of the law of a justice-seeking love.

The New Testament church's understandings of sexuality were a direct counter to today's liberal toleration of "whatever people do in private" is OK. Through baptism, according to St. Paul, Christians' bodies belong to God...are members of the body of Christ...a temple of the Holy Spirit...so that what we do with other bodies sexually is important in the community of faith. These are matters of concern to the whole body. The challenge to the community, however, is how to express that concern in ways that move beyond the controlling, power over sexuality that has so long characterized the church's guidance as a controlling parent and has helped excuse if not justify abuse and oppression. A central challenge today is how communities of faith can be genuinely helpful in helping people live out their sexuality in ways that are faithful and responsible.

Most communities of faith have a long way to go before that will become a reality, but there are glimpses of that occurring, in thousands of congregations that have begun talking about these matters. In the process they are discovering the brokenness and woundedness in their midst, and experiencing the healing presence of God in their listening and expressions of compassion toward one another. The presence of God's Spirit enables the kind of community in which communication about what matters most to us sexually can begin to occur, and thereby a new sense of what it means to be church can emerge: an image of the people of God in deep and enduring relationship with one another.

ENDNOTES

[1]Presented March 1, 1993 at the Reinhold Niebuhr Institute conference on "Sexuality, Spirituality, and Society: Issues Facing the Churches" at Siena College, Albany, NY.

[2]James Davison Hunter, *Culture Wars: The Struggle to Define America* (Basic, 1991).

[3]*National Catholic Reporter*, December 25, 1992; 9.

[4]In 1991 the Evangelical Lutheran Church in America published a study booklet, "Human Sexuality and the Christian Faith," intended for the church's deliberations prior to the drafting of a position-proposing statement. Reflections in this essay are based on some of the thousands of responses received to that study. Work is continuing on the development of a social statement expected to be acted on at the 1995 ELCA Churchwide Assembly.

[5]"Undertakings and Promises: An Anatomy of Sexual Ethics," *First Things*, 1991, 40.

[6]"Controversial Social Issues and the Evangelical Lutheran Church in America," Lutherans Say...#4 Report, ELCA Office for Research, Planning and Evaluation, 1991.

[7]Michael Kinnamon, "Restoring Mainline Trust: Disagreeing in Love, *The Christian Century*, vol. 109:21 (July 1-8, 1992), 647.

[8]"Human Sexuality and the Christian Faith," ELCA Division for Church in Society (1991), 31.

[9]Karen L. Bloomquist, *The Dream Betrayed: Religious Challenge of the Working Class* (Fortress, 1990), 52.

[10]L. William Countryman, *Dirt, Greed and Sex: Sexual Ethics in the New Testament and Their Implications for Today* (Fortress, 1988), 237f.

[11]Patricia Beattie Jung and Ralph F. Smith, *Heterosexism: An Ethical Challenge* (unpublished manuscript), 173.

[12]Thomas Laqueur, *Making Sex: Body and Gender from the Greeks to Freud* (Harvard, 1990).

[13]Laquer, 149ff.

[14]Phyllis Trible, *God and the Rhetoric of Sexuality* (Fortress, 1978), 12ff.

[15]Trible, 103.

[16] "Faithful Responses to Human Sexuality: Issues Facing the Church Today" *Chicago Theological Seminary Register* (Spring 1991), 3-4.

CHAPTER X

THE UNITED METHODIST EXPERIENCE

by

Victor Paul Furnish

I will be commenting, in turn, on some of the United Methodist Church's official actions and statements, on what is actually happening at the local and national levels in the denomination, and — very briefly — on several kinds of issues that have emerged in the discussions to date. To begin with, however, a few introductory points need to be registered.

First, no comprehensive study of human sexuality has ever been commissioned by the United Methodist Church. There is therefore no United Methodist document to compare with the general studies of human sexuality recently undertaken by some other American religious communities .

Second, official United Methodist statements about various matters of social justice and responsibility, including human sexuality, are contained in a statement of "Social Principles" that is included in *The Book of Discipline*, the denomination's "book of law" that is published every four years following a quadrennial General Conference. According to a Preface that introduces the Social Principles, these are "intended to be instructive and persuasive," and to summon "all members of the United Methodist Church to a prayerful, studied dialogue of faith and practice."[1]   Only the General Conference, at present constituted of almost 1,000 delegates — an equal number of lay and clergy — can speak officially for the denomination. It is this body that determines the contents of the Social Principles and that establishes policies and standards for the governance of the whole church, including all local congregations.

Finally, it is probably not surprising that in recent years the two subjects addressed in the Social Principles which have prompted the most discussion and debate are abortion and homosexuality. Of these, homosexuality has generated by far the most controversy, and is therefore the topic of the comments that follow.

I. OFFICIAL STATEMENTS AND ACTIONS

No American religious community remained unaffected by the social activism of the 1960's, which — given the 1954 Supreme Court decision on - school desegregation — was focused in the movement to gain full civil rights for ethnic minorities, especially African Americans. Because this movement was based largely in the black churches and benefitted from the effective leadership of a number of black clergy, it was the first to claim the attention and win the support of the American religious community in general. However, such a religious base was not readily available for those concerned about the civil rights of homosexual persons. The first two American gay rights organizations, the Society for Individual Rights and the Council on Religion and the Homosexual, were formed in 1964, but without the support of any prominent religious leaders, and with vocal opposition from many.

The turning-point for the nascent gay rights movement came five years later, on the night of June 27-28, 1969, with a riot at the Stonewall Inn, a private club located off of Sheridan Square in Greenwich Village. Because most of the club's membership was gay, the New York Police Department routinely conducted raids there. On this particular evening, however, the law officers met resistance — not only from those patronizing the Stonewall Inn itself, but also from hundreds of patrons of nearby bars and residents of the community. William Wynkoop, a 33 year old Professor of English at Adelphi College, and gay, lived nearby and was awakened by the noise. Twenty years later, recalling that evening, he told an interviewer: "There was a feeling — that I certainly felt — of glory, of inner glory, that this rebellion was going on ...."[2]

In the spring of 1968, just one year before the Stonewall riot, the United Methodist Church was formed by a union of the former Methodist and Evangelical United Brethren churches. The Uniting Conference, meeting in Dallas, had determined that a statement of Social Principles should be drawn up for the new denomination. A drafting committee chaired by Bishop James Thomas was charged with the responsibility of submitting such a statement to the 1972 General Conference.

Precisely during the four years that the Thomas committee was at work on a set of Social Principles, gay rights concerns began to surface within the United Methodist Church, not least through the initiatives of several clergy who disclosed their affectional orientation as homosexual. Up to this time no predecessor body of the newly-formed denomination had ever made any official statement about homosexuality or homosexual practice. However, Bishop Thomas and a majority of his committee were convinced that the Social Principles simply had to include some kind of statement on this topic. As a consequence, the document recommended to the 1972 General Conference by the Thomas committee included a brief statement about homosexuality. This statement neither condemned nor condoned the practice, but said only:

> Homosexuals no less than heterosexuals are persons of sacred worth, who need the ministry and guidance of the church in their struggles for human fulfillment, as well as the spiritual and emotional care of a fellowship which enables reconciling relationships with God, with others, and with self. Further we insist that all persons are entitled to have their human and civil rights ensured.[3]

At the General Conference session this statement made it through a preliminary legislative committee. However, by the time it reached the entire body there was intense opposition to it. During heated floor debate a lay delegate moved the addition of one qualifying clause to the last sentence of the committee's statement, and his motion prevailed. Thus as finally adopted, the last sentence read: "Further we insist that all persons are entitled to have their human and civil rights ensured, *though we do not condone the practice of homosexuality and consider this practice incompatible with Christian teaching*" (italics added).[4] This last clause has remained in the denominations's Social Principles ever since, despite repeated attempts to delete it, and despite certain other changes in the remainder of the paragraph. Indeed, in subsequent General Conferences support for the "incompatibility" clause increased, so that by 1988 fully eighty per cent of the delegates voted to retain it.

By 1988, given various changes over the years, the entire Social Principles statement about homosexuality read:

> Homosexual persons no less than heterosexual persons are individuals of sacred worth. All persons need the ministry and guidance of the Church in their struggles for human fulfillment, as well as the spiritual and emotional care of a fellowship which enables reconciling relationships with God, with others, and with self. Although we do not condone the practice of homosexuality and consider this practice incompatible with Christian teaching, we affirm that God's grace is available to all. We commit ourselves to be in ministry for and with all persons.[5]

By now the reference to civil rights for homosexual persons had been subsumed within a broader statement in an earlier paragraph:

> We insist that all persons, regardless of age, gender, marital status, or sexual orientation, are entitled to have their human and civil rights ensured.[6]

Although it is not possible here to provide a detailed report of United Methodist discussions about homosexuality since 1972, four specific actions are worthy of note.

First, the 1976 General Conference provided that ". . . no board, agency, committee, commission, or council shall give United Methodist funds to any 'gay' caucus or group, or otherwise use such funds to promote the acceptance of homosexuality."[7] This provision, which remains in effect, has put at financial risk any official church group, agency, or institution, that ventures to raise questions about the wisdom of the denomination's statements and policies concerning homosexuality. A sanction of this sort applies to no other topic addressed in the Social Principles.

Second, the 1984 General Conference, citing the "incompatibility" clause of the Social Principles, specified that no "self-avowed practicing" gay or lesbian person is to be ordained. The decisive statement of the matter (parts of which are reflected at several other points in *The Book of Discipline*) reads:

> While . . . persons set apart by the Church for the ministry of Word, Sacrament, and Order are subject to all the frailties of the human condition and pressures of society, they are required to maintain the highest standards represented by the practice of fidelity in marriage and celibacy in singleness. Since the practice of homosexuality is incompatible with Christian teaching, self-avowed practicing homosexuals are not to be accepted as candidates, ordained as ministers, or appointed to serve in The United Methodist Church.[8]

Third, by an extremely close vote the 1988 General Conference mandated an official four-year study of homosexuality, something that previous General Conferences had declined to do. The responsibility for this study was assigned to the denomination's General Council on Ministries, which entrusted it to a committee chaired by the Reverend Nancy Yamasaki. There were both lay and clergy members on the committee; and a number of them were chosen because

of their expertise in fields pertinent to the study. The committee's responsibility
was to:

> a) Study homosexuality as a subject for theological and ethical
> analysis, noting where there is consensus among biblical scholars,
> theologians, and ethicists and where there is not.
>
> b) Seek the best biological, psychological, and sociological
> information and opinion on the nature of homosexuality, noting
> points at which there is a consensus among informed scientists and
> where there is not.
>
> c) Explore the implications of its study for the Social Principles.[9]

When first presented for discussion, the authorizing resolution mentioned not only
the Social Principles but also the statements about ordained ministry. However,
in the interest of getting the General Conference to authorize any kind of a study,
the latter reference had to be deleted. Most delegates were unwilling to let the
ordination of homosexual persons be a matter even for study.

Finally, the 1992 General Conference received and took action on the
report that it had authorized four years earlier, and also on three
recommendations that accompanied it. The first recommendation was that the
entire Social Principles statement about homosexuality be replaced. Although the
Yamasaki committee had been unanimous in its recommendation to jettison the
old statement, it was not fully agreed about the wording of the statement that was
to replace it. The majority proposal, signed by seventeen committee members,
not only acknowledged the church's divided mind about homosexuality, but also
declared that "the present state of knowledge and insight" is an insufficient basis
for any wholesale condemnation of homosexual practice.[10] In its entirety, this
majority statement read:

We acknowledge with humility that the church has been unable to arrive at a common mind on the compatibility of homosexual practice with Christian faith. Many consider this practice incompatible with Christian teaching. Others believe it acceptable when practiced in a context of human covenantal faithfulness. The present state of knowledge and insight in the biblical, theological, ethical, biological, psychological and sociological fields does not provide a satisfactory basis upon which the church can responsibly maintain the condemnation of all homosexual practice. The church seeks further understanding through continued prayer, study and pastoral experience. In so doing, the church continues to affirm that God's grace is bestowed on all, and that the members of Christ's body are called to be in ministry for and with one another, and to the world.[11]

It will be noted that this majority statement, like the one that had been drafted by Bishop Thomas's committee in 1972, neither condemns nor condones the practice of homosexuality. Nevertheless, four members of the study committee dissented from one key sentence, and their minority version was included within the full committee report that was presented to the 1992 General Conference. In the minority version the key sentence reads: "The present state of knowledge and insight . . . does not provide a satisfactory basis upon which the church can responsibly *alter its previously held position that we do not condone the practice of homosexuality and consider this practice incompatible with Christian teaching*" (italics added).[12]

The Yamasaki committee was unanimous, however, in making two other significant recommendations. It proposed adding to the Social Principles a paragraph addressed specifically to the human rights and civil liberties of homosexual persons.[13] And it recommended authorizing the United Methodist Publishing House to develop and make available "educational study materials on the issue of homosexuality."[14]

All three of these recommendations were vigorously debated by the 1992 General Conference, first of all in the legislative committee to which they were assigned and then later in plenary sessions of the entire Conference. Ultimately, the recommendations about developing study materials and adding a civil rights paragraph were approved, with only minor amendments. The latter reads, as adopted:

> Certain basic human rights and civil liberties are due all persons. We are committed to support those rights and liberties for homosexual persons. We see a clear issue of simple justice in protecting their rightful claims where they have: shared material resources, pensions, guardian relationships, mutual powers of attorney and other such lawful claims typically attendant to contractual relationships which involve shared contributions, responsibilities and liabilities, and equal protection before the law. Moreover, we support efforts to stop violence and other forms of coercion against gays and lesbians.[15]

The Yamasaki committee's recommendation to delete the "incompatibility" clause, toned down a bit,[16] reached the floor of the Conference only as a minority report from the legislative committee in which it had been debated. To no one's great surprise, it was defeated — with 372 delegates voting for it and 594 voting against it.[17] Subsequently, the old paragraph, which in its essentials, although not its exact wording, dated back to 1972, was reaffirmed by a vote of 710 for, 238 against. Perhaps the most important of these votes, however, was the earlier one. Even though the study committee's (amended) recommendation had not prevailed, 40% of the delegates had indicated that they were in favor of replacing the old statement with a non-condemnatory one. Thus even in defeat, proponents of change were heartened, because just four years earlier (1988) only 20% of the delegates had voted to remove the "incompatibility" clause.[18] There was clearly a growing uneasiness with the rigidly judgmental language that had been in place for twenty years.

II. THE PRINCIPLES IN PRACTICE

When one turns from the principles and policies about homosexuality enacted by the General Conference to the actual attitudes and practices of United Methodist laity and clergy, the words that come to mind are *diversity, ambiguity,* and *frustration.* As demographic studies consistently show, United Methodism reflects the ideological, political, social, and economic diversity of America itself. For this reason, and also because of the distinctive "connectional" structure of the denomination, there is inevitably a certain ambiguity in how the actions of the General Conference are viewed and implemented at the local level. And of course, diversity and ambiguity not infrequently give rise to frustration in all quarters.

The topic of homosexuality has been kept alive in no small part by two unofficial caucuses within United Methodism. On the one hand there is a national caucus of evangelical Methodists ("Good News") which maintains that homosexuality is a sin, and which is therefore resolutely opposed to any change in the church's present official statements and policies. On the other hand, a national caucus of gay, lesbian, and bi-sexual Methodists ("Affirmation") has been increasingly active in trying to get the church's official statements and policies changed.

A number of people affiliated with Good News were among the 48 pastors from 18 different states who gathered in Houston, Texas in December, 1987. Mindful of the 1988 General Conference just months away, these clergy endorsed a three-part statement which commented, in turn, on "The Primacy of Scriptures," "The Trinity," and "The Ordained Ministry." The third section was devoted entirely to the matter of homosexuality. It described "homosexual practices as a sin," repudiated "all irrational fear of and contempt for homosexual persons," affirmed a ministry aimed at helping them change their "lifestyle" even if their orientation cannot be changed, and called it "unacceptable in the context of the Christian faith" that homosexual persons "be ordained to ministry or continue in representative positions within the church."[19] In January, 1992 a similar group was convened in Memphis, Tennessee. A so-called "Memphis Declaration," endorsed by 117 persons, urged the forthcoming 1992 General Conference, among other things, to reaffirm its view that homosexual practice is incompatible with Christian teaching, and therefore to reject "the report and recommendations of the Committee to Study Homosexuality and oppose further study."[20]

The Affirmation caucus originated as a support system for gay and lesbian persons within the United Methodist Church, and a number of local Affirmation groups across the country continue to function in this way. In addition, a national board has sought to mobilize support for changes in the denomination's statements and policies concerning homosexuality. In 1984 Affirmation established a Reconciling Congregation Program (which later became independent) to help local churches "consider justice and ministry issues arising from the involvement of gay men and lesbians," to support them in their ministries with and for such persons, and "to identify local churches where lesbians and gay men are welcomed as full participants in the body of Christ."[21] By 1993 more than sixty United Methodist churches, several Annual Conferences (the United Methodist equivalent of a diocese or synod), and some other official denominational bodies had affiliated with this program.

The Transforming Congregation Movement was started up later, largely to counteract the Reconciling Congregation Program, and by 1993 almost thirty local churches had joined. The stated purposes of this movement are to "affirm the biblical witness that homosexuality is a sin," to "heal homosexual persons and their families," to "facilitate God's work of healing and wholeness to those struggling with homosexuality," and to integrate all repentant, redeemed persons into full, active responsible membership in the local church."[22]

The two contrasting "congregation" movements, like the two national caucuses, demonstrate the great diversity that exists within United Methodism. This diversity accounts in part for the complex and ambiguous situation of gay and lesbian clergy in the United Methodist Church. On the one hand, as we have seen, the ordination of "self-avowed practicing" gays and lesbians is specifically precluded by church law. But on the other hand, decisions about whom to ordain, and also the actual appointment of clergy to serve in local churches (or elsewhere), are among the responsibilities of local judicatories (the Annual Conferences) and the bishops who preside over them.[23] In practice, this has meant regional variations in the way General Conference policies have been interpreted and applied. There is of course no way to know how many closeted gays and lesbians there are among the denomination's ordained clergy or among its seminary students preparing for ordination, and few bishops or other church officials have shown much heart for identifying them. Indeed, some ordained persons who are "more or less" open about their homosexuality continue to serve under appointment, although in most of these cases the assignment is to some form of ministry other than the local pastorate. Ordinarily, where a local judicatory has denied ordination to someone on the grounds of her or his homosexuality, or has required the surrender of a person's ministerial orders for this reason, some specific incident has prompted the action. One has the impression that many church officials prefer not to know who of the clergy under their jurisdiction are homosexual, and that they try to deal with specific situations pastorally and confidentially until some kind of public disclosure forces them to invoke denominational laws.

Sometimes public disclosure is unavoidable, as in the case of a retired United Methodist bishop who died of AIDS in 1987. It soon became known that, despite his public support of the General Conference's stand against homosexuality and the ordination of homosexual persons, he himself for many

decades had led a secret life as a gay man.[24] Even though his episcopal
colleagues had harbored suspicions and heard rumors for many years, they
scarcely spoke of these even among themselves, and since his death have
maintained their silence. There is no more tragic or dramatic symbol of the
present, practical situation in the United Methodist Church.

III. SOME ISSUES

It was essentially a pastoral concern which prompted the statement about
homosexuality that was recommended to the 1972 General Conference by Bishop
James Thomas's committee. As we have seen, the statement as originally drafted
included no specifically moral judgment about homosexuality or homosexual
practices. A moral judgment entered in only with the addition of the qualifying
clause about the "incompatibility" of homosexual practice with Christian teaching.
This addition was adopted without the benefit of any kind of study, either of
homosexuality itself or of "Christian teaching" about it. What had started out to
be solely an expression of pastoral concern for homosexual persons ended up
including a clause which appeared to give theological warrant to a widespread
opinion that all homosexuality is "sinful," and that homosexual persons are
dangerous both to themselves and to society.

As the "incompatibility" clause was debated in subsequent General
Conferences, the usual scriptural passages were tossed back and forth like hand
grenades, from one "camp" to another. Somewhat less often, the findings of the
empirical sciences were invoked. Primarily, however, the debate proceeded on
the basis of unexamined prejudices and misinformation, with appeals to personal
experiences with homosexual persons (pro or con), and in the service of varying
political agendas. Not until the authorization of a study committee in 1988 did
United Methodism provide for a forum wherein the issues as such could be
identified, and then considered in an informed and reasonable way. Five special

issues kept recurring as this committee conducted its investigations and discussions.

From the beginning, and then constantly throughout its work, the study committee found itself significantly divided about basic matters of biblical authority and interpretation. When, at the end of their study, committee members identified nine fundamental points on which they had been unable to achieve consensus, six of those related wholly or in part to the interpretation of the Bible.[25] There was relatively little disagreement over "what the Bible says" about homosexual practices. The more critical and disputed matter was whether, and if so, how Scripture can inform the mind of the modern church on specific moral issues like homosexuality. By the end of the United Methodist study, it had become evident that the church's clergy as well as laity need to reflect much more deliberately and carefully on the nature and authority of the biblical writings, on what procedures are appropriate for interpreting them, and on how Scripture can and cannot assist the church in thinking through ethical issues.

Another issue, closely-related to the first, was what weight should be given to the findings of the empirical sciences concerning homosexuality. On this matter, too, the committee found consensus elusive.[26] The question becomes especially important at those points where the findings of the natural and social sciences appear to call into question, or even to contradict, the church's own traditions, including Scripture. Are such findings to be accepted only when they seem to support, or at least seem not to contradict the apparent teachings of Scripture?

Third, the committee also failed to reach a consensus on what the "acceptable moral options" are for persons of homosexual orientation. A few members of the panel argued "that such persons should be committed to a life of celibacy, or else seek transformation to heterosexual orientation." Most members, however, concluded that "committed same-sex monogamous relationships" are an acceptable option for Christians of homosexual orientation.[27] However, available data suggest that most United Methodists do not approve of same-sex unions, and in several cases bishops or other church officials have specifically prohibited pastors from conducting liturgies of "holy union."[28]

A fourth question, although not specifically addressed in the United Methodist report, was nonetheless implicit in many of the panel's deliberations: On what kinds of moral issues, if any, and in what kinds of circumstances, if ever, is it appropriate for the church either to "legislate" or even to provide guiding "principles" for its members? Here one touches on the deeper questions of what the church is and of what it means for the church to function as a community of moral discernment. This issue becomes especially acute when, as in the case of human sexuality, knowledge is so extremely limited that equally sincere and informed persons can come to very different conclusions. Are there, perhaps, certain kinds of ethical issues on which it is inappropriate or unwise for the church ever to legislate, or to make general pronouncements? Can legislation and pronouncements sometimes support and inform the church's pastoral ministries? Or do legislative actions and pronouncements on matters like homosexuality inevitably hinder, or even preclude those ministries?

A fifth question, which overlaps the fourth, is specifically addressed in the United Methodist report: "How Should the Church Deal with Unresolved and Unresolvable Questions Related to Homosexuality?"[29] When the church is faced with conflicting or incomplete evidence on a subject like this, and therefore with uncertainties and different understandings, one option is simply to remain silent. A second option is the one adopted by the General Conference — to be guided by majority vote. Yet a third is the one recommended by the study committee, but only partially accepted by the General Conference: to agree in so far as possible on what the church can and cannot responsibly teach,[30] to identify and clarify the issues that remain, providing guidance on how to think them through, and in the meantime to withhold judgment.

ENDNOTES

[1]*The Book of Discipline of the United Methodist Church 1992* (Nashville: The United Methodist Publishing House, 1992), p. 87.

[2]Quoted in the *San Francisco Examiner*, June 4, 1989.

[3]*Daily Christian Advocate*, April 25, 1972, p. 484 (Calendar Item 444, Petition A-5753), and April 28, 1972, pp. 707-709.

[4]*The Book of Discipline of the United Methodist Church 1972* (Nashville: The United Methodist Publishing House, 1973), p. 86.

[5]*The Book of Discipline of the United Methodist Church 1988* (Nashville: The United Methodist Publishing House, 1988), p. 96.

[6]*The Book of Discipline . . . 1988*, p. 95.

[7]*The Book of Discipline of the United Methodist Church 1976* (Nashville: The United Methodist Publishing House, 1976), p. 337.

[8]*The Book of Discipline of the United Methodist Church 1984* (Nashville: The United Methodist Publishing House, 1984), p. 189.

[9]*The Book of Resolutions of the United Methodist Church 1988* (Nashville: The United Methodist Publishing House, 1988), p. 121.

[10]Four members of the committee opposed this proposal. Three other members did not vote: the committee's chairwoman, a staff person who also sat as a member of the committee, and an openly gay member of the committee who had to be absent when the vote was taken.

[11]*Report of The Committee To Study Homosexuality to The General Council on Ministries of The United Methodist Church* (August 24, 1991), pp. 32-33.

[12]*Report of The Committee To Study Homosexuality*, p. 33.

[13]*Report of The Committee To Study Homosexuality*, p. 33.

[14]*Report of The Committee To Study Homosexuality*, p. 32.

[15]*The Book of Discipline* . . . 1992, p. 92.

[16]In the interest of compromise, sponsors had agreed to deleting the sentence that "the present state of knowledge and insight" provides no adequate basis for retaining the "incompatibility" clause.

[17]*Daily Christian Advocate*, May 13, 1992, p. 482.

[18]Of the 946 delegates, 181 had favored removing the old language, 765 had favored retaining it.

[19]"The Houston Declaration," an undated and unpaged pamphlet [p. 4].

[20]"The Memphis Declaration — Part II," a paid advertisement in *The United Methodist Reporter*, April 6, 1992.

[21]"How to Become a Reconciling Congregation," an unpaged pamphlet dated May, 1989 [p.1].

[22]"Transforming Congregations," an unpaged reprint of a statement drawn up in October, 1988 [p.2].

[23]Thus, while Decision No. 544 of the denomination's Judicial Council (October 26, 1984) upheld the right of the General Conference to establish minimum standards for the clergy, it also affirmed that actions related to ministerial standing and appointment remained the responsibility of the Annual Conferences. See also Decision No. 542 (May 10, 1984).

[24]The most extensive published report of the matter is by Emily Yoffe, "The Gay Bishop," *Texas Monthly*, October, 1987, 102-106, 188-200.

[25]*Report of The Committee To Study Homosexuality*, pp. 25-26.

[26]*Report of The Committee To Study Homosexuality*, p. 26 ("We do not have consensus on the weight we should give scientific evidence in arriving at moral judgment[s]").

[27]*Report of The Committee To Study Homosexuality*, p. 26.

[28]So far, however, there is no General Conference action that specifically prohibits United Methodist clergy from conducting such liturgies.

[29]Report of The Committee To Study Homosexuality, pp. 27-28.

[30]See the Report of The Committee To Study Homosexuality, pp. 23-25.

PART THREE:

THE FUTURE OF THE DEBATE

CHAPTER XI

ENLARGING HUMAN FREEDOM: A FEMINIST VIEW

by

Sylvia Thorson-Smith

From a feminist perspective it is not easy to envision the future of the sexuality debate ln America's churches. My feelings are a mixture of pessimism and optimism. In this chapter I want to put those mixed feelings in perspective. Let me begin by sharing an illustration of my experiences in addressing sexuality issues within the church. It occurred on Tuesday, June 11, of 1991 in Baltimore. The General Assembly of the Presbyterian Church (U.S.A.) had concluded its decision-making on our report and my husband and I were walking from the convention center back to our hotel. Coming toward us was a young gay man, wearing a t-shirt that caught our eyes. Complete with Presbyterian symbol, on the front it said boldly: "I had sex with the Presbyterian Church." On the back we read as he walked by: "And it was awful."

For almost five years, I too had sex with the Presbyterian Church, since I served as a member of the General Assembly Committee on Human Sexuality. I have often used the word, bittersweet, to describe my feelings of this experience. Presbyterian failure to engage in churchwide education about sexuality issues and the continuing brutal defense of its exclusionary policy towards gay men and lesbians is our bitter, awful reality. This reality, however, has been sweetened for me by a network of courageous allies, who have an unquenchable thirst for justice. This is indeed the worst of times...and the best of times.

In order to convey my feelings about how this crisis of sexuality played out in the Presbyterian Church, I'd like to share some excerpts from an article I wrote shortly after the Baltimore assembly. I think it describes well the dynamics at work as the church considered our report:

> Preliminary work on our report by the Assembly was conducted by a committee of 67 commissioners and advisory delegates. Witnessing this group discuss our report was a painful exercise. I became more anguished and angry as [...] the agenda of retrenchment was relentlessly advanced. Men's voices outnumbering women's over 5 to 1 during critical decision-making sessions even though the committee was 40 percent women. Supporters of our report [...] were worn down and finally defeated in their efforts to reject hurtful actions and offer inclusive ones.
>
> At the end of the assembly committee's deliberations, one man (who had opposed our report and any language that would have been more pastoral to gays, lesbians and singles) stood and said, "We have heard your pain and we're sorry." The committee was then reminded that we need to love each other, we are all one family, so let's hold hands and pray. Several others and I left. At this moment, all I could think of was an image of institutional battering. Those who have studied domestic violence are familiar with the abuse syndrome — the abuser hurts the victim and then says, "I'm sorry, I love you." But the abuse goes on [...] (and) the policies don't change. So, while the committee prepared a pastoral letter affirming that we are all loved unconditionally by God, those who have ears to hear understand that our love for each other is set against deeply-entrenched patterns of privilege, power and control.[1]

Since June of 1991, this report has been alive and well. It continues to be studied by Presbyterians and many others. Momentum has developed to create a more just and loving church policy in some areas, particularly around issues of clergy sexual misconduct. I am glad for that and take that as a positive sign. However, policy that prohibits the ordination of open, "practicing" lesbians and gay men not only remains in force, but has recently been confirmed by a crushing judicial decision. In a vote of 12 to 1, the Permanent Judicial Commission of the Presbyterian Church (U.S.A.) ruled that the Downtown Presbyterian Church of Rochester, New York could not issue a call to Rev. Jane Adams Spahr, even though a lower court ruled 8 to 1 that since she was ordained before 1978, she was protected under a "grandfather" clause in the '78 policy. Both the vote and the reasoning are depressing to me, and that mentality does not bode well for the future of gay and lesbian persons in the Presbyterian Church (U.S.A.).

In a related decision, the Permanent Judicial Commission ruled that Lisa Larges, a ministerial candidate who has acknowledged her lesbian identity, may not be certified ready to receive call until it is determined whether or not she is "now a practicing homosexual." The schizophrenia inherent in Presbyterian policy is ably exposed in the dissenting opinion of W. Clark Chamberlain in his comments as a Judicial Commission member:

> The majority, while acknowledging her present good standing, her ministerial gifts, and her acceptability both to her calling congregation and presbytery, finds that her call cannot be fulfilled.

> The position of the majority is not consistent. If Jane Adams Spahr is a sinner, why is she not to be disciplined? If she is in good standing, why can her call not be fulfilled? If some ministers in good standing cannot do what other ministers in good standing may do, how can this be anything other than a double standard?[2]

Mr. Chamberlain's opinion raises the specter of a terrifying, but possible, next stage: if open, sexually active gays and lesbians are not in sufficiently good standing to be ordained and extended calls, should not those who are already ordained be disciplined for violating acceptable standards of ordination? How else can the church resolve this double standard when it refuses to ordain? And how will the church peer into bedrooms to determine what "practicing" means? Is it possible that the 20th century could end with a Presbyterian version of the witch trials? This is part of my fear and pessimism about the future.

My optimism, however, is grounded in the more progressive side of Presbyterian social witness. I was recently reading *Woman of Valor*, Ellen Chesler's biography of Margaret Sanger, and was reminded that American churches have long been engaged in crises over human sexuality. In 1931, a study committee of the Federal Council of the Churches of Christ recommended endorsement of contraception and met with immediate controversy. Chesler writes that liberal Congregationalists and Presbyterians affirmed the statement while conservative members, including some Methodists, protested. Disgruntled Presbyterians in the deep South briefly severed their affiliation with the Federal Council and Episcopalians and Lutherans, in "consultive connection" to the Federal Council, refused to comply. Although birth control remained a point of contention between opposing constituencies in Protestant churches into the 50s, Chesler contends that early support of liberal Protestants marked a critical turning point on this issue.[3]

As a Presbyterian, I grieve my denomination's retreat from its earlier ground-breaking positions on sexuality issues. The Presbyterian Report of 1991 stands in this progressive tradition. On justice for gays and lesbians, the United Church of Christ (those Congregationalists) and the United Church of Canada are out there without us. We can likely expect more turbulence on these issues. Strategies to change the church's position on even considering lesbians and gay men as eligible for ordination will proceed and will continue to be met by fierce resistance. In all of this, I am sustained by the unshakable conviction of Susan B. Anthony, who gave her entire life in the struggle for women's suffrage, never lived to see it, and still knew it would someday prevail because "Failure is Impossible." And Kate Millet is right after all: "The work of enlarging human freedom is such nice work, we're lucky to get it."[4] That is the vision of the future that inspires me, and to which I want to commit myself.

ENDNOTES

1Thorson-Smith, Sylvia. "I Had Sex With the Presbyterian Church." *Presbyterian Life and Times*, October 1991, 4.

2Chamberlaln, W. Clark, dissenting opinion ln the decision of the Permanent Judicial Commission, as subsequently reported in *More Light Update*, February 1993, 12.

3Chesler, Ellen. *Woman of Valor* (New York: Simon & Schuster, 1992), 319-20.

4Millett, Kate. *Sexual Politics* (New York: Simon & Schuster, 1969), xii.

CHAPTER XII

THE NEED FOR NEW MODELS OF MANHOOD: CAN THE MEN'S MOVEMENT HELP?

Something is happening with men in this country. It's relatively young, and it encompasses psychology, mythology, politics, sexuality and the workplace. And when men get together and howl at the moon or make wooden masks or pound drums or steam in Native American sweat lodges; when they talk about how it feels to raise a daughter and watch her develop into a woman, or to be in competition with another man; or any of the other things that men feel all the time but never thought they could talk about — in some small way they feel they are changing their culture's ideas about who men are, and who they should be. *Changes*, Sept.-Oct. 1990, p. 29

One thing is very clear as a result of the sexuality debate: men need to change. As the benefactors of patriarchy, men need to change. As the perpetuators of violence and abuse against women, men need to change. As the specie inclined to view women as objects of sexual conquest, men need to develop different sexual mentalities and attitudes. As persons molded by intrigue with competition, violence, and machismo, men need different models of masculinity. The Presbyterian report sought to articulate many of these concerns in its chapter on "Male Issues." In this chapter, I want to explore the newly emerging men's movement and see what potential it has as a way of changing male consciousness. Can church men learn from this movement? Does it promote healthier images of manhood? Can it help us in the broad quest for sexual justice?

My work with the Presbyterian report prompted me to take the men's movement more seriously than I had before. Actually, I had known since 1975 that there was a movement afoot to reappraise the problems of men. I had read Herb Goldberg's book *The New Male*; Jim Dittes' book *The Male Predicament*; and many articles in the secular press. I recognized that much of this early literature about the dilemmas of being male was created by perplexity and anger at the women's movement. Since the women's movement caused many women to move away from traditional gender roles and ways of relating to men, men obviously needed to do something to reappraise their masculinity and psyches. From 1987 to 1990 I was aware of this growing body of literature but not really existentially involved with it. It was only when the Presbyterian Sexuality Committee decided that we needed to include a chapter on men's issues that I got seriously drawn into the concerns, visions, and perplexities of the literature of the men's movement. I am still not an authority on this literature or the movement, but I have learned much from my work in this area and thought it might be helpful to bring some of the fruits of my research into the discussion about the future of America's sexuality debate. Although most of the men's movement has taken place outside of the formal structures of the church, it is worth noting that a new men's caucus has been approved by the American Academy of Religion, and the literature generated by the men's movement seems to be growing weekly. This chapter is organized into five sections: (1) the beginnings of the men's movement and what spawned it; (2) a diagnosis of what the men's movement says about the male condition; (3) a consideration of the creative answers which have been offered from the men's movement about men's health, growth, and well being; (4) tensions within the movement including critiques from feminists, nonparticipating men, and Christian ethicists; and (5) the significance of this movement for the Christian sexuality debate.

THE BEGINNINGS OF THE MEN'S MOVEMENT

Most scholars would date the beginnings of the men's movement to some of the early writings of Eugene Bianchi, Jim Dittes, Herb Goldberg, and Warren Farrell. Bianchi's volume, *From Machismo to Mutuality* (Paulist Press, 1975, co-authored with Rosemary Ruether) was one of the first books to reflect on male experience, patriarchy, hierarchical gender roles, and male intrigue with violence. Although Bianchi's work reflected his Roman Catholic background and reflected some theological themes, he nonetheless named important issues for most men. Goldberg's important volume *The Hazards of Being Male* was published in 1976 and *The New Male* was published in 1979. Warren Farrell's book, *The Liberated Man*, appeared in the early 1980s and his book *Why Men Are the Way They Are* came out in 1986. These early writers discerned the threat that feminism posed to the traditional male self images of the strong, macho man who is intrigued with competitiveness, violence, pro football, war, and the conquest of women. They began to recognize some of the strange paradoxes of American masculinity: that men live somewhere from seven to nine years less than women, that men have few friends, that men seem to have their priorities wrong about taking care of their bodies, that men have deep fears about the aging process and their sexual potency, and that men are confused as to how to relate to women and to their children. These early themes continued to shape much of the early assessment of men. James Nelson subsequently put many of these issues into a cogent and theological perspective in his book, *The Intimate Connection* (Westminster Press, 1988). It is to Nelson's credit that he also moved the discussion away from the psychological and bodily anxieties of men, and related the questions of male sexuality to masculine spirituality. Nelson, of course, had contributed in a major way to the understanding of male sexuality in his classic book, *Embodiment*, published in 1978, and has recently published a potential best seller *Body*

Theology (Westminster/John Knox, 1992). He is one of the few Christian ethicists to be seriously engaged with the men's movement, along with Eugene Bianchi, Merle Longwood, and Marvin Ellison, Jr.

A second wave of interpretation came to the men's movement through the various writings of Robert Bly, a nationally known poet long before he turned his attention to issues of maleness and masculinity. Bly's book, Iron John (Addison-Wesley, 1990), became a best seller despite the fact that his poetic style makes his arguments about manhood and maleness difficult to follow. Bly is the best known of a cluster of poets and clinical psychologists who have contributed much to the movement. As early as 1975 the first National Conference on Men and Masculinity was held, and the sixteenth annual meeting was held in Tucson, Arizona in May of 1991. The National Conference on Men and Masculinity is sponsored by the National Organization of Men Against Sexism (NOMAS) which was formerly called the National Organization of Changing Men (NOCM). The motto of NOMAS is tripartite: to be pro-feminist, gay-affirmative, and enhancing of men's lives.

Some subsequent books which have enriched this movement along include: John Stoltenberg's *Refusing to be a Man* (1989); Sam Keen's *Fire in the Belly* (1991); David D. Gilmore's *Manhood in the Making: Cultural Concepts of Masculinity* (1990); Robert Moore and Douglas Gillette's *King Warrior Magician Lover: Rediscovering the Archetypes of the Mature Masculine* (1991); Aaron Kipnis' *Knights Without Armor* (1991); Dan Millman's *No Ordinary Moments: A Peaceful Warrior's Guide to Daily Life* (H. J. Kramer, Inc., 1992); and Geoff Mains' *Gentle Warriors* (Knight's Press, 1989). The national movement has also been enhanced by the journal *Wingspan*, published in Manchester by the Sea, Maine. *The Journal of Men's Studies* has been founded and many other materials shared nationally in mimeograph or xeroxed form. Regional conferences and local meeting groups have popped up around the country. One of the best known in the last five years has been the Rocky Mountain Men's Conference, held on the campus of the University of Colorado in Boulder. Because of my work with the Presbyterian Sexuality Report, I was invited to attend the Rocky Mountain Men's Conference ln October 1991. That was my first exposure to this complex and ever-widening movement.

DIAGNOSIS OF THE MALE CONDITION

The men's movement now embraces men of diverse backgrounds. At Boulder I was struck that most of the participants seem to be men who are single, men who have been wounded in previous relationships, men who have not had previous support groups, and for the most part, men who are unchurched. I came to realize that the broadening movement incorporated special concerns for gay men, Afro-American men, native American men, and even has an internationally-minded group that explores special problems for men in the Soviet Union. There were also special efforts made in Boulder to transcend class and vocational distinctions. A surprising number of women were present, I assume because of their interest in understanding and helping men who are trying to refocus their identity. Leaders in the men's movement include poets, story tellers, ecologists, musicians, anthropologists, drummers, psychologists, and outdoorsmen. In every issue *Wingspan* (which incidentally has a circulation of over 60,000) lists conferences, events, and weekends all over the country that are designed to help men.

Is there anything that all of these men can agree upon? Do the diagnosticians of this movement have a common angle of vision? Perusal of the literature of the movement would suggest that most of the men who write about it agree that as men we are wounded, and that all is not well in our masculine psyches. Aaron Kipnis, in fact, in his book *Knights Without Armor* thinks that this "confession of failure" is the first step towards health for men. Evidences of this wounding would include workaholism; lack of emotional sensitivity to those who are closest to us; obsession about sex (usually joined with fantasies of conquest); loneliness; fear; and an inability to express the deeper concerns of our lives. There is a recognition that the traditional gender roles for men which include toughness, a taciturn quality, and competitiveness all take deep tolls on our lives, health, and well being. We at the same time have been conditioned to look down upon men who do not share those values, calling them "wimps" or "effeminate." Military training is of course notorious for reinforcing this mind-set. We incorporate into ourselves the cultural bias of homophobia, and often have a fear of close male friendships. We are often afraid of, or distrustful of women. Kipnis says about this:

> "The hero is one sided and one dimensional. Perhaps we needed this arch type more in a world at war with nature than other nations. Now the time for peace and healing is upon us-time to welcome home the hero, attend to his wounds, and then help him create a more cooperative world between men, women and nature."[1]

The admission that we are not all strong, tough, healthy, proud and confident is the first step in a virtual twelve-step process towards health for men. Marvin Ellison, Jr., a Christian ethicist from Bangor Seminary in Maine, adds that men also need to break their silence about the abuse of male power (it is one thing to personally acknowledge this and another to speak out against it), and to commit themselves to work for a far different world, one that is without patriarchal privilege and devoid of violence.[2]

Thus far Christian ethicists can agree with the diagnosis that as men we have lived a lie; we have embraced traditional gender roles when we many times had deep questions about them; and we have been silent about the reality and abuse of male power. Perhaps the most dramatic part of the men's movement, however, lies in its prescriptions as to what can be done to help men find health, wholeness, and identity.

CREATIVE ANSWERS

The limited focus of this chapter mandates that I only list a few of the interesting and creative answers that have emerged out of the men's movement. The first and very major assumption is that we need to recover something deep in our natures which has been lost. The answer for men is not the feminist plea that we become "softer" by developing our own feminine sides. Robert Bly notes:

> "The male in the past twenty years has become more thoughtful, more gentle. But by this process he has not become more free....I see the phenomenon of what I would call the 'soft male' all over the country today....They are lovely, valuable people — I like them — and they're not interested in harming the earth or starting wars or working for corporations. There is something favorable toward life in their whole general mood and style of living. But something's wrong. Many of these men are unhappy: there is not much energy in them. They are life preserving but not exactly *life giving*."[3]

Bly's answer, of course, is well known. It is also worth noting that this assessment is merely Bly's opinion, for which he offers no empirical evidence save his impressions from his travels. Bly thinks that men need to recover a mysterious depth of manhood, which he describes in his book *Iron John*. It is the strength that men come to only when they can separate from their mothers and live independently. It is the strength of the "hidden warrior" within us that enables us to know when to be kind, when to be protective, and when to be fierce. Bly's answer, of course, reflects his interest in German folktales. He does point to an interesting phenomenon, however: the "inner core" of man which constitutes masculinity at its best. Bly stresses that this care is a primordial fierceness, which is related to the image of warrior. Sam Keen broadens this base considerably, and suggests that we can learn from many different exemplary models of manhood: we need the passion of the Dionysian man, the vision and integrity of prophetic men, and the loyalty and commitment that we see in Jesus of Nazareth, which remind us that we are created in the image of God. Other writers such as Jungian psychologist James Hillman and the psychologist Aaron Kipnis agree with this goal of reaching a deeper level of masculine consciousness, and agree with Keen that we should draw on a variety of models. Sam Keen stresses that any new identity will require a pilgrimage into difficult emotional depths; the new, healthy man will be a Pilgrim, not a homesteader.[4]

For some men this quest takes them into drumming. I had a first-hand experience of this in a two-hour drumming seminar while I was in Boulder. Men brought different drums and those of us who arrived without were provided with different types of drums. There is both a charm and a mystique about developing a special kind of drum that suits one's own personality. There are Latin American drums, native American drums, African drums, drums from the continent of India, and from southeast Asia. My drumming seminar was led by a professional drummer who helped our group develop various cadences and urged us to be attentive to what happens when one drums in rounds. (The idea being that the whole is greater than the sum of its parts.) Much to my surprise, several women joined our drumming circle until we had approximately twenty-five people. Groups were formed of treble drums, bass drums, and deep bass drums. After an exhausting two hours in which we tried different drum beats, people present talked about the experience. It was clear that some people who came were professional drummers and are most interested in being a part of a rhythmic group. Others admitted that they drummed to release anger and frustration. A third group acknowledged that they drummed because they thought

It was a primordial religious way to evoke the spirits. A good bit of serious discussion followed that about experiences in Africa and with American Indian tribes where drumming created its own hypnotic state and produced an altered sense of consciousness. Most people acknowledged that the drumming was a form of therapy, and got them out of a rational mode of being.

On the negative side, one must note in passing how drums have been so important to the military, and how drums were used so effectively by the Nazis at night rallies of the Nazi party. Many women look with some dubiousness at this drumming phenomenon, feeling that it is too close to the old image of man as warrior to be comfortable for them. Nonetheless, all over this country on virtually every weekend, men's groups are gathering to drum.

Closely related to that is the experience of a sweat lodge, which takes place in a tent erected in a friendly field and heated by rocks or steam. Men take off their clothes (all of this is something similar to a sauna or steambath experience), feel the comfort and or pleasure of their sweat glands opening, and of their being close to each other and to nature. The sweat lodge, of course, is historically linked to native American cultures who used experiences like this for the purification of warriors. Men who have shared this experience generally say that it is a liberating experience, enabling them to get closer to each other and to their bodies. Both drumming and sweat lodges demonstrate an intrigue that at least one stream of the men's movement has with native American cultures. Implicitly at least, these men believe the Indian brave is a good model for authentic manhood: the brave was a provider, protector, physically fit, and a guide for his sons.

Chanting is another technique used for male solidarity and transcending of the rational. Chanting can induce an altered state of consciousness. It can synchronize the left and right hemispheres of the brain, and change the rates of respiration, heartbeat, and brainwave activity. Different parts of the body are resonated when men chant, and adherents claim that this vibrates both the physical body and the energy fields of the body.[5] It is mystical, and deepens our sense of reality.

Three other techniques have been developed in the men's movement and are sponsored weekly in virtually all areas of the country. One of these is the wilderness trip, where one can sign up for a long weekend (or sometimes for as long as a week) to go out with another group of men to live in the wilderness. This can be a camping experience, a canoeing experience, a raft experience down white-water rivers, mountain climbing, or rock climbing. In these instances, somewhat similar to the philosophy behind Outward Bound, the idea is that we also learn much about ourselves and bond with the people with whom we share the experience. In the context of these experiences men are encouraged to be more open about their own life histories and to reflect on the stories of others. Related to these wilderness trips are the tracking weekends led by tracker John Stokes and some of his associates in New Mexico. Somewhat similar to the way in which many of us went out on Boy Scout camping weekends and tracked animals, trackers feel that when we go out in nature and see the balance of life and death, we can get beyond the duality in nature and discern a force that holds us all together. When we learn something about predator-prey relationships we learn about the symbiosis of nature and the place of carnivores.

Some leaders in the men's movement would prefer to stress the ecological lessons of these experiences and, in fact, there is one stream of the men's movement developing more literature on "Ecomasculinity."[6] Still another variation of this intrigue with nature comes in the work of some men in doing "placemaking." The idea behind this is to lead men into isolated spaces and encourage them to try to create a sacred space. This includes helping men to be more attentive to nature, more perceptive about the nuances of nature, and how to confirm our relationship with the earth. Many people these days, including ethicists and feminists, have special interests in ecology, and it is interesting that this is taken to be a priority for the men's movement as well.

Elsewhere in the movement one finds intrigue of Haitian voodoo rituals, Indian initiation rights, and the importance of storytelling. Deep in all of this, however, lies the theme of getting into a new consciousness, moving beyond rational modes of life and experience, and discovering something that is latent in us as men. Most of the therapies advocated in the men's movement are experiential, and I am struck with how strong the influence of Carl Jung is in this movement as opposed to Sigmund Freud.

On the positive side, one has to note the interest in helping white, middle-class, heterosexual men develop better relationships with gay men, with Afro-American men, and with working-class men. All of these have historically been areas of conflict and suspicions that have been reinforced by business, cultural, and religious institutions. There are also special therapy groups at most national meetings where men can discuss their ambivalent or painful histories with their own fathers, their difficulties in separating from their mothers, and the difficulties that they have in understanding and relating to their own sons. One technique that I have seen in meetings is that men introduce themselves as "John, son of Edmund, father of William." This is a male bonding technique to circumvent the influence that women have had on our development. Virtually every national meeting also has some discussion group on men's legal rights, vocation, problems of male single parents, underemployment, and child care.

INTERNAL TENSIONS

We come now to assessment of the men's movement. The first thing to say is that its diversity brings many types of persons under the same tent. Broadly speaking there is a tension between the "mythopoetic advocates" (to borrow a term from Mark Muesse) and the politically active participants in the movements. The poets such as Robert Bly and James Hillman see the goal of the men's movement as seeking identity, roots, inwardness, spirituality, and ritual peace. If men can find these things, they believe that other things will fall into place. The political activists, while recognizing the importance of the poets agenda, are also concerned about the difficult problems of male violence, male intrigue with war, men as perpetuators of rape, men who suffer from drug and alcohol addictions, and the dilemmas of poor men who live on the streets. These men are more concerned about the impact of patriarchy on our society, about homophobia, and about men who regard women as the enemy. John Stoltenberg, Marvin Ellison, Jr., James Nelson, and James Dittes would fall in this category. I would add that there is a third group of men who are more interested in environmental, ecological, and out of doors experiences; they bring a third agenda into the broad movement. Thus far the general fluidity of the movement and its lack of structure enable persons of different interests and persuasions to find help and companionship with their own agendas. No one has to be squeezed out, but on the other hand everyone does not come with the same goals and interests. It must be stressed, however, that there are diverse models of manhood emphasized, and the choice is *not* between being a "wildman" or being a "wimp." We must be careful lest we oversimplify what is going on and what is being said in this diverse and creative movement.

Feminists tend to be rather dubious about the entire men's movement. I say this in spite of the presence of a number of women in Boulder who seemed to want to help men in this quest. Most feminists I know, however, take a rather dim view of this movement lifting up the image of men as warriors, the image of Indian braves, and of activities such as drumming and marching. These experiences do not enhance or support the qualities of manhood that feminists think need to be recovered.[7] Feminists are also apprehensive about the separateness which characterizes some streams of the men's movement, although most public documents indicate a welcoming of women to conferences and meetings.

Feminists are also notably less sympathetic to the male claim that men have been exploited and are bearers of pain. If it is true that men bear some scars from traditional gender roles, feminists think that women bear even deeper scars.[8] Women are not moved by Robert Bly's nostalgic stories of the days of King Arthur when men spoke in verse and had feelings of affection for each other. As Judith Mirkinson observes "Arthurian Knights, as far as I know, were not known for their libertarian view of serfs or of women for that matter. I believe it is fair to say that feminism desires a new style of manhood but it is unclear to most feminists that the men's movement is really committed to identical goals."[9]

Not all women agree on these matters, of course, but some critiques by women indicate that the only thing that happens when a man goes off on a "warrior weekend" is that when he comes home he is even more taciturn, and just grunts while he sits in front of the television set. On the whole, I think the men's movement is still conflicted about how to understand and deal with women, just as the women's movement is conflicted about men. Bly's work, in my judgement, is finally anti-female (in spite of his earlier support for "the feminist principle"), and Keen feels that men have their own work to do before they should worry about women.[10]

From a male standpoint, a number of other criticisms emerge. The romanticizing of native American culture seems to overlook the male-dominated imperialism and colonialism that crushed these cultures. The analysis that most modern men are intrigued by the violence of sports concentrates on the "Super-Bowl Culture," and disregards the positive influence that sports have had on male identity and development. Not all sports are violent: men enjoy tennis, golf, racquetball, slow pitch softball, table tennis, archery, track and field events, skiing, swimming, diving, pick-up basketball games, and a host of other competitive activities. We should be cautious lest we assume that male interests in sports equates to a delight in violence or to a monosyllabic vocabulary. Many men would say that their interests in sports have broadened them, taught them something about teamwork and effort, and made them better persons. Athletics has been the source of deep friendships and lasting relationships for many men, and that has not been a bad thing.

The point here is to be reminded of the complexity of analyzing the "male predicament." Men experience pain and confusion in different ways, but not all men are jocks, beer-guzzlers, or exploiters of women. Even if most men need to work at friendship, we have also had good experiences of friendship. If we have been workaholics, we have also gained satisfaction from work. If we have been perplexed by women, we have also been blessed by them and have learned much from them. If we have benefitted by patriarchy, we also know that morally we need to work for a more just society. The analyses which have shaped the men's movement, in other words, describe some men but not all men. There are different types and styles of maleness, as well as many paradoxes about maleness, and we need to remain sensitive to that.

IMPLICATIONS FOR ETHICS AND SEXUALITY

A penultimate concern in this chapter is what Christian ethicists should say about this movement. I find myself intrigued by it because it is so much more bold, creative, and visionary than what comes out of most denominational offices on men's work. Offices of men's work have been notoriously slow in recognizing the deeper changes that are afoot in American culture and the pains that men bear. Much of the church's interests in men are still geared to help men to become better ushers, better deacons, or more responsible trustees of church property. Major efforts are still made to get men out to breakfasts and out for workdays on church property. The men's movement reminds ecclesiastical leaders that a great revolution is under way, and that as Christian men we need to take far more seriously problems of our irrational selves and our struggles for identity. Fortunately we are seeing some changes in denominational approaches. Jim Dittes has argued that if churches take this movement seriously they might produce some new visions for ministry, help men channel their new-found commitments into spiritual channels, and give all men a more vital sense of "God the Father."[11] I have no empirical way of knowing this, but lt has certainly been my impression that most of the men who come to this movement are not involved in churches, and if anything have negative senses about traditional religious communities. If denominational leaders as well as ethics can build a bridge to these men, listen to them and learn from them, it might well open whole new frontiers for the church's understanding of male pain, needs, and hopes.

Christian ethicists interested in this dialogue will bring to it interests in male-female mutuality and relationships. Christian ethicists would stand against the male separatists and ally more with the pro-feminist element. They will remind men that they have responsibilities to daughters as well as to sons, and that the religious themes of covenant and fidelity are important in our relationships. The fluidity of the men's movement means that all of these issues are still being debated, and we can make a difference.

As far as the sexuality debate is concerned, I believe we can learn much from the men's movement. It does remind men that their sexuality is linked to deeper and broader concepts of personhood. It can help men learn to talk to each other and to identify with different types of men. It boldly encourages men to think through the old (and inadequate) myths about masculinity. Most of the men I have known who have been involved in the men's movement have developed greater insights into themselves and are more open in relationships. Generally speaking I think the men's movement reduces homophobia because it facilitates interaction between straight men and gay men. It at least recognizes the identity crisis that troubles so many men and encourages them to name their anxieties. If the men's movement is not the final word for men, it is at least a creative way to begin a new process, and, as Marvin Ellison has pointed out, it can help men envision and work for sexual justice.

I invite male and female Christians to take the men's movement seriously. If the male determination to find new models for manhood can be enhanced by a vision of male-female mutuality, not only our generation will benefit, but our sons and daughters as well.

ENDNOTES

[1]Aaron R. Kipnis. *Knights Without Armor.* (Los Angeles: Tarcher, Inc., p. 34.

[2]See Ellison's essay, "Refusing to be 'Good Soldiers': An Agenda for Men" in Susan E. Davies and Eleanor H. Haney, *Redefining Sexual Ethics* (New York: Pilgrim Press, 1991), pp. 189-198.

[3]Keith Thompson. "The Meaning of Being Male: A Conversation with Robert Bly." *L. A. Weekly,* August 5-11, 1983.

[4]Sam Keen. *Fire in the Belly.* (New York: Bantam, 1991), pp. 125-128.

[5]See Jonathan S. Goldman. "Drumming and Chanting: Vibration and Consciousness." *New Age Retailer,* October 1991, and the cassette entitled "Gateways: Men's Drumming and Chanting" by Jonathan Goldman and *Spiritsounds,* available from Spirit Music, P. O. Box 2240, Boulder, CO 80306-2240.

[6]See Gary Snyder. "Ecology-Ecomasculinity on the Rise," *Wingspan,* Summer, 1990. pp. 4-5.

[7]A sharp exposition of this view is found in Jill Johnston's article, "Why Iron John is No Gift to Women." *New York Times Book Review,* February 22, 1992. pp. 1, 28-33. and in Jill P. Baumgaertner's, "The New Masculinity or the Old Mystification?" *The Christian Century,* May 29-June 5, 1991, pp. 593-596. The best source for a broad appraisal of the men's movement by women is Kay Lelgh Hagan's, *Women Respond to the Men's Movement: A Feminist Collection.* (San Francisco: Harper, 1992).

[8]See Susan Faludi's critique of this in *Backlash* (New York: Crown Publishers, 1991). pp. 300-312.

[9]"Men 'R' Back," *Breakthrough,* Winter, 1991.

[10]See Keen's book, *Fire In the Belly,* pp. 23-24 on "Saying Good-Bye to Women."

[11]See Dittes' "A Men's Movement for the Church?," *The Christian Century*, May 29-June 5, 1991. pp. 588-590.

CHAPTER XIII
ISSUES TOO HOT TO HANDLE

Readers of this book are well aware that the sexuality debate in the churches raised difficult and emotional issues. As one who was in the eye of the storm it is hard for me to believe that the controversies could have been more intense. Issues of "moral absolutes," sex and singleness, sexual violence and abuse, love and legalism, gays and lesbians, and the naming of patriarchy and homophobia as controlling ideologies in American culture seemed to many people to challenge the very foundation of our traditional moral values. It seems clear in retrospect that the raising of all these issues at one time was more than any institution could process. It will come as a surprise to many, therefore, for me to say that in addition to the complex issues listed above the Presbyterian Committee recognized another whole group of problems that we came to regard as "too hot to handle" — i.e., too complex, too morally ambiguous, or too theologically borderline to include in our report. There were, after all, limits as to what a Presbyterian General Assembly might be expected to consider. I commented on some of these issues in my August 19, 1991 article for *Christianity and Crisis*, entitled "Sexuality: What We Couldn't Say." As we consider the future of the sexuality debate however, it seems appropriate to consider these issues in more detail.

It needs to be said initially that it is not the task of the Churches alone to solve these complex problems. They mirror broader dilemmas in our culture, and involve persons outside the churches as well as inside the churches. It seems reasonable, however, that as concerned Christians we should be aware of these issues, recognize their subtlety, and provide contexts where they can be discussed and better understood. Acknowledging them is also a reminder of the many nuances of human sexual behavior — an important corrective to the popular tendency to oversimplify human sexuality. Some reasons why Christians have had a hard time acknowledging these deeper issues relate to historic theological convictions about God's will in male-female dynamics. Many of these difficulties are related to the historic Christian sense of sin; some are tied to the primacy of the Ten Commandments in Christian ethical reflection, and to the tendency of the church to refer to moral absolutes. Still other difficulties are tied to the negativism and suspicion with which Christianity has traditionally viewed sexuality. Scholars working in the field of human sexuality know that there are some recurrent patterns in sexuality that could never be thoughtfully and critically discussed in a church context: sadomasochism, transvestism, swinging, communal living experiments, pederasty, and bestiality, to name but a few. Conventional Christian ethics has tended to regard all of these as aberrant and pathological, and instead focused attention on what are deemed to be more proper, appropriate, and constructive modes of sexuality. Even within this tighter and more conventional agenda, however, our research identified five problems which have been virtually undiscussable in Christian contexts. There may be others which will occur to readers of this book.

1.   The first topic is **bisexuality**. Most persons in a society, of course, appropriate cultural gender roles and incorporate those roles in their personal development. How we relate to each other as males and females is a difficult, but not impossible, topic to study. To introduce the concept of bisexuality, however, and thereby a deep ambiguity about gender and bonding patterns, seems to be more than most church members can cope with. Closely related to the question of bisexuality is the awareness that all of us carry certain masculine and

feminine characteristics, and that self designations as "male" and "female" have to be elastic enough to allow for wide varieties even within those parameters. We found that the majority of church persons prefer their ethical analyses clearly stated, and moral boundaries clearly defined. Bisexuality cuts across the familiar categories and introduces ambiguities into familiar gender categories. Other than acknowledging it as an observable phenomenon, we decided we could not really deal with it in any detail in our study.

Bisexuality is ethically and theologically an important topic, however, when we recognize that many men and women have some same-sex experience but basically regard themselves as heterosexual persons. The original Kinsey Report of 1948 indicated that 50% of the male population had experienced homosexual genital relations at some time in their lives, and for 37% of them it was orgasmic behavior after puberty.[1] The subsequent Kinsey study on females (1953) demonstrated extensive female same-sex experience. Although the Kinsey findings were controversial they were also pioneering in American sex research. Subsequent researchers have challenged Kinsey's findings by criticizing his methodology and statistical conclusions, but most agree that Kinsey did at least point to many of the deeper complexities of human sexual behavior, and especially to the frequency of same-sex genital experience. It is a generally understood axiom today among sex researchers that the vast majority of persons are not exclusively heterosexual or homosexual, and that most of us have more bisexual capacities than we have been allowed to acknowledge in a society shaped by rigid gender roles.[2]

Feminist ethicists have frequently stressed that love and fidelity are the essential components of a bonded relationship, and that the object of love can be of either sex. Mary Habgood has recently pointed out that "the intensity of erotic union is determined not by gender difference but by the connection one makes to a core aspect of a truly distinct self."[3] Many women seem to be able to live with equal satisfaction with male or female partners. "Both types of relationships have their advantages and disadvantages," a bisexual woman told me. The ethical focus is on the nature and quality of the partner as a person, not on gender; the assumption is that at least some persons have the ability to relate affectionately to either sex.

Clearly this way of understanding the flexibility of the self raises important questions for Christian ethical thinking. Whatever else, bisexuality cannot be dismissed as incongruent with Christian life or witness. It does not help to dismiss bisexual persons as "sinners." It may be that the recognition of our own capacity for bisexuality underlies much of the homophobia in our society, especially among men.

2.   The second undiscussable problem is **the relationship between monogamy and fidelity**. Many studies document that both single and married people have "sexual friends" — relationships with persons where the ties are historic, affectionate, and strong, but not a person's primary relationship. Sociological data suggest that many people feel that some expression of sexual intimacy is appropriate in such relationships. This phenomenon is something other than persons having mistresses or lovers: it might be closer to the phenomenon described in the movie, "Same Time Next Year," or what John Cuber and Peggy Harroff described in their book, *Sex and the Significant Americans* (Baltimore: Penguin Books, 1965). Although some of the persons who are in these types of relationships are married and church members, it is difficult to find a category to describe this that fits within a Christian framework of sexuality. The issue is critical and emotional: must monogamy be at the heart of a sustaining relationship? Is it the one critical ingredient for a marriage or bonded relationship? Or in stressing this norm, have the churches put the emphasis at the wrong place?

Few topics could be more volatile than this in a church discussion of love, sex, and marriage. Knowing that we would be facing many other complex issues anyway, the Presbyterian Committee decided that this sensitive issue should not even be raised.   Our report therefore assumed monogamy as a normative component of marriage but argued that fidelity is a value which is broader and richer.   We were aware that some recent literature attempts to separate monogamy and fidelity, by arguing that fidelity implies a long-term loyalty and commitment to another person, and that this may or may not include monogamy. It is possible, as one of our members acknowledged with a poignant story of his own parents, for a couple to live together monogamously but without fidelity — i.e., without personal sensitivity, support, encouragement, assistance, tenderness, or mutuality. Fidelity means a commitment to the total well-being of another. Ethicist Margaret Farley has argued that fidelity is a way of being that expresses a continuing commitment in a relationship. It is more than duty or constancy. It is, she says,

> ...a kind of "being there," being present to those to whom I am committed. We can express this in personal *spatial* terms like being "with," being "near to," "before,'' in the presence of "you whom I love" and being "here" in the activity I perform. We can also express it in terms of personal time: being present "now," *holding together the past and the future in a present process.*[4]

Fidelity is the critical ingredient for long-term relationships. It counteracts staleness, boredom, the fading of earlier hopes and visions. Our report stressed that it is other than, and more than, monogamy. A monogamous relationship without fidelity is unnourishing and ultimately defeating. Relationships without fidelity can work; they can continue with partners living in detachment from each other, but such relationships are without love or even tenderness. Women can be (and are) abused in monogamous relationships.

Feminist ethicists have argued that monogamy as a norm in relationships has too often been advocated for women and not for men, and that its real roots lie in the possessive mentality of capitalism. Mary Habgood maintains, for example, that the traditional marriage model of a working husband and a domesticated, monogamous wife fits into the ideology of capitalism because it supports the notion of the inequality of labor, condones hierarchical domestic relationships (similar to those in the industrial sphere), endorses the idea of possessiveness of persons, and both demeans and limits significant friendships with the opposite sex.[5] Monogamy has value, she argues, not when it is superimposed ideologically but only when it is freely chosen. Carter Heyward, in her influential book *Touching Our Strength*, links not only monogamy but all of heterosexism to capitalism and its related cultural assumptions. Are there hidden and unspoken assumptions behind our historic stress on monogamy?

Clearly there is more to this issue than the Christian community has been willing to talk about. The professional literature abounds with reflections on this problem. People can have monogamous relationships without fidelity, and faithful committed relationships without monogamy. The church's interest is in helping people learn how to have both. We do need, however, to be more sensitive to the feminist critique that traditional Christian marriage patterns support men more than women, and in the emerging phases of this discussion we need to encourage relationships of all kinds to be based on partnership and equity. Letty Russell's writings on partnership are a good starting point for this discussion.[6]

3.   **Cohabitation** is another vexing problem. Most church persons do not understand nor approve of patterns of people living together without benefit of marriage. There is often a "generation gap" in families about this phenomena. Some parents have reluctantly had to accept this as they have seen it in their children; others are angered at middle-aged persons who cohabit without benefit of marriage, and they do not understand why everyone does not want to be married. There is also a good bit of perplexity about older adults who choose to

live together for economic, legal, or inheritance reasons. Given the strong priority of marriage in Christian theology and custom, cohabitation seems to threaten its views about the divine intent for male-female bonding, and introduces difficult issues for a Christian ethical system.

This topic requires more analysis and honesty than Christian communities have been willing to undertake. It intertwines with the issues of sex outside marriage, our theologies of marriage, and the relationship of love and law. It reminds us that sex and marriage are different experiences, and that indeed a person can have one without the other. Cohabitation reminds us how differently a younger generation lives, an anxiety-producing phenomenon in its own right to the middle age culture. Many Christians of middle years have had to reappraise their earlier moral judgments when their own children choose to live with a "significant other." Many adult Christians do some reappraising when (frequently after a divorce) they decide to live with another person for a period of time before marriage. Other adults, who grew up in a religious culture that said only marriage made sex "acceptable" and legitimate, frankly envy young people today their opportunity to live together and to test out a relationship. Every married person comes to realize that there is much more to a serious relationship than sex; we recognize that there is something ethically valuable for couples being able to understand that before they take the legal step of marriage.

The increasing phenomenon of cohabitation makes most ministers realize that there is a difference between the Christian blessing of a relationship and the state's interests in the legal contract of marriage. Practically every minister or priest knows persons in their congregations that are living together without being married. Cohabitation includes gay and lesbian couples as well as heterosexual couples, of course, and it involves people at all chronological stages of life.

There is a great deal of literature on this phenomenon in sociological, counseling, and family life circles. What should the churches say about this?

Should it be ignored, like the unspoken shame of unmarried pregnant daughters of previous generations? Should it be condemned as a threat to the moral fabric of our society, as conservatives claim? Is it true, as I have heard in various debates around the country, that if the churches even tacitly support these unmarried couples no one will ever again have any incentive to get married? Just what stake does the church have in marriage as a social and legal institution, particularly if it endorses an ethic of love rather than law, of substance rather than form? Can or should the churches, in our diverse society, continue to stress that marriage is God's ideal norm for how people should live (this, of course, is the view of Roman Catholics and of conservative Protestant churches), or can they be more flexible in their ministry to persons?

Cohabitation is not an easy answer to the problem of living with another person. Critics note that without a strong commitment, it is easier for couples to split than to work through hard times. Studies show that the splitting of unmarried couples produces many of the same traumas as divorce. Some feminists have noted that this phenomenon enables heterosexual men to enjoy female companionship without any long-term commitment. But marriages break up, too, and a formal public ceremony is no guarantee of a nourishing life-long partnership. Much clusters around this issue, and it will clearly have to be on the future sexuality agenda.

4.   **Deeper nuances of the gay and lesbian subcultures** were another impossible topic. It would be enough, we concluded, if we could raise the consciousness of Presbyterians about the cruel stereotypes in the heterosexual culture, and to frame the issue of gays and lesbians in the church as a "justice-love" issue. Even that, of course, was more than the Presbyterians (and most other church bodies) were willing to acknowledge.

People who study sexuality issues know, of course, that the gay and lesbian cultures are not monolithic, but have many variations. Among gay and lesbian couples there still exist hierarchical patterns of dominant-subordinate relationships; there are male patterns of one-night stands; of leather and bondage subcultures; of male prostitutes; and the stratification of men by age, profession, and social class. The gay world has its own graphic pornographic literature and films. There are special problems for Afro-American gays, as the 1992 PBS documentary pointed out. A major strand of lesbianism is political and does not identify with the debate over genetic vs. social conditioning as causes of same-sex preference. Lesbians have divided over how to treat bisexual women (are they collaborating with the enemy?) and over the condemnation of what some women call sadomasochistic practices.[7] (What is one person's sadomasochism is another's source of fantasy and pleasure.) Older gays and lesbians have separate needs and sub-cultures. Finally there are those segments of the broad gay and lesbian world that find satisfaction in transvestism and in pursuing relationships with children. The gay and lesbian community itself is sharply divided over these life-styles. These are the behavior patterns that cause so much fear and stereotyping in the heterosexual culture. Clearly the Christian community, with an ethic of common decency, has something to say about these internal disputes in the gay and lesbian cultures.

Most of these sub-cultures have kept themselves well distanced from the churches, but they are known to virtually all gay and lesbian persons. There are three salient issues here for concerned Christians: (1) to recognize that the world of gay and lesbian persons is diverse and divided over a number of issues, just as heterosexuals are divided over issues; (2) to realize that understanding the multiple gay and lesbian subcultures is far more complex than just raising theological arguments for grace and justice; and (3) to clarify what Christian people should advocate as ethical norms and models for all people. We need to be reminded as we acknowledge these deeper levels of perplexity in gay and lesbian life that the heterosexual culture also has its own dimensions of problematic behavior.

5.   A fifth impossible topic to discuss was the **close relationship between so many of our churches and middle-class culture.** Soren Kierkegaard said one time, speaking of 19th century Denmark, that the greatest problem is "to encourage people to become Christians when they live under the illusion that they already are Christians." It is difficult to help many Christian people see that the claims of the Gospel offer a different value system than that which is affirmed and passed on by middle-class culture. Our work in sexuality has sharpened our awareness of how much of our main-line church members have their religious values shaped by middle class culture. Our work has confirmed the famous "Herberg thesis" of 1955 that middle class Americans do not primarily find their identity through their religious heritage as through their embracing of "the American Way of Life."[8] We had hoped that the call for justice-love would have evoked a more prophetic consciousness in our churches.

A frequent charge made against the Presbyterian Report was that it simply capitulated to the culture's satiation with sex. "If you follow the guidelines of this report," opponents said publicly, "anything goes." It was difficult to clarify that what we advocated was not a capitulation to the culture but a thoughtful, compassionate approach to sexuality that followed an even higher ethical model of responsibility. The minority report alleged that this capitulation to the culture was the result of our ignoring clear Biblical mandates. The reply to that charge might better be given by an outside observer. Karen Lebacqz, in her review in *Christianity and Crisis* noted:

> The committee is charged with ignoring Scripture. The minority report accuses the majority of a "wish for accommodation" to the culture, and urges that Christians "live by the authority of God's word in sexual matters." The assumption of the minority is that God's word simply requires monogamous, heterosexual marriage. Any acceptance of sexual relations outside

of this form must therefore be an accommodation to culture. But it is the minority group, not the majority, that has accommodated to culture. The minority reads Scripture with eyes that have clearly accommodated to the 20th century. Why else could it proclaim that "the total picture of human sexuality" as given in Scripture is captured in the "lifelong commitment of husband and wife to each other"?

Only eyes blinded by 20th-century nuclear families could ignore the practice of polygamy among ancient Israelites and the affirmation of nonmarital sexual love in the Song of Songs ("Holy of Holies"). Only eyes blinded by 20th-century homophobia could assume that the church has spoken with a "single voice" on Issues such as homosexuality. Only eyes blinded by 20th-century assumptions about the "privacy" of sexuality could so ignore the links between sexuality and violence in this culture, and the need for a true return to the core of biblical witness: the movement of the spirit in overcoming cultural purity claims in order to place sexuality within a context of justice.

The committee, with its call for ever more demanding standards for sexual relating, has not accommodated to culture. The minority has, with its failure to allow 20th-century assumptions to be challenged by Scripture. The committee, with its return to the core Gospel message of right relation, has not neglected Scripture; the minority has, with its neglect of the total biblical record and context of biblical passages. (Although I commend the Presbyterian Church for its consistent commitment to publishing minority reports, this minority report is an embarrassment to the church.)[9]

The reason this charge was too sensitive in the public debate is that it is hard to make this allegation without sounding self-righteous or without condemning so many of the congregations of the Presbyterian Church (U.S.A.). For purposes of persuasion and changing minds it is better to treat the issue of cultural accommodation indirectly, and as an issue that is not confined to America. But the haunting reality remains: does Peter Berger's prophetic condemnation of main-line churches, as articulated in his 1961 book *The Noise of Solemn Assemblies* (Garden City: Doubleday) still hold true? Have the majority of our churches lost their ability to transcend and critique our culture? Do the words of Amos apply to our congregations just as they did to ancient Israel?

This chapter is a reminder that however far we have come in this debate, the future will take us into new, and basically uncharted, waters.

ENDNOTES

[1]See Alfred C. Kinsey, et. al., *Sexual Behavior in the Human Male* (Philadelphia: W. B. Saunders, 1948) and *Sexual Behavior in the Human Female* (Philadelphia: W. B. Saunders, 1953).

[2]Recent studies by the Alan Guttmacher Institute have indicated, however, that today only about 1% of American males consider themselves exclusively homosexual, and that only about 2% reported some homosexual experience. Kinsey in 1948 had estimated that about 10% of men were exclusively gay, and his estimates have been used over the years as a basis for calculating the gay and lesbian population in America. The new figure has political consequences but does not bear on the point about bisexuality that we are making here. The Guttmacher study was funded by a $1.8 million grant from the National Institute of Child Health and Human Development. For a fuller report of the study see *The New York Times*, April 15, 1993, pp. A1, A9.

[3]"Marriage, Market Values, and Social Justice: Toward an Examination of Compulsory Monogamy," in Susan E. Davies and Eleanor H. Haney, eds., *Redefining Sexual Ethics* (Cleveland: Pilgrim Press, 1992), p. 125.

[4]*Personal Commitments* (San Francisco: Harper and Row, 1986), p. 46.

[5]*Op. Cit.*, pp. 124-25.

[6]See her book *The Future of Partnership* (Louisville: Westminster/John Knox, 1979) and *Growth in Partnership* (Louisville: Westminster/John Knox, 1981)

[7]An organization of lesbians called Samois has defended sadomasochism on grounds of sexual freedom; some heterosexual women have argued that dominance in men is exciting. For a further discussion see Sandra Lee Bartky, "Feminine Masochism and the Politics of Personal Transformation," in Alan Sable, ed., *The Philosophy of Sex*, 2nd ed. (Savage, MO: Rowman and Littlefield, Inc., 1991), pp. 219-242. Her essay contains an extensive bibliography of this debate.

[8]See Will Herberg, *Protestant-Catholic-Jew: An Essay in American Religious Sociology* (Garden City, NY: Doubleday Anchor Books, 1955), especially

Chapter V, "The Religion of Americans and American Religion," pp. 72-98. This "American Way of Life" includes a belief in democracy, in free enterprise, in egalitarianism, and in idealism. It believes in self-reliance, individualism, and progress, and tends to see moral issues in plain and simple, black and white categories. See pp. 78-79.

⁹*Op. Cit.*, p. 175.

CHAPTER XIV
THE DEBATE IN RETROSPECT AND PROSPECT

From the standpoint of 1994, many things are now clearer about American churches and the crisis in human sexuality. Developments in the various denominations have shown that the "main-line" churches — overwhelmingly white, heterosexual, and middle-class — have not found it easy to acknowledge or to discuss sexuality issues. A state of denial still persists, and church leaders would clearly prefer to have all of these complex problems disappear without further debate or acrimony. Controversial issues are bad for church morale: they impact on membership, congregational giving, and church budgets at all levels. Controversy polarizes people and leaves residual scars. Presbyterians, for example, declined an opportunity to publish a book about their internal debate, declined through the Louisville Seminary-based Institute for the Study of American Protestantism to fund a research project which would examine how Presbyterians dealt with these issues, and have refused to advertise in any medium the continuing availability of the sexuality study. But the issues of the sexuality of young people, singles, persons with disabilities, gay and lesbian persons, and older adults remain with us. Medical complexities — AIDS, sexually transmitted diseases, new reproductive technologies — continue to vex the nation's medical and ethical communities. We are hearing more, and not less, about clergy sexual abuse and sexual violence. Feminists and persons of color are not going to stop naming the sins and consequences of a predominantly patriarchal society. So in spite of denial and a changing ecclesiological climate

(Presbyterians, for example, are now worrying about finances and structural reorganization) the issues of sexuality still linger and await resolution. The genies, we might say, are out of the bottle, and they are not going to go back in.

A RETROSPECTIVE LOOK: SEVEN LESSONS LEARNED

Some lessons have emerged from the continuing debate. It now seems that the Presbyterian (U.S.A.) report was too long, written (in spite of ourselves) in too technical a style, and was too ambitious to be assimilated by people in the pew. Few people read the whole report, and fewer still understood it. The Lutheran report, by contrast, was more modest in scope, more focused, and prepared better as a study guide. The Lutherans also conveyed that their report would be the first step in a long process; the Presbyterian report, despite being offered as a study document for two years, was perceived by many people as being a "Here it is, take it or leave it" document. Methodists, perceiving (either wisely or unprophetically) that the time was not right to bring a wider range of issues to their constituents, at least narrowed their discussion to one issue and focused most of their discussion to an editorial/juridical issue in their *Book of Discipline*. Presbyterians should have prepared a study guide that high-lighted major themes and issues. If time had allowed, a penultimate version of the report should have been field tested in a number of diverse churches. The progressive wing of the church should have been better organized. Most of these problems were created by the tight time-frame for the writing of the report, and the need to make it available to commissioners of the General Assembly. The important lesson here is that given the complexity and the emotion which surround sexuality issues, they should never be presented to denominational constituencies without an ample time for review, discussion, and opportunity for revisions. The Lutheran strategy could serve as a model for all denominations.

The ELCA published a second edition of its initial study document in

October of 1993. The 21-page document, entitled "The Church and Human Sexuality: A Lutheran Perspective" is irenic in tone, balanced in its consideration of diverse theological viewpoints, and includes guidelines for local congregations which might want to use the document for study. It acknowledges that "through the ages the Church too often has overlooked the created goodness of sexuality," and sets the discussion of all sexuality issues in the framework of the community of the baptized.

What Lutherans will eventually do with this fresh draft about sexuality issues remains to be seen, but I can note here that it has the advantages of brevity, clarity, and of not being issued in a time of denominational political strife. It recognizes the special problems of teenagers, single adults, and gay and lesbian persons. It does not advocate a single approach to gays and lesbians in the life of the church, but it considers three different responses which are all set in the Christian context of "love of neighbor." The document is clear that Christian people need to stand against "whatever violates, harms, or demeans persons and relationships" (p. 17); this includes adultery, promiscuity, sexual abuse, spreading sexually-transmitted diseases, discriminatory behavior toward others due to their sexuality, prostitution, pornography, and commercial exploitation of sexuality in advertising and media. Most of these concerns, the document points out, have implications for public polity, and concerned Christians of all denominations will need to be advocates for legislation which furthers justice and human rights.

The Lutherans continue to exemplify a careful and thoughtful process. Even the October 1993 draft is offered for discussion and field testing; congregations are asked to reply by June 30, 1994 and those replies will form the basis of still another theological statement. To the extent that other denominations still wish to be helpful to their constituents, we can learn from the Lutherans both in theological tone and in process.

A second lesson is that sexuality issues are hard to talk about. Simply naming the issues and gathering statistical data does not necessarily facilitate discussion about the matters which concern us most deeply. Time and again as the Presbyterian Committee broke up into sub-groups to visit with local churches we were met with a strong silence after we explained the interests and concerns of our Committee. Yet when our formal meeting was over, people would corner us and ask if they could speak with us individually and confidentially. If we reflect on it, husbands and wives often have a hard time talking about sexuality. Parents have difficulty talking with children and vice versa. People who are close friends often never discuss sexuality problems. In group contexts or general church discussions, people do not ask the questions that are most important because just asking a question sometimes reveals more about our personal lives or family circumstances than we want to reveal. Many times sexuality problems require professional insight rather than group support. There is a special art, therefore, in knowing how to help people. This requires an expertise in ministerial counseling and a familiarity with community resources. Minimally for congregations it entails a sensitivity to the wide scope of sexuality issues, and not a state of denial about the scope of the problems. Pastors need both knowledge of the issues and skills in group dynamics.

A third lesson relates to the gap between the churches and the academic academy in areas of Biblical studies, theology, and ethics. After the Presbyterian Church (U.S.A.) refused to accept the report of its Special Committee on Human Sexuality as a study document, the Society of Christian Ethics decided to focus on the report at its national meeting in Philadelphia in January of 1992, and the Ethics Section of the American Academy of Religion sponsored a panel discussion on "Sexuality and the Churches" at its 1992 annual meeting in San Francisco. The Society of Biblical Literature held a session on "The Bible and Homosexuality" at its 1992 annual meeting. Recognized caucuses of gay men and lesbians openly and frankly discussed matters of concern in these professional contexts that they could not discuss in virtually any ecclesiological context.

Most dramatically, one sees this knowledge gap in the field of Biblical studies. Members of the academy are now talking about feminist criticism, ideology criticism, deconstructionism, reader-response criticism, hermeneutics of suspicion, and fantasy criticism; all of that presumes familiarity with source criticism, textual criticism, and form criticism. Biblical scholars and teachers presume familiarity with a wide range of archaeological, textual, and historical information. Literary categories of myth, legend, epic, story, and folklore form a common frame of reference. Methods of exegesis and alternative hermeneutical perspectives are debated as to details but recognized to be essential in Biblical studies.

Against this background stands the wide range of Protestant lay people with virtually no awareness of critical Biblical study at all. Discussions in presbyteries and congregations around the country revealed countless numbers of persons who, though not really being fundamentalists, still spoke as though 150 years of Biblical scholarship has not taken place. Thousands of churches do not use denominational study materials. Thousands of Christians simply presume that the Bible undergirds middle-class life and culture. Should we expect lay people to understand the word "exegesis?" Is it too much to presume that our people should know something about the great themes of the Bible, and try to relate specific texts to those themes? Why do eyes glaze over when we speak of *interpreting* the Bible? Why should the Presbyterian emphasis on "Justice-Love" as an interpretive norm for the Bible come as such a shock to lay people and ministers alike? (One layman in the Midwest wrote to me, "What is all this justice crap? What does that have to do with the Presbyterian Church?".)

I was aghast when in the course of the Presbyterian debate six former moderators of the Northern and Southern streams of the church published a document claiming that the Presbyterian (U.S.A.) Sexuality Report was "unbiblical" because in an interpretive statement I had written that a guiding principle for the Committee was that "Biblical ethics and Christian ethics for the church today are not the same thing." The point, of course, was to clarify the ethical dilemma created by the assumptions of ancient cultures (women as property, ritual uncleanness, etc.) that our modern society does not share. (All of these matters are considered in detail by William Countryman in his book *Dirt, Greed and Sex: Sexual Ethics in the New Testament and Their Implications for Today* [Fortress, 1988].) Granted that church moderators are generally chosen for their administrative service to the church and not because they are scholars, churches nonetheless deserve better from their former leaders. The embarrassment of the first statement of former moderators was off-set by a subsequent statement of twelve former moderators which acknowledged the legitimacy of the Sexuality Report and its consideration by the General Assembly. But the gap between the academic academy and the churches has been exposed as vast and embarrassing, and we need to find ways to diminish it.

The matter of how we read and interpret the Bible is one of the major underlying controversies in this debate, as Victor Furnish points out in his Appendix to this volume. If one is to move beyond prooftexting from Leviticus or even from Romans I, one has to have some broader perspective (a "hermeneutic," as scholars say) from which to understand various Biblical writings. Frankly as Presbyterian, Lutheran, and Methodist scholars we had expected more sophistication from lay people, ministers, and even church leaders. There are, of course, legitimate theological differences of opinion in this area, such as how the Bible is to be used as a guide in Christian Ethics, and how we are to understand the authority of Biblical texts and terms, but those ought to be discussable among Christians of good will. On the whole, the level of the debate about the Bible has not been conducted on a very high level. We have collectively failed in a major task. How to do better in the future should be an educational priority for all main-line churches.

A fourth lesson is related to the way that the issue of gay and lesbian persons overshadowed all of the other matters which surround human sexuality. Much of that, as I have noted earlier, was due to media emphasis and distortion. It became clear that the discussion of gay and lesbian ordination is not a rational or even theological matter. It was also clear that appeals for justice for gays and lesbians in our churches and in our societies do not follow the same lines as earlier appeals for justice on civil rights matters. Many liberals and moderates who took courageous stands on civil rights have expressed serious reservations about gays, lesbians, and the lifestyles they represent. The black community, the Hispanic community, and the Korean community in the U. S. all reflect wide-scale apprehension about gays and lesbians, somewhat because of their special cultural histories, somewhat due to their theological conservatism, and somewhat out of fear that too much attention on the gay and lesbian issue overshadows their deeper concerns about racism and discrimination of minorities. Not all persons who are troubled about the place of gays and lesbians in the churches deserve to be dismissed as "homophobes," but the church community needs to move beyond stereotypes if progress is to be made on this issue. We need to talk more about grace and compassion in the Church. Better seminary education on these matters would be a first step in the right direction. And, as Marvin Ellison has noted, we must keep working to remind church constituencies that there are other dimensions of the sexuality debate.

A fifth lesson is that the churches' debate of sexuality issues quickly becomes involved with the broader cultural debate over diversity and inclusiveness. That debate, as we all know, challenges our curricula in schools and colleges; our political visions as to what is the right future for America; our ideologies of race, class, and gender; and deep-seated convictions about the relationship of the church to the broader culture. What should Christians do, say, and advocate in a society that is moving away from the old nuclear family into many forms of bonded living units? Should that be lamented, or should it expand our understanding of what families are? Should the Church be an exclusive or inclusive community? Have Christian models for life, sexuality, and marriage been an authentic witness to divine norms, or have they mirrored the ideological interests of a privileged group? Who has benefitted from the traditional value system? Of course these are threatening questions, but they need to be raised.

The voices of liberation theologians — feminists, womanists, black men, advocates of the poor — come into the debate at this point. No matter how impressive or insightful these voices seem when they are discussed in seminary classes or seminars, they are clearly anxiety-producing to most middle-class persons in our churches. Small town and rural America finds these perspectives especially anger-producing. The issue seems to come down to this: can main-line churches be instruments of new sight? Can pastors who work on the front lines help their people to recognize and see through the ideologies that shape us? Or are our churches so deeply embedded in those ideologies that we are unable to transcend them? Are our churches part of the answer or part of the problem? To be effective molders of conscience and centers of "spiritual presence" (to borrow a term from Paul Tillich) I believe we will need to develop a new ecclesiology, both at the denominational and congregational levels. Some suggestive works are already appearing: Lettie Russell's *Church in the Round* (Westminster/John Knox, 1992) stresses partnership, egalitarianism, and hospitality in the Christian community; her vision is consistent with her previously published work on partnership. Most feminist writings, in fact, offer a serious alternative to the predominantly male hierarchical models that have shaped denominational structures, and gave us new theological foundations as well. The time may be at hand for caring people to explore alternative models of Christian community. We can learn much from the "Base Community" movement in Central and Latin America. The German Lay Academy movement is an example of how teaching can be directed at those who live on the margins of established churches. Intentional communities can be formed in the spirit of the "Faith and Life" communities that once existed in Austin, Texas and in Chicago. Local support groups and house churches can and will enable people to find nurture and acceptance apart from official Christendom. Computer networking enables people of like mind to communicate quickly and easily with each other. Let us be clear on this: the movement for renewal in the churches will find a way to express itself, inside or outside of our present denominational structures.

A sixth lesson is that our churches need to move away from platitudes and theological abstractions to dealing with actual sexual experience. We need to be concrete and specific as to what sexuality is and how it impacts on people's lives. Great joy and great pain are intertwined in human experience, along with much fear and vulnerability. As ethicist James Nelson puts it:

> We need to listen carefully to women's stories; we need to hear of the actual experiences of those who have been oppressed by sexual violence; we need to listen to the gospel speaking profoundly through gay and lesbian experience; we need to hear the voices of men struggling for a richer and more just sexuality; we need to pay attention to teenagers yearning for the church to stand with them; we need to heed the voices of single persons who feel both neglected and condemned by the church in their struggle for responsible sexual expression.[1]

Less pontificating and a little more honesty would give our churches more credibility in sexuality discussions. Time and again I have heard from my own friends and from people around the country that if they ever wanted help with any sexuality-related problem the *last* place they would go would be the church. Too many people perceive that the church's historic convictions do not fit with the ambiguities of their lives. There are times in the church's life to proclaim and times to listen. In the contexts of today's "paradigm shifts," it is time to listen.

A seventh lesson is that we need to become wiser and more realistic about American media, both in its print forms and in television. Janet Fishburn has documented the many distortions the media interjected into the debate, and I could add many of my own observations to hers. As I noted in Chapter III, it was sobering to me to realize that virtually no newspapers or popular magazines provided depthful and fair coverage of the Presbyterian report. The biased interpretations of both *TIME* and *Newsweek* coverage, along with the distorted interpretations of Peter Steinfels in the *New York Times*, disillusioned me of any thoughts I ever had about clarity or fairness in the media. This same tendency was demonstrated again in October 1993 when the revised Lutheran statement ("The Church and Human Sexuality") was published. Despite all of the careful and balanced theological language in that statement, headlines in America's newspapers screamed "Lutherans to Encourage Masturbation" and "Sell Condoms to Teenagers, Say Lutherans." Let's face it: American main-line Christians cannot, and should not, expect the popular press to treat their issues in a balanced way. Sensationalism, not accuracy, sells newspapers.

But how can stories be told fairly and clearly? Can we rely on or own denominational journals and press offices? Clearly, not always, as Presbyterians can testify. How can we counteract bias in the media? There is no way to control, of course, what reporters write, or the "spin" that various journals choose to put on documents or events. I do not have an answer to this, but I can say that theologians, ethicists, and church leaders need better skills in telling our stories to the lay public. Maybe we should learn from the TV assumption that the average attention span of an adult American is three minutes. That may say something about sermons and speeches. It certainly underscores the need for brevity and clarity for church committees!

It is sobering to realize, as Tex Sample has pointed out in his *U. S. Lifestyles and Mainline Churches* (Westminster/John Knox, 1990), that the "cultural left" in American society is by and large not found in our churches. The progressive element in our society has, for various reasons, given up on the churches. Some have found other religious communities and some have found meaning-giving groups in environmental, peace, or gender-specific communities. What they share is a sense that the critical issues of our culture have gone beyond the churches, and a study such as Sample's confirms that even the more progressive of the main-line churches retain a substantial residue of social conservatism. This may explain why so many people who have left the churches have applauded the effort of the churches sexuality studies to name the problems and to offer some alternative ethical perspectives. An on-going theological task will be to increase social consciousness in middle-class churches, which have traditionally thought of religion in individualistic terms.

THE FUTURE AGENDA

It is risky to predict the future, of course, but I believe that developments in the past year have underscored several topics that will demand theological attention in the future. Two preliminary observations need to be made before we look into any crystal ball. The first is that I do not expect any major "media event" to arise again in the churches over sexuality issues in the next decade. The intense, semi-hysterical reactions of 1991-92 were unique in timing and social context. They dissipated much energy from both extremes in these discussions. Whatever the future brings, it will set these debates in more reasoned contexts, and I expect that moderates will play a more influential role. The second observation is that the topics I have outlined in Chapters XII and XIII will have to be a part of any evolving work in the churches on sexuality issues: the struggle for new models of masculinity; bisexuality; creative discussions and workshops on marriage; the phenomenon of cohabitation; and the relationship of the churches to the culture. They are too important to ignore, and will come to the discussion table as uninvited guests.

These matters being noted, what other issues will have to be dealt with? Four are discernible and others will doubtless emerge. The first is the problem of clergy sexual misconduct. The Catholic experience has already underscored the scope and cost of out-of-court settlements and legal fees. All of this dispute, however, is not about money or legal issues. It also impacts on the integrity of the professional ministry, the name and reputation of the denomination, and on the sensitivities of church leadership. There are related issues as to standard of conduct for single Protestant clergy (Is it ever appropriate to date a parishioner?) and even as to what constitutes sexual harassment in staff situations or church related agencies.[2] Episcopalians have promulgated a sexual harassment policy and Presbyterians have just recently approved such a document. (The Presbyterian document had over 20 revisions and was worked on for over two years by a writing team.) Major tensions are raised between the legitimate complaints and pain of survivors and the need for the accused to be assured of due process. There is also the sensitive professional problem that a clergyperson, once accused, might be ruined for life even if subsequently cleared of charges. Representatives of survivors and clergy often do not agree on what time limit should apply to any statute of limitations. Recent court decisions which hold national Church bodies liable in cases of sexual misconduct have given these cases a dramatic urgency. In 1992 a $1.2 million civil judgment was rendered against an Episcopal bishop in Colorado and his diocese because a woman had been sexually exploited by a priest under the Bishop's authority. The courts, as Donald C. Clark, Jr., has pointed out, have stepped into this arena because of the

unwillingness of virtually every domination to act promptly and adequately.[3]
Legal and financial factors have drastically changed the ways that churches handle
these matters, that is for the better.

Secondly, denominations will continue to struggle with issues raised by
gay and lesbian persons. The emphasis may well shift from controversy over
ordination to discussion of blessing ceremonies for same-sex unions. This is
often done quietly now; making such events public becomes emotional for many
people, and raises the question of the relationship of such church blessings to the
state's legal attestation of marriage. (Episcopalians are working on such a
liturgical form now.) Conceivably denominations will also wrestle with the
question of whether gays or lesbians in church employ may designate their
partners as beneficiaries for health or pension benefits. The gay and lesbian
community has learned that there is no social change without pressure, so it is
unrealistic to assume that amid the broader cultural movement there will be less
pressure on the churches. The more strident mood of the April 25, 1993 march
on Washington — estimated by the National Park Service to have been the fourth
largest demonstration in Washington, D.C. in our nation's history — was an
obvious indication that gays and lesbians are determined to claim their civil rights
in the 1990s. Leaders of that march were quoted as saying "We are not going
to ask for our rights; we are going to take them." Inasmuch as the broader
strategies of the gay and lesbian movement are a barometer of the climate for the
churches, we can anticipate continuing pressure on the churches for full
acceptance of gays and lesbians as members and as church leaders. A 20 year
old female marcher from Tallahassee, Florida was quoted as saying "We are a
part of this society, and people are going to have to deal with us — and a lot
sooner than they want to."

A third agenda item in the future will be an expansion of church-related
sexuality issues into matters of public policy. This will be true especially for

women's issues.   Sex education in the schools is one example; others might
include programs to educate the public about the range of sexual abuse; measures
to protect the civil rights of all persons regardless of their sexual orientation; and
legislation to change provisions in pension plans, social security, welfare
payments, and tax codes which financially penalize those who wish to marry.
The persistent inequity of women's pay as opposed to men's pay should be
addressed by communities of faith.   Can and should the churches advocate for a
compensation scheme for women who do housework and raise children?   Some
years ago Beverly Harrison argued that "there will never be genuine economic
justice for women until greater justice prevails between domestic labor and labor
outside the home."[4]   To have one's consciousness raised about the roles of
women in a patriarchal society is to likewise raise questions about the social
structures that undergird these societies.   I have commented on that in Chapter
XIII; here I simply note that it is bound to be a part of the future discussion of
sexuality issues.

      A fourth issue deals with strategies for social change.   Even if the
theological axis of the churches can be tilted towards a more evolutionary mode
of thought — Tex Sample's suggestion of a "journey theology" is a rich model,
where faith is seen as a process, not as an arrival — we still need more precise
strategies for social change.   Sociological analyses of how people change their
minds and their behavior can be helpful to church leaders who are serious about
moving the churches in new directions.   Most people, for example, do not change
their minds when they are attacked or ridiculed.   Most people need positive
examples, encouragement, and exposure to incremental change.   Church leaders
at all levels need to be mindful of the pain and perplexity of most sexual issues,
and should strategize as to how to create supportive contexts for people to learn.
Church strategies might involve new and better sexuality curricula for both youth
and adults; better continuing education programs for clergy; how to get required

academic work on sexuality into seminary curricula; how to build bridges with men's support groups in any given community; how to utilize other professional expertise (medical, social work, counselors, gerontology specialists) in local church programming.

It seems clear that in terms of realistic expectations of institutions the Presbyterian report asked too much too soon. If the "shock" phase is behind us, however, we need now to be wise about incremental change. We need to have clear priorities. The Lutheran document of October 1993 is a good model for this. What can (and should) be done first? How can planning be realistic without losing the long term prophetic vision of a more compassionate church? How do visions become programs?

The future of the sexuality debate remains unclear. Trends in most denominations are not encouraging. The different political agenda of the Clinton administration may well create a more open cultural climate that will encourage change and growth in our churches, but the resistance to his plan for allowing self-acknowledged gays and lesbians to serve in the military shows how deep-seated the opposition is. The collected voices of women that call for a new social paradigm of a "partnership" model for life (see Diane Eisler's *The Chalice and the Blade* [Harper, San Francisco, 1987]) will continue to create a pressure on theological and ethical thinking. We will probably see church splits, realignments, and new communities formed. Progressives may simply give up. Mainline denominations may well continue to shrink in size as people leave for very different reasons. My distinct impression is that denominations *per se* will not be the shaping influences on American people as we struggle with the sexuality issues that are so deep in our culture. I suspect that what constructive help people find will be found at the congregational level, and there only in contexts of trust, friendship, and support. The Lutheran attempt at denominational guidance needs to be watched carefully; it is a positive and constructive effort but it is going against the stream of anti-denominational bias. Financial problems, internal reorganization and anti-ecumenism in major denominations these days do not make denominational headquarters likely places for helpful guidance on sexuality issues.

We have much at stake, however, to help our denominations preserve some prophetic vision and compassion. We finally have to trust that the Spirit will give us cohesion and courage. But such a future is not self-evident. The major Protestant churches are all showing signs of becoming more exclusive, parochial, and comfortable, becoming advocates for the privileged majority. Will we have a church that yearns for yesterday, or will we have a church with a vision of tomorrow? And what would a church of tomorrow look like?

ENDNOTES

[1]"Needed: A Continuing Sexual Revolution," in *Sexual Ethics and the Church* (Chicago: The Christian Century Foundation, 1989), p. 66.

[2]These issues have been raised thoughtfully by Karen Lebacqz and Ron Barton in their book *Sex in the Parish* (Westminster/John Knox. 1991).

[3]"Sexual Abuse in the Church: The Law Steps In," *The Christian Century*, April 14, 1993, p. 397.

[4]"Sexuality and Public Policy," in Carol S. Robb, ed. *Making the Connections* (Boston: Beacon Press, 1985), p. 95.

CHAPTER XV

THE CHURCH OF YESTERDAY AND THE CHURCH OF TOMORROW

The place was Burlington, North Carolina. The date was March 2, 1991. The occasion was a special called meeting of Salem Presbytery in North Carolina, and the meeting place was the sanctuary of the First Presbyterian Church of Burlington. The sanctuary was packed; over 500 people gathered in a sanctuary that was designed to seat about 400 people. Visitors and official representatives sat on the floor in front of the first pews, in the choir stalls, and stood along the sides of the church. I had been asked to come to speak about the Majority Report of the Presbyterian Sexuality Report; my colleague, Marilyn Washburn, was invited to speak about the Minority Report. I opened the meeting by discussing how the General Assembly Special Committee on Human Sexuality came into being; what problems we found; what visions we shared; and why we wrote the type of report that we did. Marilyn Washburn followed by affirming many things in the Majority Report, but also indicated where and why she dissented from that report.

After Marilyn spoke, the moderator called for general discussion. The mood was intense. After about a half hour of various questions, a man arose and gave an impassioned speech. He said that as a churchman, he was bewildered and angry about this report. "Why", he asked, "are we now calling for change and something new? Aren't Christian values eternal? Isn't it hard enough to assimilate the traditional values that we have been taught?" "What," he asked, "has happened to the church of my childhood that gave me a clear vision for life?" Then looking at Marilyn and me, he said: "As far as I am concerned, I would like to hear less from people like you and more about how we can recover that church of yesterday!" Most of the people in that sanctuary applauded, and about half gave him a standing ovation.

I

Well, what about that church of yesterday? Was this impassioned speaker correct in saying that the recovery of that church should be our highest priority today. Even when we allow for some nostalgia and selective memory, what can we say about that church of yesterday? I confess that I share some of that speaker's nostalgia. I can still get choked up when I think about my home church in Fort Wayne, Indiana. I remember, as a little boy, being a part of the Mission Band. I remember the people who taught me in Sunday school (not very learned people, and certainly not professional teachers), but they taught me that the church is a good and safe place to be. I remember singing gospel hymns in Sunday school, and being a member of Christian Endeavor. If that church of yesterday was so appealing and satisfying, why does the report on Sexuality call for some change in our hearts, values, and priorities? Let's reflect on that church of yesteryear, the Protestant churches from 1930 to 1970. There are some common things we can say about all of mainline Protestant churches that nurtured us while we were young.

1.   The first thing that we have to note is that the church of yesterday was *exclusive*. It was for most of us almost exclusively white; it was predominantly middle-class; it was made up mostly of married people; and it was smugly Protestant. The church of yesterday was tightly organized along denominational lines. If we think back on our experiences, we realize that the church of previous generations had little concern for Black persons; most of us

had little contact with Roman Catholics; and the church was highly suspicious of Jews. We believed that we had God's blessing on our way of life, and we certainly affirmed the status quo of middle-class America.

It is embarrassing to realize that many of our churches strongly resisted the civil rights movement of the late 1950s and early 1960s. I arrived in Tallahassee, Florida, in the summer of 1960 when the sit-in movement among Black students was growing. Tallahassee was the center of that activity in the state of Florida. Many mainline white churches in Tallahassee employed off-duty policemen to stand at their doors and be sure that no Black persons presented themselves for worship. We can think of some heroes and prophetic figures of those days, but on the whole, particularly in the south, the witness of the churches was not impressive. Most protestants in the church of yesterday voted Republican and really believed with "Engine Charley" Wilson of General Motors (later appointed as President Eisenhower's Secretary of Defense) that "What is good for General Motors is good for the country."

The church of yesterday invited us to think about Christian missions, and many of us can still remember bringing dimes to our Sunday school classes to support the mission work of the church. But if the church would go around the world, it would not go around the corner. Few of us can remember significant commitments to social justice in our local communities that were advocated by our churches.

But since those days, the world has changed and the church is in the process of changing. Our society has now become more aware of diversity. We are mindful that both our society and our churches are made up of Afro-Americans, Asian Americans, Middle-Eastern Americans, Hispanic Americans, and Native Americans. The Presbyterian church merged in 1983, bringing together northern and southern streams of the Presbyterian heritage to create a new family. In that family today are persons of different ethnic backgrounds, as well as a sizeable number of gay and lesbian persons and people from various socioeconomic levels. We have become more aware of single people, and of the integrity of singleness as a life style. We are now aware of the special needs of older adults, of widows, widowers, and Gray Panthers. In our work on the Sexuality Committee, we noted that the median age of members in the Presbyterian church is 55, and that nearly one third of all of the members of the Presbyterian church are over age 65.

So we are now aware that the church is called to be an inclusive community. We cannot go back to the smugness, the homogeneity, or the parochialism that once shaped the protestant churches of America.

2.   Secondly, the church of yesterday was *moralistic and judgmental*. In the church of an earlier generation (as well as throughout our society), the greatest social stigma was to be a pregnant, unmarried young woman. Families hastily and embarrassingly arranged "shotgun" weddings. The church saw issues of sexual morality in black and white terms. As Nathaniel Hawthorne wrote in *The Scarlet Letter*, and as Allen Payton wrote in *Too Late The Pharalope*, and as Theodore Dreisser wrote in *An American Tragedy*, the deepest and most shame-filled sins were of a sexual nature. Young people were reminded of the sin of premarital sex; many people today still bear the scars of guilt about that. We were persuaded that the people of God were heterosexual, middle-class and married.

If gay and lesbian persons were ever acknowledged or discussed, it was done in hushed, harsh, and unrepeatable terms. Propriety was a high value of the church of yesterday. Overtones of judgment and Pharisaism were dominant. We talked much about moral absolutes, the rightness of our faith, and the superiority of our culture and of our way of life.

But now, with the theological and social developments of the last 25 years, we know that all cultures are relatively conditioned. We recognized that what we once proclaimed as absolutes are tinged by the interests of our own social and cultural contexts. In the process of our own intellectual growth and geographical moves, most mature adults recognize that what we once thought was absolute was in fact shaped by the parochialism of a specific time, place, and social class. When we are honest we recognize that sin lurks in all of us. We have learned from our children who cohabit before marriage, and from gay and lesbian persons whom we know to be good, decent, and God-loving human beings. We learned that human goodness is found in many ethnic groups as we got to know racial ethnic persons who have lived in different cultural patterns. We have come to recognize that there is more of God's grace in compassion than in judgment and condemnation.

So the report on human sexuality invites us to a broader vision of compassion, and to an awareness of those who have borne great pain in our society. That vision is a decidedly more biblical stance than the judgmental view of the old church.

3.   Thirdly, the church of yesterday was *basically negative in its understanding of human sexuality.* The Christian tradition has a long heritage of regarding human sexuality as a part of our lower, or animal, nature. Sexuality was thought to be "redeemable" in the married state, but generally our tradition has said that what is good about us is above the waist (our hearts and our heads) and what is problematic, sinful or demonic about us is found below the waist. Married Victorian women who worried about this duality were advised that in performing their conjugal duties, they should shut their eyes, clench their fists and think of England.

The church of yesterday spoke much about Agape, but it did not tell us much about Eros, that love of skin against skin, and the human experiences of delight, pleasure, and ecstasy. The church of yesterday was wise in recognizing that our sexuality is closely related to our vulnerabilities, and that many people bear great pain through memories of abuse, exploitation, and shame. It was more difficult, however, for the church of yesterday to also recognize that the gift of sexuality also has great promise for joy, fulfillment, and human happiness.

The churches that most of us grew up in had fixed gender roles for men and women. They unquestioningly affirmed the use of masculine language for the divine, and for generations most of us felt that male experience was synonymous with all human experience.

Now, however, we are living in a church that has heard the need to respond to feminist critiques of our masculine orientation. Churches around the country are becoming more sensitive to inclusive language. New theological paradigms that express the feminine sense of the divine help us to understand deeper mysteries about God. As we try to relate our sexuality to our spirituality, it has become clear that we now need a positive sense of human sexuality. We need a constructive theology of our bodies, a way to affirm sexuality as a gift of God to be enjoyed responsibly, thoughtfully, and faithfully. These new perspectives will lead us to the church of tomorrow, and not move us backward to the church of yesterday.

II

For all these reasons, the church does need to change and to address new communities of people in our midst. In that process, we need an ethic of the spirit and not of the law. We need to have a vision of positive sexuality. The church that will equip us for a creative future will be a church that is more honest; more thoughtful; more diverse; more flexible in its dealings with human diversity. It will be a church that will be more ecumenical, more egalitarian, and more compassionate than the church of yesterday.

We can find a Biblical model for this type of openness to the future in the apostle Paul. Centuries ago while he was in prison, he wrote to the church at

Philippi that had supported him in his missionary endeavors. Paul talked about pressing on to a new future. He wrote to them "Forgetting what lies behind and straining forward to what lies ahead, I press on toward the goal for the prize of the upward call of God in Christ Jesus." When Paul wrote those words, he did not know what the future would bring, but he did know that God is best served as we look ahead and not as we look behind.

So the impassioned speaker in Burlington was wrong to look backwards. It is good to have appreciation for the past, but we need to recognize that the creative spirit in the church in every age has pulled the church forward, in courage, compassion, and faith. Paul reminds us that God will support us in that venture, and the church in the process will become more faithful and more humane.

That is basically the vision of the church advocated by the Majority Report of the Presbyterian Committee. In that spirit I invite readers of this book to be open to a bold and exciting future. May our churches always be beacons of light and places of compassion for all who come through their doors.

POSTSCRIPT: A PARABLE

I indicated in Chapter I of this book that much of the conflict over sexuality issues is related to two different models of Christian ethics. These models start in different places and prioritize different values about the Christian life. For the theological generations from 1930-1970 the two polar alternatives were represented by the Swiss theologian Karl Barth and the German-turned-American theologian Paul Tillich. Barth stood for Biblical authority and the clear identity of the Christian community. Tillich represented the effort to understand the human situation, the complexities of culture, and how to bring Christian answers to these problems. Barth proclaimed; Tillich began by listening. Much of the controversy over human sexuality in our churches and in our culture from 1988-1993 can be traced back to those theological and ethical alternatives.

At the 1991 annual meeting of the North American Paul Tillich Society in Kansas City, Langdon Gilkey, Shailer Matthews Professor of Theology, Emeritus, at the University of Chicago, recounted a story about Barth and Tillich. It was Tillich's version of what he thought about Barth, and how each of them had opposed the Nazi regime in Germany. Gilkey also tells this story in his book *Gilkey on Tillich* (New York: Crossroad, 1990), pp. 204-205. My recounting here follows Gilkey's oral version of the story.

> One evening in Tillich's apartment we asked Tillich to tell us about his relation to Barth. After Tillich had carefully opened a bottle of wine, he settled back, and began to answer our questions.

"When you're fighting against a tyrant, then Barth is the best man to have on your side. He drives a sharp wedge between heaven and earth, between the gospel and culture. And that is good when culture becomes demonic and claims the authority and power of heaven. With Barth's sharp separation of church and culture, he gives to us the power to resist the tyrant who represents *Kultur*, has in fact swallowed *Kultur* whole, for there is then *in Kultur itself* no place to stand. That is why Barth's theology had such power in these days. It gave power to all those who wanted to resist Hitler and found in German culture no place from which to resist. Barth's message was appropriate for that *Kairos* — more appropriate than mine. I respect and have always respected Barth, not only for the originality and power of his theology but also for the clarity of his insight into the idolatry of Hitler and his courage for declaring it." Tillich paused, and then began again in an even firmer voice:

"But," and here Tillich looked at each of us with weighty seriousness and yet also with great vulnerability. He spoke with deliberate emphasis, pausing with great care at each point:

"But, I was right about the relation of culture to theology, even a theology of resistance against culture. Theology has to understand what is happening in a culture and to critique that culture. And, in last analysis, Barth and I fought for different things. Barth and his friends fought for the freedom of the Evangelical pulpit. I fought...for the Jews.

She/he who has ears to hear, let them hear.

HOMOSEXUAL PRACTICES IN BIBLICAL PERSPECTIVE*

by

Victor Paul Furnish

INTRODUCTION

"What does the Bible say about homosexuality?" This question is repeatedly asked, not only in churches (and synagogues), but also in various kinds of public forums, including the news media. Thus formulated, however, the question itself can mislead. First, it fails to take account of the fact that the word "homosexuality," as well as the very concept, is an anachronism when applied to the Bible, and to the ancient world in general (see below). Second, it overlooks the fact that the Bible is actually a collection of writings, representative of many different authors, times, and places. It is therefore wrong simply to presume that "the Bible says" just one thing about any given subject. Finally, those who put the question this way often fail to realize that determining what the biblical writings say is only part — indeed, the easiest part — of the task. It is imperative always to ask, as well, why these writings say what they do. This

---

*An abridged version of a paper first presented to The Committee to Study Homosexuality of The United Methodist Church (1990; revised in 1991 and again in 1992). Discussions within that committee, and also with individual members of it, have influenced to a considerable extent both the scope and the content of this essay. To my colleagues on that panel I am deeply indebted. The views presented here are strictly my own, however, and should not be regarded as those of either the Study Committee or of the United Methodist Church.

requires the careful examination of each text in all of its appropriate contexts — literary, historical, theological, etc. And for those of us who regard the writings of Old and New Testaments as Scripture, there is yet a third critical question: How, if at all, may these ancient texts inform our understanding and give us moral guidance in today's world?

The first part of this study is devoted to an examination of the biblical passages that are most often invoked in discussions of homosexuality. The attempt will be to understand each of these in the light of its own particular contexts. In the second part, some suggestions will be made about how the Bible can — and cannot — inform and guide the church today as it seeks for clarity about this matter.

I. TEXTS AND CONTEXTS

Terminology

It is important to recognize that "sexuality" is an abstract concept for which we are indebted to modern psychological investigations and theories. The same is of course true for the concepts of "heterosexuality," "homosexuality," and "bisexuality." There were no such concepts and no terms for them in the ancient world. It was universally presupposed that everyone was "heterosexual," in the sense of being inherently ("naturally") constituted for physical union with the opposite sex. Thus there is no biblical text about "homosexuality" understood as a "condition" or "orientation."[1]

It is also important to know that the word "sodomite" appears nowhere in the Hebrew text of the Old Testament, not even to mean "a resident of Sodom." The Hebrew term that was translated as "sodomite" in the King James Version (Deut 23:17-18; 1 Kings 14:22-24; 15:12; 22:46; 2 Kings 23:7, Joel 3:3) refers to a (male) temple prostitute, as virtually every modern English version properly recognizes. Nor does the word "sodomite" ever appear in the Greek text of the New Testament, although the English word is employed twice in the New Revised Standard Version (1 Cor 6:9; 1 Tim 1:10).[2]

Genesis 19:1-25

This story about the men of Sodom is still the one most people think of when the topic of the Bible and homosexuality is being discussed. However, it is not a story about homosexual behavior in general, and certainly not a story about homosexual acts performed by consenting adults. It is a story about the intent to do violence, and had that taken place, it would have just happened to be the rape of two males by a mob of other males.[3] The men of Sodom were "out for a 'wilding,'" and Lot's vulnerable victims came along as a handy target.[4] This is recognized in Ezekiel 16, where Sodom's sin is described without explicit reference to the rapacious intent of the men of the city: "This was the guilt of your sister Sodom: she and her daughters had pride, excess of food, and prosperous ease, but did not aid the poor and needy" (v. 49).

Significantly, not one of the biblical references to the story makes a point of the "homosexual" character of the intended rape. It is sometimes claimed otherwise about Jude 7 and 2 Pet 2:10 (the writer of 2 Peter is here, as elsewhere, dependent on Jude).[5] However, the evil that is in view in these passages is not the violation of males by other males, but the violation of *angels* by mere mortals; for Lot's guests were really angels in disguise.[6] As for the two statements about Sodom attributed to Jesus (Matt 10:15 [par. Luke 10:12] and Matt 11:23-24), these refer to the city only generally, as an example of what happens to those who disobey the will of God.

Leviticus 18:22 and 20:13.

These two statements prohibiting male homosexual activity occur in the so-called "Holiness Code" (Leviticus 17-26), probably a compilation of several distinct collections of laws and regulations.[7] This Code had achieved its present form by the time of the Exile (6th century B.C.E.). The two statements, however, stand in two distinct parts of the collection, each of which has its own tradition history.[8] Overall, the Code as we have it reflects ancient Israel's concern for *purity*, which was understood in a quite objective, "physical" sense. To be "pure" meant to be an unblemished specimen of one's kind, whole in oneself and unmixed with any other kind (which would be pollution). Within this context, "defilement" does not mean moral defilement, but pollution in a literal, physical sense. This is why, according to the Holiness Code, animals must not be allowed to "breed with a different kind," a field must not be sown "with two kinds of seeds," and one must not wear any clothing "made of two different materials" (Lev 19:19).

Similarly, a male must not have sex with another male, since that would mean — as the Hebrew text literally says — that one of the partners must "lie the lyings of a woman." Because his male-ness is thereby violated, he is no longer an unblemished specimen of his kind. This is what is defiling about the act. There is no specific concern here for what is "good" or "just" or "loving," but only for *purity*, understood in an objective, physical sense. This is also why the prohibition is so absolute and unqualified. It does not matter who the males might be, how old they are, what their relationship, or whether there has been mutual consent. It matters only that one or both of them will be physically polluted by taking the part of a female.

Some, in a case like this, would invoke what I have called "the law of diminishing [or: varying] relevancy": The *more specifically applicable* an instruction is to the situation for which it was originally formulated, the *less specifically applicable* it is to any other situation. Thus if the Levitical taboo regarding homosexual behavior does not address or even envision the situations and issues confronted by the 20th-century church, then it cannot be specifically applicable to those.

To be sure, there are interpreters who believe that it is inappropriate to invoke any such "law of diminishing relevancy" here, even though our concerns and presuppositions are different from those on which the Holiness Code rests. In their judgment it is important that *every* biblical reference to homosexual behavior is negative in one way or another (a point that can be readily granted).[9] Therefore, they argue, the Levitical proscription of homosexual practice is not just an expression of Israel's concern for purity. It must be an expression, finally, of God's will for every time and place. As confirmation of this they point to the Genesis creation accounts, especially to 1:26-28 (in the later, Priestly account) and 2:24-25 (in the earlier, Yahwistic account).[10]

Genesis 1:26-28

According to one interpretation of these verses, the statement about being created "male and female" (v. 27b) is connected just as closely with the preceding statement about being created in God's image (vv. 26-27a) as it is with the following statement about procreation (v. 28).[11] If so, then it would seem to follow that "heterosexuality" is part of what it means to bear "the image of God," and that any kind of homosexual relationship would be a violation of that divine image. Thus the "purity" with which the Holiness Code is concerned would have to be understood in a less restricted and particular sense. It would involve maintaining not just the physical state of one's body, but one's God-given "heterosexuality."

Others[12] believe that more attention must be paid to the context, and they make these points:

(i)   Genesis 1 is about *nature and humankind in general* (e.g., the

Hebrew word *adam* is a collective term here, referring to humankind; and "male" and "female" are biological terms, not sociological). It does not deal with culture or particular individuals, with historical circumstances, or with ethical issues, but is interested only in what is typical of all humankind.

(ii)   This is an aetiological account; that is, told in order to explain why things *are* as they are, not to prescribe what *ought* to be.[13] Specifically, in this account the Priestly writers were intent on explaining why species and kinds are properly kept separated (the basis of the Priestly system of ritual purity — because they were created separate; and in particular why the sabbath day is special — because on the seventh day God had rested.

(iii)   The statement about creation in God's image is meant to emphasize that humankind is set apart from the rest of creation by reason of its special relationship to God. This relationship is shared by all members of the human species (male and female).

(iv)   Nothing is said about *how* humankind is like God, only that this "likeness" is what distinguishes humankind from other species.

(v)   The distinctiveness of humankind is therefore not that it has been created "male and female" and enabled to reproduce itself. Precisely in these respects humankind is *like* every other created species and *unlike* God. There is certainly no suggestion that the differentiated sexuality and reproductive capacity with which every created species has been endowed is shared by God. Indeed, of all of the deities of the Ancient Near East, only Israel's God was regarded as *asexual*.

Genesis 2:24-25

Some interpreters find in these two verses a provision for essentially all of the "constituent parts of marriage," including its monogamous, covenantal, and heterosexual character.[14] A number of interpreters, however, make the following points (among others):

(i)   One must also recognize the aetiological character of the Yahwistic account. Here the special concern is to explain why men and women have distinctive roles and tasks in society, and why people (typically) view the opposite sex as they do. Thus the question in view in Genesis 2 is not whether it is "morally right" to become one flesh with a person of the same sex. It is, rather, why a person from one family leaves his or her blood kin in order to become one flesh with someone who has left her or his blood kin.[15]

(ii)   Nothing at all is implied in this passage about a "marriage" relationship, and certainly nothing about "monogamy." Although the word "wife" appears in most English translations of these verses, the Hebrew word itself (issha) means only "adult woman." Whether in a given passage it refers to a "married" woman has to be determined entirely on the basis of the context; and there is nothing in this particular context to justify that translation.[16]

In summary: One interpretation of Genesis 1-2 holds that heterosexuality alone is God's intention for humankind, intrinsic to creation, and part (at least) of what it means to have been created in the image of God. As a consequence, it is argued, homosexual relationships are fundamentally evil, a perversion of the created order, and contrary to God's will. According to another interpretation, however, the biblical accounts of creation do not command heterosexual behavior but only explain it. On this view, the Genesis creation accounts are not about God's will for individual members of the species but only about what is typical of the species as a whole. For this reason, they take no account of the physically or mentally disabled, of the celibate, of the impotent — or of those who in modern times have come to be described as "homosexual."

This second interpretation is supported by the fact that there is no appeal to these creation accounts in either of the Old Testament passages that are concerned with specific sexual practices (e.g., Leviticus 18 and 20). It has been claimed, however, that for Christians the New Testament texts must be the decisive ones; specifically, that Paul's negative view of homosexual practices can be shown to rest, ultimately, on his conviction about God's design for creation. It is therefore to the New Testament, and above all to Romans, that we must now turn.[17]

Romans 1:26-27

The following adaptation of the NRSV translation will give a better idea than most English versions of how these verses read in Paul's Greek:

> [26]For this reason God gave them up to degrading passions, for just as their women exchanged natural intercourse for unnatural, [27]so also the men, abandoning natural intercourse with women, were consumed with passion for one another, men committing shameless acts with men and receiving in their own persons the penalty required by their error.

a.   Grammatical and syntactical observations. (i) In Greek there is just one sentence here. (ii) This is a sentence in the indicative mood; i.e., it is in the form of an *assertion*, not in the form of a question, command, or prohibition. (iii) The subject of this sentence is "God" (v. 26a). (iv) The direct object of the sentence is "them" (v. 26a), meaning the Gentiles (the Gentile world overall, not individual Gentiles); these have been in view since v. 18. (v) The indirect object of the sentence is "degrading passions" (v. 26a).   (vi) The references to homosexual behavior (vv. 26b and 27) make the phrase "degrading passions" more specific.

b.   The function of the assertion within Paul's argument.   The grammatical and syntactical observations alert us at once to two important points. First, no specific moral instruction or commandment concerning "homosexuality" is being issued here.   Second, "homosexual" activity is not even the topic of this sentence. The topic of the sentence is God, and specifically — as it has been since 1:18 — "the revealing of God's wrath." One is therefore required to consider the function of this sentence within its context.

Verses 26-27 stand within the first major section of Paul's argument in Romans, 1:18-3:20. The subject of this section is not Christian behavior (the specifically moral instructions and appeals of the letter are clustered in chapters 12-15) but the human predicament. As interpreters have long recognized, Paul's argument here, both in form and in content, bears the imprint of his Hellenistic-Jewish heritage.[18] The "bottom line" is summed up by the apostle himself in 3:22b-23: "There is no distinction [Paul means: between Jew and Gentile], since all have sinned and fall short of the glory of God."

What Paul understands by sin is made clear in 1:18-21. Although humanity *can know* God through what God has created (vv. 18-20a),[19] knowing God is not enough. God must also be acknowledged as the One from whom all life has come and by whom all life is claimed. "Sin" is the refusal to do this, the refusal to glorify [NRSV: "honor"] God and to give God thanks (v. 21).[20] Sin means trying to go it alone without God, refusing to let God be God. It means seeking to be one's own god, attempting to live out of one's own finite resources. Sin is the presumption that one exists as a self-generated and self-sustaining individual. Sin is the refusal to accept one's creatureliness, the refusal to accept one's life as a gift from Another.[21] This is the folly that Paul sees manifested in pagan idolatry (vv. 22-23); those who fashion the idols, refusing to acknowledge their own mortality, end up worshiping lifeless images that are inferior even to themselves.[22]

Thus in Rom 1:24-32 Paul is not enumerating specific "sins" but listing some representative *consequences* of sin. His Hellenistic-Jewish heritage is especially evident here, e.g., in the notion that "one is punished by the very things by which one sins" (Wisd 11:16). He also shares the view that the failure to acknowledge God leads to a fundamental "confusion over what is good [θόρυβος ἀγαθῶν]" (so expressed in Wisd 14:26), and that sexual immorality is an especially telling symptom of this.[23] In short, the refusal to let God be God sets something like "Murphy's Law" in operation — "everything that *can* go wrong *does* go wrong." Alienation from God brings the breakdown and de-formation of every other relationship. Paul makes it clear that this is not only the case among the Gentiles. In Rom 2:23-24 he illustrates how also the Jews have fallen short of God's glory (cf. 1:21), so that "there is no distinction." In Rom 1:18-3:20 he is writing about the predicament of humanity as a whole.

Having completed this description of the human predicament, he goes on to proclaim that the source of humanity's salvation is God's grace, as that is received by faith in Christ (3:21 through chapter 8). This helps to underscore the fact that the earlier paragraphs have not been written to "condemn sinners," to frighten them into repenting, or to specify what one should and should not do. Rather, Paul's concern in 1:18-3:20 has been to emphasize that the whole of humanity shares a common plight, and by emphasizing this to prepare for the message of 3:21ff. — that salvation comes as God's gift (e.g., 5:6-8).

c. What Paul is presupposing about "homosexuality." What is said here explicitly about homosexual behavior is fairly minimal: it takes place between females as well as between males;[24] it is an expression of "degrading" and self-destructive passions; it is "unnatural"; and it results in an appropriate penalty. All of these points are present as well in Hellenistic, including Hellenistic-Jewish literature of Paul's day, often in the context of specific discussions of the topic. One may therefore reasonably expect to get a somewhat fuller idea of what Paul has in mind by determining what those sources say about homosexual practice.[25] Some essential results of such an investigation can be summarized as follows.

(i)   It was universally presupposed that, except in cases where one person was victimized by another, homosexual practice was a matter of one's own choosing. This presupposition is reflected in Paul's use of the verb "exchanged" (μετήλλαξαν) in Rom 1:26, to which "abandoning" (ἀφέντες) in 1:27 is parallel.[26] There was of course no inkling of any biological, psychological, or sociological factors that might predispose one to such behavior.

(ii) The possibility of enduring, "committed" homosexual relationships that are accommodated to societal structures seems not to have been entertained. The literature of this period, including the works of the "secular" moralists, by and large views homosexual relationships as expressive only of unbridled lust.[27] One reads most often, although not exclusively, about pederastic relationships (typically involving a boy in his early teens and an older male). The pederastic relationships most discussed — and in Paul's day usually condemned — are those between masters and slaves and between youthful male prostitutes and their customers.

(iii) When Paul's contemporaries, like the apostle himself, described homosexual behavior as "contrary to nature," they seem to have had two things in mind above all: that it disrupts what is self-evidently the way human beings reproduce,[28] and that it inevitably diminishes the properly superior status which "by nature" belongs to the male.[29] These two points may also explain why male homosexual practice is much more frequently mentioned than female homosexual practice.[30] Yet the second point could also lead to the condemnation of "lesbian" activity; time and again one sees the argument that when women engage in homosexual behavior they are "overstepping the bounds of the female, passive role" to which they were assigned in Greco-Roman culture.[31]

d. Theological considerations. The concern for what is and is not in accord with "nature" had its origin in Hellenistic (e.g., Stoic) thought, and from there it was taken over into Hellenistic-Judaism, which was Paul's own specific religious background. These points are not generally disputed, and they have led some to conclude that Paul's attitude toward homosexual behavior simply reflects the view that was prevalent in the Hellenistic (and Hellenistic-Jewish) culture of his time and place.

Others believe, however, that whatever cultural influences his description of homosexual practice may reflect, Paul's negative view of it has distinctly theological roots, and is therefore a matter of principle.[32] It is argued, in particular, that he calls homosexual practices "unnatural" because he believes they violate God's created order, specifically God's creation of humankind as both male and female (Gen 1:27-28). On this reading of Romans 1, a timeless moral imperative underlies the apostle's listing of same-sex intercourse as one (perhaps the prime) example of the debaucheries that have been visited upon the Gentiles. It is therefore held that Paul would not be able to condone *any* kind of homosexual relationship, including one between consenting, committed adults. Any such relationship would contravene God's created order.

Advocates of this interpretation support it primarily by appealing to the context, especially Rom 1:18-25. There, unquestionably, both creation and God's role as Creator are clearly in view, not least in the comment that immediately precedes Paul's reference to homosexual behavior: "[idolaters] exchanged the truth about God for a lie and worshiped and served the creature rather than the Creator" (v. 25). From this it is concluded that the concept of "nature" implicit in vv. 26-27 is specifically the *biblical* concept of creation as found, especially, in the accounts of Genesis 1-3.[33] This view runs into difficulties, however, at three points in particular.

(i)   Rom 1:18-32 contains neither a quotation from Genesis 1-3 nor a single identifiable allusion to any part of those creation accounts.[34] Creation is of course in view, but not because Paul wants to emphasize what God brought into being or God's *intentions* for creation. Rather, in this passage his emphasis is almost entirely on *God as the Creator*, because his concern is to show the folly of pagan idolatry. For this purpose Paul would have found the creation accounts themselves less directly pertinent than other parts of Scripture. Thus in Rom 1:18-32 he seems to be relying mainly on chapters 13-15 of the Hellenistic-Jewish book, Wisdom of Solomon; and behind these chapters lie not the accounts of creation in Genesis 1-3, but such passages as Psalm 115 (especially vv. 1-8), Isaiah 40 (especially vv. 18-26, 28), and Isaiah 44 (especially vv. 9-20).

(ii)　　　Although there are numerous references to homosexual behavior in the Hellenistic-Jewish texts that are roughly contemporary with Paul's letters,[35] there is seldom any indication that the author is condemning the practice on the basis of God's created order.[36] It is generally condemned for the same kinds of reasons given by non-Jewish authors of the period.

(iii)　　　No such "creation theology" as that alleged for Rom 1:26-27 is evident in any of Paul's other references to what is "natural" or "unnatural" ($\kappa\alpha\tau\grave{\alpha}\ \phi\acute{v}\sigma\iota\nu$, $\pi\alpha\rho\grave{\alpha}\ \phi\acute{v}\sigma\iota\nu$, etc.). The most significant of these (with respect to the present topic) occurs in 1 Cor 11:2-16, where he is trying to show why women who pray or prophesy during worship should do so with their long hair neatly bound up on the top of their heads, like a covering.[37] There his appeal to what "nature itself" teaches (vv. 13-15) is nothing else than an appeal to social convention — to the practice with which he himself is familiar and which he therefore regards as self-evidently "proper."[38] It should not be overlooked that this argument from "nature" follows and in effect replaces a curiously convoluted argument that had drawn on the creation accounts in Genesis (vv. 7-10).[39] Paul himself had made a corrective comment in vv. 11-12, plainly concerned lest he be read as sanctioning the use of Genesis 1-3 to prove the inferiority of women.[40] He must have realized, however, that the "correction" rendered his whole argument from creation problematic; and so he offered the argument from "nature" as decisive. The second argument in no way derives from or assumes the first.

1 Corinthians 6:9; 1 Timothy 1:10

These are the only other passages in the New Testament in which homosexual behavior comes specifically into view. In both instances we are dealing with a simple listing of behaviors that were generally regarded as unacceptable in Greco-Roman society at large. Nothing is said about why the things listed are wrong. Such lists, which appear frequently in the moral tractates of the time, "secular" and Jewish as well as Christian, were drawn up only as reminders or examples of what any respectable person would want to avoid.

In 1 Cor 6:9 the fourth and fifth words in the list are the pertinent ones, but there is some dispute about how exactly they should be translated. The first edition of the RSV (1946) rendered them with just one term, "homosexuals." In the second edition of the RSV (1971) that was changed to the phrase, "sexual perverts." In the New Revised Standard Version (1989) they are translated, respectively, as "male prostitutes" and "sodomites."[41] The 1946 translation is very misleading, both because "homosexuals" is an anachronism in a first century text, and because it does not take into account the fact that Paul himself uses two different words. The 1971 revision is also misleading, both because Paul's two nouns are rendered by an adjective and a noun, and because the Greek words are unable to encompass all kinds of "sexual perverts." The most recent translation is some better, but can still mislead. The first of Paul's words was often, but not always used to slander "male prostitutes," and the word "sodomites" is at once too general and too specific. It is too specific because it imposes a reference to Sodom that is not implied by Paul's term; and it is too general because, in current English usage, "sodomites" has a broader range of meanings than the Greek word can bear.

The literal meaning of the first Greek term (μαλακός) is "soft," and it came to be used frequently to mean "effeminate," in the pejorative sense. By further extension it was sometimes used to describe the more passive male in a homosexual relationship — the one who, according to ancient moralists, was degraded by assuming (or having to assume) the woman's usual role. As for the second term (ἀρσενοκοῖτος), its earliest known occurrence is in this list. It combines two Greek words, one for "male" and one for "bed," both of which are found, juxtaposed, in the ancient Greek translation of Lev 18:22 and 20:13. It is therefore probable that the second of the two words in 1 Cor 6:9 is of Hellenistic-Jewish origin, and had been coined to describe "a male who lies with a male."[42] This is the same word that is listed in 1 Tim 1:10.[43]

Exactly how Paul is using the two terms remains in dispute, however. For example: Is he thinking of all kinds of homosexual relationships, or only of pederasty? Or only of male prostitution? For this reason, and also because one is dealing only with a list, 1 Cor 6:9 can be of little help in ascertaining Paul's attitude toward homosexual practice.[44] For Paul's view, as indeed for the entire New Testament, Romans 1:26-27 remains the key reference.

II. DISCERNING THE WILL OF GOD

In the first part of this study we have had to take account of both the antiquity and the diversity of the Old and New Testament writings. Now we must take account of their status as Scripture within the church. In doing so we are confronted with fundamental and complex hermeneutical and theological questions. What interpretive procedures most fully respect both the historical character and the scriptural status of these writings? In what sense can they be "authoritative" for the church's life and thought? More specifically, even if a "critical mass" of biblical scholars could agree on the interpretation of the biblical passages discussed above, would the church then be able to declare what the will of God is respecting homosexuality? To explore such questions in any detail would carry us quite beyond the scope and focus of the present essay. As a start, however, and with special reference to the topic of homosexuality, the following theses are offered for consideration.[45]

1.   *The Bible bears witness to the word of God, but the words of Scripture do not themselves constitute "the written word of God.*"[46] Nowhere in the Bible itself is God's word identified with the words of Scripture. The prophets, more than others, refer to God's "word" (usually called an *oracle* [or *utterance*] from the Lord), and they regularly set this over against the words of the law, which was their "Scripture." In the New Testament one saying attributed to Jesus does indirectly identify a specific commandment of the Decalogue as "the word of God."[47] More typically, however, the Synoptic evangelists portray Jesus as, in effect, the Lord of Scripture.[48] Other New Testament writers, especially the apostle Paul, associate the word of God closely with the (oral) gospel about Jesus as the Christ.[49] And the Fourth Evangelist identifies Jesus himself as the word of God.

2.   To decline to identify the Bible as "the written word of God" is not to diminish the authority of the Bible but to preserve the sovereignty and freedom of God. This is in accord with Scripture itself, for no biblical writer suggests that the scope of God's word is limited in either time or place.

3.   The subject matter of the Bible is the history of salvation as documented by the history of faith. What lies before us in the various and varied writings of the Old and New Testaments is, first of all, documentation of the faith and witness of ancient Israel and the earliest church. Yet in and through these documents the church is constantly re-introduced to the "mighty acts of God," as the writers and the religious communities of which they are representative had experienced those taking place in their midst.

4.   While revelations may occur in and through the Bible, revelation as such does not constitute the subject matter of the Bible. Revelation is not an

inert "subject matter" that can be "deposited," "learned," "taught," and "believed." It is an occurrence, an event. It is, as the Greek word itself indicates, an "un-veiling" ($\dot{\alpha}\pi o$-$\kappa\alpha\lambda\dot{\upsilon}\pi\tau\epsilon\iota\nu$), a "dis-closing" and "dis-covering" of a reality that is otherwise hidden from view. Of course revelation reveals *something*, it does not just "occur." But what it reveals can never be defined apart from the act of perceiving, thus never without reference to those for whom the dis-covering takes place. They are necessarily part of the revelation event.

5. *The fundamental reality that is dis-closed in and through the Bible is the reality that we are creatures of God's grace, and that we live only by God's grace.* In the Bible, both the gift of life and its continuing renewal, both creation and the new creation, are regarded as manifestations of God's grace. While we are still sinners (presuming, vainly, to live by our own strength and merit), God's love enfolds us to reconcile and transform.

6. *The biblical witness to God's grace attests that it is at once a gift and a claim.* To live by grace means to allow the reconciling, transforming love of God to find expression in our daily lives. Above all, Scripture defines the claim of God's grace with reference to the Great Commandment to love God and neighbor, expanding the concept of "neighbor" to accord with the inclusiveness of God's own love for us.

7. *The authority of Scripture for Christian faith and witness derives from its historical, not from its "superhistorical" character.* Scripture is the one channel of access to the apostolic witness to Christ, and thus to the norm by which an authentically "Christian" understanding of God and human existence can be shaped. Therefore, in different but closely related ways both Scripture and the apostolic witness to which it gives access are "authoritative" and "normative" for Christian faith and practice. However, it remains the case that, according to Scripture itself, the source of all authority (including that of Scripture) is God alone, as definitively revealed in Jesus Christ.[50]

8.   *The specific moral rules, teachings, and advisories of Scripture are an integral part of the history of faith.* They reflect the effort of God's people, in the midst of the vicissitudes and contingencies of particular times and places, to be faithful to the God by whom their existence as human beings has been graced and claimed. It is therefore not surprising that the specific laws and moral counsels of the Bible are very diverse, often in tension with one another, sometimes even contradictory. This is not a "flaw" in Scripture but evidence of the moral seriousness of the faith communities within which the biblical writings were produced. To be specifically relevant a moral directive or appeal has to address the particular situation; and to be intelligible and credible it has to be expressed in a way that is meaningful within the particular social and cultural setting. Since the situations and settings of the biblical writings were varied, so are the specific moral directives and appeals they contain.

9.   *The moral rules, teachings, and advisories of Scripture do not in themselves constitute "the revealed will of God," nor can normative principles for "Christian ethics" be extracted from them* (e.g., on the basis of some particular reconstruction of what Jesus did and said). To the extent that they are specific to the times and places for which they were variously formulated, they cannot be taken over automatically as God's will for all other times and places.[51] And to try to fashion from them something more generally "normative" would require the kind of selective and constructive procedure that only extra-Scriptural criteria could possibly effect.[52]

10.   *To affirm the primacy of Scripture is not the same as to affirm its sufficiency.*[53] The church properly affirms the primacy of Scripture, because it is only in and through its witness that access has been given to the One by whom believers have been constituted and are continually renewed as a community of faith. Only in and through the witness of Scripture can this faith community find and appropriate its identity as the body of Christ and the people of God. But for

deciding what is required of believers in concrete ways and in specific instances, Scripture alone cannot suffice. Just as the biblical writers themselves often drew on non-scriptural, including (what we might call) "secular" sources of knowledge and insight, so must the church in our day.

11. *Scripture attests not only the integral relationship between being and doing ("indicative" and "imperative"), but also the importance of reasoning when it comes to particular cases of "doing."* This is especially evident in the letters of Paul, who writes more than once about "searching out" what the will of God is (Rom 12:1-2; Phil 1:9-10; cf. 1 Thess 5:21-22). The process suggested by Paul's term (δοκιμάζειν) includes the examination and critical appraisal of all available evidence and every reputed "good," in order then to make a reasonable decision about what is best.[54] Paul's appeal to "search out" God's will is the more striking when compared with his comments in Rom 2:17-21. There he is sharply critical of those who believe that all knowledge and truth are deposited in the law (Scripture!), and who boast that since they are well instructed in that law, they definitely "*know* [God's] will" and are therefore able to "determine what is best" from case to case.[55]

12. *It is within the context of the community of faith that the "searching out" of God's will properly goes on.* This is the presupposition of Paul's appeal in Rom 12:1-2, and also of his prayer in Phil 1:9-10. The faith community listens for the word of God as it interprets Scripture, as it offers up its prayers and supplications, as it weighs (διακρίνειν) what is said by the prophets in its midst (1 Cor 14:29-32), as it takes critical account (λογίζεσθαι) of "whatever" thoughtful people in general regard as true, noble, just, etc. (Phil 4 8),56 and as each of its members is challenged, through word and sacrament, to consider what it means to belong to the body of Christ (cf. 1 Cor 11:27-29).

13. *One of the most fundamental responsibilities of ecclesiastical structures, officers, and legislation is to support and safeguard the type of*

community in which this "searching out" of God's will can take place. The apostle Paul may again be our guide, especially as we see him appealing and working for this in 1 Corinthians. There as elsewhere Paul's word for such community is *koinonia*, for which "fellowship" is much too weak a rendering. The *koinonia* of which the apostle writes (1:9; 10:16) is a community that is called and bound together by the crucified Lord (1:18-2:5), who thereby provides the norm for its faith and its witness, including its congregational life (e.g., 8:11). Paul's own convictions about various specific moral questions, and even cases, are clearly stated and commended as authoritative. But he does not draw on Scripture for specific rules of conduct,[57] nor does he draw up his own "apostolic" rules for the community's life.[58] While he does invoke Jesus' prohibition of divorce (7:10, 11b), he not only tolerates an exceptional situation (7:11a), but even counsels that, for one whole category of marriages, the Lord's word should sometimes be set aside (7:12-16). Paul's concern is not to spell out the will of God for the Corinthians, but to remind them of who and Whose they are in Christ, and to guide them in their own searching out of what is best in particular circumstances.

CONCLUSION

The church must attend to the witness of Scripture as it seeks to discern the will of God in the matter of homosexuality. Scripture provides access to the apostolic witness, wherein the believing community finds the norm by which appropriately *Christian* faith and conduct, including sexual conduct, may be ascertained.

It would be a simple matter if this norm could be found in what Scripture provides by way of specific rules, teachings, and advisories concerning homoerotic relationships. But that is not the case. However pertinent they may have been for the various times and circumstances within which they were originally formulated, the biblical injunctions and teachings on this topic presume much that can no longer be presumed about human sexuality. It is certainly true that our present understanding of homosexuality is incomplete and undergoing constant revision. Yet our knowledge of this subject is vastly superior to that available in ancient Israel and the early church. Moreover, we can appreciate the complexity of the issue, as well as the incompleteness of our understanding of it, in a way that the ancient world could not.

Therefore, it is not what "the Bible says" about homoerotic relationships that constitutes the witness of Scripture to the church on this topic. Rather, in this instance as in every other the witness of Scripture is that human existence, like the whole of creation, is the gift of an omnipotent, just, benevolent, and caring God; that God's purposes are shaped and accomplished by God's love, over which nothing in all creation (including humanity's rebelliousness) can finally prevail; that the people of God are repeatedly summoned to walk in the same love from and in which, by God's grace, they properly "live and move and have their being"; that the claim inherent in God's love is no less boundless than the gift; and that it is in Christ that women and men of faith will find, at last, both the saving power of God's gift of love and the strength to follow where it leads.

ENDNOTES

[1]The word "homosexual" was not coined until 1869, by a Hungarian physician (Karoly M. Benkert) who, writing in German, used it with reference to "male or female individuals" who "from birth" are erotically oriented toward their own sex. According to the Oxford English Dictionary, the word appeared for the first time in English only in 1912. See Petersen (1986, 188-89). The word "homosexual" was not used in any English Bible until 1946, when the first edition of the Revised Standard Version employed it in 1 Cor 6:9. Greenlee's remarks on this subject (1979, 97-100) show that he has not understood what is at stake here; the ancient world could and did distinguish between types of sexual behavior, but it had no conception of different types of sexuality.

[2]For comments on 1 Cor 6:9 and 1 Tim 1:10, see below.

[3]Thus, e.g., Wenham (1991, 361); Parker (1991, 6-8), and many other interpreters.

[4]Parker (1991, 6).

[5]Stott, e.g., calls the verse an "unequivocal statement" about homosexual behavior (1985, 221).

[6]Commenting on Jude 7, Bauckham (1983, 54) points out that "σαρκὸς ἑτέρας, 'strange flesh,' cannot, as many commentators and most translations assume, refer to homosexual practice, in which the flesh is not 'different' (ἑτέρας); it must mean the flesh of angels."

[7]In what follows I am indebted in certain respects to both Bird (1990a) and Countryman (1988, esp. 22-28). See also Thurston (1990).

[8]Parker (1991, 13).

[9]E.g., Gaiser (1990, 165) observes that "unlike dietary laws, which are specifically overturned in the New Testament, the proscription of homosexual activity [in Leviticus] specifically remains in the New Testament."

[10]Note Stott's comment that "the *negative* prohibitions of homosexual practices in

Scripture make sense only in the light of its *positive* teaching in Genesis 1 and 2 about human sexuality and heterosexual marriage" (1985, 226, his italics; similar comments on p. 232).

[11]E.g., Oswalt (1979, 69-71), whose comments on Genesis 1-3, however, are quite brief and general. A more moderate version of this interpretation is offered — but also quite briefly — by Gaiser (1990, 162-63); cf. Stott (1985, 227-29).

[12]Here I am especially indebted to Bird (1987; also 1990a, 1990b).

[13]This point is stressed by Bird (1990a, 1990b). Similarly, Jacobson cautions that narrative materials in general are "descriptive" not "prescriptive" (1990, 157).

[14]Thus Stott (1985, 229).

[15]Note von Rad's comment (1972, 85; italics added), that in Gen 2:24 "the entire narrative so far arrives at the primary purpose toward which it was oriented from the beginning. This shows what is actually intended. The story is *entirely aetiological*, i.e., it was told to answer a quite definite question. A fact needs explanation, namely, the extremely powerful drive of the sexes to each other." Seamands (1991, 8) believes otherwise, holding that v. 24 is "a moral directive."

[16]Again von Rad (1972, 85): "One must emphasize . . . that our narrative is concerned not with a legal custom but with a natural drive. So no recognition of monogamy should be read out of the word" [i.e., out of this verse]. Seamands, however (1991, 9 n. 1), holds that the possessive, "*his* woman," permits the inference that a marital relationship is in view. Stott (1985, 228-29) finds the whole "institution of marriage" presupposed here, including monogamy and "a public social occasion" to recognize the making of "a loving, cleaving commitment or covenant, which is heterosexual and permanent."

[17]None of the sayings attributed to Jesus deals explicitly with the matter of homosexual practice, including the two that refer to Sodom (see above, p. 255). This holds as well for the saying about "eunuchs" in Matt 19:11-12, which is a rejoinder to the negative comment about marriage that is attributed to the disciples (v. 10): In addition to the obvious cases of those who are born without the requisite sexual organs or who become sexually disabled, singleness is appropriate only for those [males] to whom celibacy is "given" (v. 11) for the purpose of serving God's kingdom more fully (v. 12). Deming's argument (1990) that Mark 9:42-48 (cf. Matt 5:27-32) refers metaphorically to pederasty, masturbation, adultery, and lustful glances is intriguing, but finally not persuasive. Nor does

homosexual behavior seem to have been a standard *topos* in the moral teaching of the earliest church. There is in fact more attention paid to it in non-Christian, including Hellenistic-Jewish texts of the day. It would of course be unwarranted to conclude from this relative silence of the New Testament texts that both Jesus and the early church were generally tolerant of homosexual behavior. One can only conclude that it seems not to have been a topic with which either Jesus or the church was preoccupied.

[18]See in particular chapters 13-15 of the Wisdom of Solomon. This is a Hellenistic-Jewish writing of the late 1st century B.C.E., part of what most Protestants call "the Old Testament Apocrypha." These writings were included, however, in the Greek version of the "Old Testament" that was used by the early church (including Paul), and were considered scriptural.

[19]Cf. Wisd 13:5.

[20]Compare 2 Esdras 8:59b-60 (90-100 C.E.): "For the Most High did not intend that anyone should be destroyed; but those who were created have themselves defiled the name of him who made them, and have been ungrateful to him who prepared life for them now" (NRSV).

[21]Note the rhetorical question with which Paul challenges the Corinthians (1 Cor 4:7): "What do you have that you did not receive? And since you have received (everything), why do you boast as if you have not?"

[22]See Wisd 15:15-17: "For they thought that all their heathen idols were gods, though these have neither the use of their eyes to see with, nor nostrils with which to draw breath, nor ears with which to hear, nor fingers to feel with, and their feet are of no use for walking. For a human being made them, and one whose spirit is borrowed formed them; for none can form gods that are like themselves. People are mortal, and what they make with lawless hands is dead; for they are better than the objects they worship, since they have life, but the idols never had" (NRSV).

[23]See, e.g., Wisd 14:12: "For the idea of making idols was the beginning of sexual immorality [$\pi o \rho \nu \epsilon \acute{\iota} \alpha$], and the invention of them was the corruption of life" (NRSV, modified). One of the vices listed in 14:26 is "interchange of sex roles [$\gamma \epsilon \nu \acute{\epsilon} \sigma \epsilon \omega \varsigma$ $\dot{\epsilon} \nu \alpha \lambda \lambda \alpha \gamma \hat{\eta}$]" (trans. Winston [1979, 269, 280]), although Countryman (1988, 63) questions the translation, and thus whether this is really a reference to homosexual practice at all.

[24]This is the only specific reference in either the Old or the New Testament to

female homosexual activity; but the reference to the "interchange of sex roles" (Wisd 14:26) seems to be inclusive.

[25]Relevant texts are cited and discussed by, e.g., Scroggs (1983, 17-98), Brooten (1985), and Furnish (1985).

[26]Schrage (1991) 436. Hays would perhaps dispute this (1986, 200).

[27]E.g., in referring to the Sodomites Philo mentions their addiction to strong drink, delicate foods, and "forbidden forms of intercourse" (including adultery) as but varied manifestations of their lustful nature (On Abraham 135)

[28]Not only because homosexual intercourse will yield no offspring, but also because it renders the (male) partners sterile. See, e.g., Philo, *On the Contemplative Life* 62; *On Abraham* 135-136; *Special Laws* 3.29.

[29]Philo's remarks are typical of the way Hellenistic-Judaism expressed this concern: "[The wicked man] not only attacks in his fury the marriage-beds of others, but even plays the pederast and forces the male type of nature to debase and convert itself into the feminine form, just to indulge a polluted and accursed passion" (*Special Laws* 2.50); "In fact the transformation of the male nature to the female is practiced by [pederasts] as an art and does not raise a blush. These persons are rightly judged worthy of death by those who obey the law, which ordains that the man-woman who debases the sterling coin of nature should perish unavenged, suffered not to live for a day or even an hour, as a disgrace to himself, his house, his native land and the whole human race .... [The pederast] pursues an unnatural pleasure ..." (*Special Laws* 3.37-39). Lilja (1983, 135) makes a similar point about attitudes found generally in the literature of Republican and Augustan Rome.

[30]As regards the first point, in the ancient world procreation was understood only with reference to the role of the male (there was total ignorance of the female reproductive system). As regards the second point, it should not be forgotten that the ancient sources introduce us almost exclusively to the male point of view.

[31]Lilja (1983, 122, n. 150); Brooten (1985, 70 *et passim*).

[32]Hays (1986, esp. 191-94) provides an unusually well-informed and carefully reasoned argument to this effect. Cf. Stott (1985, 233), followed by Seamands (1991, 8).

[33]Thus Hays (1986, 194): "Though he offers no explicit reflection on the concept

of 'nature,' it is clear that in [Rom 1:26-27] Paul identifies 'nature' with the created order. The understanding of 'nature' in this conventional language does not rest on empirical observation of what exists; instead, it appeals to an intuitive conception of what ought to be, of the world as designed by God."

[34]I therefore do not understand on what basis Hays can say that Paul's association of "nature" with "the created order" is "clear" in Romans 1 (see preceding note). And what is there in that passage that could warrant (or explain) Hays's reference to "an intuitive conception . . . of the world as designed by God"? Cf. the criticism of Hays by Countryman (1988, 114-15 n. 20).

[35]Among these are: Wisd 14:26; the Letter of Aristeas 152; Pseudo-Phocylides 3 and 190; the Sibylline Oracles 3:185-87, 596-600, 764; 4:33-34; 5:166, 386-93, 429-31; the Testament of Naphtali 3:1-4; and the following Philonic essays: *On the Cherubim* 92; *On Abraham* 135-36; *Special Laws* 1.325; 2.50; 3.3742; *On the Contemplative Life* 59-62.

[36]Testament of Naphtali 3:4 is a significant exception, if indeed homosexual behavior is in view there: "In the firmament, in the earth, and in the sea, in all the products of his workmanship discern the Lord who made all things, so that you do not become like Sodom, which departed from the order of nature [ἐνήλλαξε ταξιν φύσεως αὐτῆς]" (trans. Kee [1983, 812]). See Eron (1990). It is possible, however, that the crossing of the line between earthly (the men of Sodom) and heavenly (Lot's angelic visitors) is in view, as in the very next sentence (3:5, alluding to Gen 6:1): "Likewise the Watchers departed from nature's order ...." See Countryman (1988, 63-64), and the comment on Jude 7 in n. 00 above.

[37]It is not entirely clear why Paul is concerned about this. Perhaps the Corinthians' interpretation of the affirmation that in Christ "there is no longer male or female" (Gal 3:28) had led some of them to adopt certain practices (in dress, hairstyles, etc.) that Paul thought inappropriate. According to a few interpreters (e.g., Murphy-O'Connor, 1980), Paul fears that the Corinthian Christians could be mistaken for people who engage in homosexual behavior.

[38]In addition to the commentaries, see Furnish (1990, 147-48).

[39]There are allusions in these verses to Gen 1:27a, 2:22-23, and 2:18. It should be observed, however, that Paul does not base his argument on God's creation of two different *sexual* beings ("heterosexuality"). The terms for "male" (ἄρσην) and "female" (θῆλυς) do not occur in this passage (he uses them only in Rom 1:26-27 and Gal 3:28), nor is there any allusion to Gen 1:27b-28. Rather, Paul

bases his argument on the fact that man was created *before* woman and that woman was then created from man.

[40]The chapters were commonly used that way in Jewish teaching.

[41]Some other renderings: while the NEB had "homosexual perversion," the REB has "sexual pervert"; while the JB had "catamites, sodomites," the NJB has "self-indulgent, sodomites"; while the NAB had simply "sodomites," the revised NAB has "boy prostitutes" and "practicing homosexuals."

[42]Thus Scroggs (1983, esp. 85-86).

[43]With most biblical scholars (who employ the accepted procedures of critical-historical research), I share the view that 1, 2 Timothy and Titus were not written by the apostle himself. They are often dated ca. 125.

[44]The same two difficulties obtain in the case of 1 Tim 1:10, although it is clear that this particular writer identifies all of the persons listed as breaking the Mosaic law (see vv. 8-9, which reflect a distinctly un-Pauline view of the role of the law).

[45]In several of the following theses the wording is drawn in part from Furnish (1991, 10).

[46]The passage most often cited to support some concept of scriptural "inspiration" (2 Tim 3:15-17) refers to Scripture as the "sacred writings" ($\iota\epsilon\rho\grave{\alpha}$ $\gamma\rho\acute{\alpha}\mu\mu\alpha\tau\alpha$) but not as God's Word. As for the reference in this passage to the inspiration of Scripture, the following points should be observed: (a) the writings in view are only those of the Old Testament; (b) the adjective "inspired" ($\theta\epsilon\acute{o}\pi\nu\epsilon\upsilon\sigma\tau o\varsigma$ — literally: "God-breathed") is applied metaphorically to the texts themselves (thus, to inanimate objects; this is not the case in 2 Pet 1:21, where it is said that the *authors* of Scripture were "moved by the Holy Spirit" and "spoke for God"; cf. 1 Pet 1:10-11; Acts 28:25, etc.); (c) the consequence of inspiration, according to 2 Tim 3:16-17, is the *utility* of Scripture "for teaching, for reproof, for correction, and for training in righteousness, so that everyone who belongs to God may be proficient, equipped for every good work" (NRSV); (d) this utilitarian view of Scripture is in accord with the comment in v. 15 that Scripture's role is to instruct ($\sigma o\phi\iota\acute{\zeta}\epsilon\iota\nu$) about the salvation that comes "through faith in Christ Jesus" (not through "faith" in Scripture itself!); (e) nowhere in this passage are inferences drawn about the "inerrancy" or "infallibility" of Scripture.

[47]See Mark 7:13 (parallel: Matt 15:6), which presumably has in view "the

commandment of God" mentioned in v. 8 (parallel: Matt 15:3).

⁴⁸Matt 5:17-20 ("I came not to destroy the law but to fulfill it," etc.) may be a partial exception. In any case, this distinctively Matthean passage — which is notoriously difficult to interpret (see Luz, 1989, 255-69) — is followed immediately by a set of distinctively Matthean antitheses in which Jesus' word is set over against that of Moses (5:21-48).

⁴⁹E.g., 1 Thess 2:13 ("We also constantly give thanks to God for this, that when you received the word of God that you heard from us, you accepted it not as a human word but as what it really is, God's word, which is also at work among you believers" (NRSV, modified).

⁵⁰My formulation of this thesis has been influenced by the position argued by Ogden (1982, esp. 86-105; see also Ogden,1986).

⁵¹Cf. my "law of diminishing relevancy" (above, pp. 256-57).

⁵²If I understand him correctly, Hays would argue that where scriptural teaching is "univocal" about a given matter, then it is "prudent and necessary" in that case to let Scripture "order the life of the church" (1991, 21). But what does "univocal" mean? For example, is it possible to speak of the "univocal" scriptural testimony about homosexuality (as Hays does) when the scriptural references and allusions reflect such different cultural and theological contexts? And how is one to relate what may be the "univocal" testimony of the New Testament to that of the Old? (Hays himself seems to accord less authority to the specific teachings of the latter; see his remarks about Leviticus on p. 18.)

⁵³See Birch and Rasmussen (1989, 152-58).

⁵⁴Space precludes repeating, or even summarizing, the exegetical substantiation of this that is offered in my study of God's will according to Paul (1989, esp. 213-17, 221). For the more general question of faith and reason in Paul's letters, Bornkamm's essay remains important (1969).

⁵⁵καὶ γινώσκεις τὸ θέλημα καὶ δοκιμάζεις τὰ δοαφέροντα κατηχούμενος ἐκ τοῦ νόμου (2:18). In this context δοκιμάζειν can only mean "determine with certainty."

⁵⁶The virtues listed are typically Hellenistic, not specifically Christian.

⁵⁷Furnish (1989, 148-49).

[58]His direction about the incestuous man (chapter 5) does not constitute a standing rule, but pertains to a specific instance. Even so, Paul presumes that the congregation itself will deliberate the matter when it assembles (v. 4).

WORKS CITED

Bauckham, Richard
 1983 *Jude, 2 Peter.* Word Biblical Commentary, 50. Dallas: Word Books.

Birch, Bruce C., and Larry L. Rasmussen
 1989 *Bible & Ethics in the Christian Life.* Revised and expanded edition. Minneapolis: Augsburg.

Bird, Phyllis A.
 1987 "Genesis 1-3 as a Source for a Contemporary Theology of Sexuality," *Ex Auditu* 3:31-44.

 1990a "Memorandum on O. T. passages most often cited as bearing on the discussion of homosexuality," privately circulated.

 1990b "The OT as a resource for a Christian approach to homosexuality," privately circulated.

Bornkamm, Günther
 1969 "Faith and Reason in Paul," *Early Christian Experience* (trans. by Paul L. Hammer; New York and Evanston: Harper & Row) 29-46.

Brooten, Bernadette J.
 1985 "Paul's Views on the Nature of Women and Female Homoeroticism," *Immaculate and Powerful: The Female in Sacred Image and Social Reality* (ed. by Clarissa W. Atkinson, et al.; The Harvard Women's Studies in Religion Series; Boston: Beacon) 61-87.

Countryman, L. William
 1988 *Dirt, Greed, and Sex. Sexual Ethics in the New Testament and Their Implications for Today.* Philadelphia: Fortress Press.

Deming, Will
1990   "Mark 9.42—10.12, Matthew 5.27-32, and *B. Nid.* 13b: a First Century Discussion of Male Sexuality," New Testament Studies 36:130-41.

Eron, Lewis John
1990   "Early Jewish and Christian Attitudes toward Male Homosexuality as Expressed in the Testament of Naphtali," *Homophobia and the Judaeo-Christian Tradition* (Gay Men's Issues in Religious Studies, 1; ed. by Michael L. Stemmeler and J. Michael Clark; Dallas: Monument Press) 25-49.

Furnish, Victor Paul
1985   "Homosexuality," *The Moral Teaching of Paul: Selected Issues* (2d ed., revised; Nashville: Abingdon Press) 52-82.

1989   "Der 'Wille Gottes' in paulinischer Sicht," *Jesu Rede von Gott und ihre Nachgeschichte im frühen Christentum. Beiträge zur Verkündigung Jesu und zum Kerygma der Kirche. Festschrift für Willi Marxsen zum 70. Geburtstag* (ed. by D.-A. Koch, et al.; Gütersloh: Mohn) 208-221.

1990   "Belonging to Christ. A Paradigm for Ethics in First Corinthians," *Interpretation* 44:145-57.

1991   "Understanding Homosexuality in the Bible's Cultural Particularity," *The Circuit Rider* 15/10:10-11, 12.

Gaiser, Frederick J.
1990   "Homosexuality and the Old Testament," *Word & World* 10:161-65.

Greenlee, J. Harold
1979   "The New Testament and Homosexuality," *What You Should Know About Homosexuality* (ed. by Charles W. Keysor; Grand Rapids: Zondervan) 81-114.

Hays, Richard B.
    1986   "Relations Natural and Unnatural: A Response to John
                 Boswell's Exegesis of Romans 1," *Journal of Religious
                 Ethics* 14:184-215.

    1991   "Awaiting the Redemption of Our Bodies," *Sojourners*,
                 July: 17-21.

Jacobson, Diane
    1990   "Biblical Perspectives on Sexuality," *Word & World*
                 10:156-60.

Kee, Howard Clark
    1972   "Testaments of the Twelve Patriarchs," *The Old Testament
                 Pseude-pigrapha*, 1 (ed. by J. H. Charlesworth; Garden
                 City: Doubleday) 775-828.

Lilja, Saara
    1983   *Homosexuality in Republican and Augustan Rome.*
                 Commentationes Humanorum Litteratum, 74. Helsinki:
                 Societas Scientiarum Fennica.

Luz, Ulrich
    1989   *Matthew 1-7: A Commentary.* Trans. by W. C. Linss.
                 Minneapolis: Augsburg.

Murphy-O'Connor, Jerome
    1980   "Sex and Logic in 1 Cor 11:2-16," *Catholic Biblical
                 Quarterly* 42:482-500.

Ogden, Schubert M.
    1982   *The Point of Christology.* San Francisco: Harper & Row.

    1986   "The Authority of Scripture for Theology," *On Theology*
                 (San Francisco: Harper & Row) 45-68.

Oswalt, John N.
    1979   "The Old Testament and Homosexuality," *What You
                 Should Know About Homosexuality* (ed. by Charles W.
                 Keysor; Grand Rapids: Zondervan) 17-77.

Parker, Simon B.

1991   "The Hebrew Bible and Homosexuality," *Quarterly*
               Review 11/3:4-19.

Petersen, W. L.
   1986   "Can ΑΡΣΕΝΟΚΟΙΤΑΙ be translated by 'Homosexuals'? (I
               Cor. 6.9; I Tim. 1.10)," *Vigiliae Christianae* 40:187-91.

Rad, Gerhard von
   1972   *Genesis. A Commentary.* Revised edition. Philadelphia:
               Westminster.

Schrage, Wolfgang
   1991   *Der erste Brief an die Korinther, 1 (1 Kor 1,1-6,11).*
               Evangelisch-Katholisher Kommentar zum Neuen Testament,
               VII/1. Zürich and Braunschweig: Benziger   Verlag;
               Neukirchen-Vluyn: Neukirchener Verlag.

Scroggs, Robin
   1983   *The New Testament and Homosexuality.* Philadelphia:
               Fortress Press.

Seamands, David A.
   1991   "A Common Thread of Opposition to Homosexuality Runs
               Through the Bible," *The Circuit Rider* 15/10:8-9, 12.

Stott, John R. W.
   1985   "Homosexual Partnerships?" *Involvement, vol. 2: Social*
               and Sexual Relationships in the Modern World (Old
               Tappan: Revell) 215-44.

Thurston, Thomas M.
   1990   "Leviticus 18:22 and the Prohibition of Homosexual Acts,"
               Homophobia and the Judaeo-Christian Tradition (Gay
               Men's Issues in Religious Studies, 1; ed. by Michael L.
               Stemmeler and J. Michael Clark; Dallas: Monument Press)
               7-23.

Wenham, Gordon J.
    1991   "The Old Testament Attitude to Homosexuality,"
                Expository Times 102:359-63.

Winston, David
    1979   *The Wisdom of Solomon.* Anchor Bible, 43. Garden City:
                Doubleday.

NOTES ON CONTRIBUTORS

THOMAS G. BANDY is the national officer of Congregational Mission and Evangelism for the United Church of Canada. He has been an ordained minister for 20 years, with extensive experience in Church Development and Ecumenical ministries in the United States and Canada. He has lectured in academic and public contexts in ethics, professional ministry, and the theology of culture, and is the author of various articles related to the faith and mission of the church. He did his theological training at Princeton Theological Seminary, and wrote his doctoral dissertation on the thought of Paul Tillich at the University of Toronto. He currently lives near Toronto, Ontario.

KAREN L. BLOOMQUIST is Director of Studies of the Commission for Church in Society of the Evangelical Lutheran Church in America. She did her theological studies at the Pacific Lutheran Theological Seminary in Berkeley, California and served as a pastor in Oakland, California and in Brooklyn, New York. She received her Ph.D. degree from Union Theological Seminary and Columbia University in New York, and has before assuming her present position taught at the Lutheran School of Theology in Chicago. She is the author of *The Dream Betrayed: Religious Challenge of the Working Class* (Fortress Press, 1990). She chaired the Lutheran Committee on Human Sexuality, and lives in the greater Chicago area.

JOHN J. CAREY is the Wallace M. Alston Professor of Bible and Religion and Chair of the Department of Bible and Religion at Agnes Scott College in Decatur, Georgia. He was on the faculty of Florida State University for 26 years (1960-86) and served as Chair of the Religion Department, Director of Graduate Studies in Religion, and as Director of the Peace Studies Program at that institution. He served as President of Warren Wilson College in North Carolina from 1986-88. He received his B.D. and S.T.M. degrees from Yale Divinity School and received his Ph.D. degree from Duke University. He has edited and written nine books, and chaired the Presbyterian Special Committee on Human Sexuality. He is an ordained Presbyterian minister and a member of the Presbytery of Greater Atlanta.

MARVIN M. ELLISON is Bass Professor of Christian Ethics at Bangor Theological Seminary in Bangor, Maine. He was a member of the Presbyterian Special Committee on Human Sexuality. He did his theological training at the University of Chicago and his Ph.D. at Union Seminary in New York and Columbia University. He has authored numerous scholarly articles. He is an ordained Presbyterian minister and a member of the Presbytery of Northern New England.

JANET F. FISHBURN is Professor of Teaching Ministry at the Drew University Theological school in Madison, New Jersey. A member of the Presbyterian Committee, she has special academic interests in Christian education and American religious history. She holds the Ph.D. degree from the Pennsylvania State University and is the author of *Confronting the Idolatry of Family* (Nashville: Abingdon, 1991).

VICTOR PAUL FURNISH is University Distinguished Professor of New Testament at the Perkins School of Theology at Southern Methodist University in Dallas, Texas. He was a member of the United Methodist

Committee to Study Homosexuality. He is the author of *Theology and Ethics in Paul* (1968), *The Moral Teaching of Paul* (1979, 2nd ed. 1985), *II Corinthians* in the Anchor Bible Commentary Series (1984) and *Jesus According to Paul* (1993). He did his theological studies at Garrett Evangelical Theological Seminary and his Ph.D. at Yale. He was the President of the Society of Biblical Literature in 1993, and is an ordained minister of the United Methodist Church.

EPHRIAM RADNER is an Episcopal priest who is currently doing Ph.D. studies in theology at Yale. He did his M.Div. studies at Yale Divinity School and has served as a missionary in Africa. He lives in Stamford, Connecticut.

GEORGE SUMNER, JR. is an Episcopal priest who is currently doing Ph.D. studies in theology at Yale. He did his theological studies at Yale and served as a missionary in Africa and in Navaho territory in Arizona. He has been a parish priest in Worcester, Massachusetts. He lives in New Haven, Connecticut.

SYLVIA THORSON-SMITH is Lecturer in Religious Studies and Sociology at Grinnell College in Grinnell, Iowa. Long active in women's advocacy groups in the Presbyterian Church (U.S.A.), she was the principal author of the study on pornography done by the denomination. She holds the M.A. degree in Sociology and Women's Studies from Wichita State University, and was a member of the Presbyterian Special Committee on Human Sexuality. Her academic interests are in gender studies and human sexuality.

SYMPOSIUM SERIES